With best is ,
Allan A. Laver

GW00701546

COBWEBS
ON THE OCEAN
FLOOR

Allan Alphonso Lowen

VANTAGE PRESS
New York

Published by Vantage Press, Inc.
516 West 34th Street, New York, New York 10001

Manufactured in the United States of America
ISBN: 0-533-10773-3

Library of Congress Catalog Card No.: 93-93521

0 9 8 7 6 5 4 3 2 1

To my mother, Virginia Graneau Lowen

Foreword

Millions of people inhabit this world, people of different races, hues, religions, creeds, and customs. Some of us are born in large cities and die in large cities, not knowing or caring about the vast number of others who dwell in far-off, unheard of places. Others are born, live, and die in these small places, some content with the life they live, never knowing anything about the larger places on earth. Still others, adventurous creatures, seek other places where they hope to better their conditions, some forced to journey to far corners of the globe to get away from oppression and unscrupulous governments.

Another few, though born wealthy, are never satisfied; they journey from place to place, seeking peace and quiet away from the hustle and bustle of cities and the demagogues who dwell in and sometimes rule them.

We in the United States of America never hear of the small cities in other parts of the world, except when wars or other catastrophes occur. Then we become temporarily acquainted with other people of the world.

This story begins in one of these smaller places on this earth, a small island in the Caribbean Sea named Dominica. Dominica was discovered by Christopher Columbus, who thought he had discovered a western route to the East Indies; therefore, the name given to the group of islands containing Dominica was the West Indies.

The West Indians we know today differ from those who

immigrated to the United States before the First World War. For economic reasons they did become united, but they remained different spiritually and morally as they held onto their original beliefs and teachings.

To American Negroes, especially those who came from the South, the West Indian was a source of ridicule to be laughed at. He was called a "monkey chaser," although many never saw a monkey before they visited a zoo or went to a circus.

There were many West Indians whose education in the islands was on a much higher level than those black American youngsters who were not able to obtain quality education due to flagrant racial oppression. The strict parental training the West Indian children received manifested itself in the manners and scholastic aptitude of these children.

Dominica, an island situated in the Caribbean Sea between Guadalupe and Martinique, was blessed with a deepwater harbor. In the year 1766, the British government passed the Free Port acts and opened up the port of Roseau, the capital of Dominica, and Portsmouth, the second town and its Port Prince Rupert.

Four masted boats, brigantines, and large schooners dropped anchor a few feet off shore in the port of Roseau. Sloops, launches, and canoes came alongside to load and unload passengers and freight from the free ports from all over the world.

Dominica has never lost the influence of the French regime that ruled the island before its loss to the British in battle in the year 1782.

The island still retains the accents, dress, superstitions, customs, and doctrines of the early French and patois, broken French, which is the native tongue of the poorer people.

Roseau has one of the most beautiful botanical gardens

in the Leeward Islands and the display of colors in the homes of the natives emphasizes the French influence.

Portsmouth has no deep-water harbor and large steamers that did drop anchor to take on cargo did so a far distance from the shore, due to the shallow water.

The land here was flat. Grave fear was felt for those who lived near the shore as gigantic waves that accompanied habitual storms swept inward several hundred yards. A few rivers and streams divided Portsmouth and relics of the early settlers could be seen far up their courses. The legend of the "white cross" was told by the older people:

Many years ago a little French girl afflicted with an incurable disease was being taken up the river in a canoe to an obeah, a voodoo doctor, by her father, who had tried every other means to cure her. A storm approached and they took refuge in one of the sheltered coves. The strong tide swept them into an underground river, and they came across a white cross with a statue of Christ nailed to it. The girl and her father prayed, and she was cured of her illness. They came out of the cove and told their story to the people. They were not believed. Others tried to find the underground river with no success, and the father and the girl were branded as liars and voodoo worshippers. Many generations passed. An earthquake caused a split in the rocks of the river and as the high waters receded, a bright, shining cross was seen by many on the side of the mountain. Some will still swear that if one looked close enough they would see a man and a young girl before the cross.

The harbor of Portsmouth was full of fishing boats and schooners that made trips to and from the neighboring islands. The clear, cool water that flowed smoothly over the pebbles and the black sandy beaches was used as a large bathtub by the poorer natives. They learned to swim while still young, and it was not at all surprising to see little boys, four years old, cavorting happily in water over eight feet deep.

The schools here were conducted by the French and English teachers. The government fostered elementary education for the poorer natives, but private schools were there for those who could afford to pay.

Women hustlers trudged along the narrow streets, using their heads as a platform for the large baskets, which were heavily laden with their wares, and in loud chants advertised their merchandise. A large multicolored handkerchief ingeniously twisted served as a cushion for their baskets that balanced perfectly as they moved along, seeking out the only means they knew to making an honest livelihood.

A mixture of odors wafted up the streets and alleys to the center of the town, where quaint houses built many years before reminded one of the dwellings in a French village. The botanical gardens farther into the city were the main attraction for the children and after church Sunday strollers. The iron railing surrounding the park was adorned by row after row of hibiscus and the many colored plants and shrubberies were kept in magnificent condition by the natives.

On Thursday afternoons, the stores were closed and the employees took time off to participate in the cricket matches. Band concerts were held in the park on Sunday afternoons and evenings. As the people of the upper classes left for home, the drivers of the hansoms, decked out in long coats and top hats, waited in line to assist their employers in climbing aboard their conveyances.

As one walked along the streets on Monday mornings, after the shops were opened, one would see a vast assortment of people whose ancestors and forefathers had come from all parts of the world. There were dark- and light-skinned Portuguese in the rum shops, Arabs and East Indians in the dry goods stores, Bacras in the larger department stores, colored men in the tobacco shops and drug stores, and black laborers pulling or pushing drays to and from the jetties and warehouses. All were making a living together, an attestment to the handiwork of God and civilisation.

The third town, Veille Case, was a village in reality, the abode of a hundred superstitions, for some the home of witchcraft. Ville Case was situated high on a clearing on the mountainside where no automotive machine was able to travel. Dirt roads and well-trodden paths were the streets. Pretentious buildings were the one-room post office, the two-room police station, and the three rum shops. Bananas were loaded into large ships and shipped to other British possessions.

The breadfruit, coconut, and mango trees shaded the homes of the rich as well as those who dwelt in huts and grass-covered shacks.

Here also were the homes of God-fearing individuals, fanatically religious Catholics, and their opposites, the devil worshippers. Here were the dwelling places of the *suckomer*, human flies at night, whose wings rustled in the air as they "flew" to and from their meeting places. Here were the *jablesse*, who could transform themselves into any animal by pouring certain liquids over their bodies. Here was the home of the Caribs, a tribe of Indians who were as mysterious and savage as they were beautiful.

Uncanny events happened here. Small, live snakes were taken out of human arms and legs, supposedly put there by the victims' enemies. Locks of hair were vomited the next morning by women who lost them at night while they slept. Impressions of one's enemies could be obtained from seers who went into profound trances. The deserted lands of the large estates were considered to be the meeting places of the devils at night. Coffins confronted late walkers on the deserted roads, and yet amid these eerie surroundings there stood a magnificent edifice of stone and mortar, the Roman Catholic church and its seminary.

As the clean trade winds from the Caribbean Sea blew across the island, they carried in their flight willowy, creepy swishlike sounds that floated and murmured through the trees like human voices whistling through the air. When the heavens opened, a mighty barrage of peal and flash seemed to be warning the good and bad of the power of the almighty God.

Indeed, the natural surroundings on this part of the island were mysterious and bizarre. The hills and mountains on a moonlit night appeared to stand out like legendary giants, guarding their offspring. The consistent breaking of the huge waves far below seemed to one standing on the projecting cliffs like echo after echo of some sound made by an invisible ogre, sweeping the cobwebs of the ocean floor with rhythmic accuracy.

Veille Case was the home of primitive folk, of full-blooded races, of mixed breeds, of a sprinkling of black people, and a preponderance of brown men and women numbering about 300.

Nature had outdone herself in this village, the green vegetation was now greener than ever. It was April in the nineteen-hundredth year of our Lord.

COBWEBS
ON THE OCEAN
FLOOR

Chapter One

April 1, 1900

Veille Case was the home of the Mondeaus and their ancestors for many generations. Pierre Mondeau, now an old man, stood at the threshold of his home with his clay pipe in his mouth, one hand shading his eyes, no longer strong enough to face the brilliance of the rising sun. This miracle captivated his fancy ever since he was a child, and now, although an old man, he never ceased to wonder each morning at this phenomenon: the beginning of a new day.

Slowly the large, orange-colored ball peeped above the edge of the blue-gray water and began to spread its rays over the island. On this beautiful morning, Pierre stood before his home, built by himself, the clay pipe dangling from his lips, trying to stare at the surrounding body of water, the Caribbean Sea: a vicious, deceptive, secretive body of water when angry; clear, calm, and beautiful when undisturbed.

Pierre was well acquainted with the whims of this body of water for he had been born here, the offspring of an East Indian Christian maiden brought to the island from India and a white man from the south of France whose forebears had settled here over a hundred years ago.

Pierre was not yet six years old when his father died and he became heir to a large coffee and cocoa plantation, the largest in the area. He was very gruff and firm to his friends and relations, but this was only superficial, for within himself he possessed the fine and determined character of his mother, who had seen that he was properly trained to become a gentleman. He'd attended a private school and at home he'd had a tutor to teach him etiquette and to instill in him the fear of God. Pierre had been baptised and confirmed in the Roman Catholic church and grew up to be a staunch and steadfast Catholic who obeyed the laws and rules; he was one of the many fanatical religious persons in the village.

His long thin nose, thin lips, and deep-set black eyes were physical features he'd inherited from his mother. The methodical and forceful manner with which he accomplished his tasks was attributed to his paternal side. At the age of twelve he'd showed signs of becoming a strong and virile man, and as he grew to manhood, no one in the village could ever boast of having defeated him at any sort of personal combat. One, he swam almost six miles to shore when a schooner on which he was a passenger overturned in a storm. There were many times when he'd wandered too far out to sea in a canoe, dreaming of what lay beyond those waters so beckoning and challenging.

He emptied his pipe against his wooden leg and once again the memory of a certain trip to South America haunted him. It was here on the wooden steps of his house that he made plans for the day, and seldom did his plans go awry, for he was a man of grim determination. Here he would review and pass judgment on any kinsmen or foe who dared to cross his path.

It was from here, many years ago, that he'd decided to go to South America. It was in Cayenne that he'd found gold. He'd also found a curse, and he'd brought both back to Veille Case. He had become the benefactor of the village. He'd purchased and paid for the installation of the organ that replaced the old one in his beloved church. He remembered the doctors whose services had been paid for by him, who'd travelled on horseback from the far town of Portsmouth to administer to those who became ill when chicken yaws developed in the village.

As he looked at his wooden leg, he closed his eyes and saw a beautiful girl in Cayenne. She had come there from France with her mother to settle the estate of her father who had passed away. There wasn't any one thing that he could think of that was responsible for what had happened. He remembered that they were on a beach not far from where he lived. When he had realised that he was being seduced by a girl of seventeen, goaded on by her mother who knew that he was a wealthy man, he'd refused to marry the girl, though he'd promised to support his offspring if there was one. The girl's mother cursed him and had sworn vengeance for his having wronged her daughter. The child the girl had borne was beautiful.

Finally, Pierre had left Cayenne and returned to Dominica. He remembered the day he boarded the boat and again the curse the girl's mother had put on his descendents. He'd become concerned a few months later when a dark spot appeared on his leg and continued to grow larger. He remembered how the doctors he'd visited had expressed amazement and advised him to visit the island of Barbados for additional examinations.

Another picture crossed his mind: over forty years before, Maribelle, the girl who later became his wife, bathing unashamed and nude in the river. She had long black hair that covered her large hips, and as she tried to hide her virginal innocence, he'd decided to make her his wife. Later, however, he found it was not so easy a thing to do. Her parents were East Indians, who had settled in a smaller village a few miles from his estate many years before. They still held to many of their traditions.

They'd consented after much deliberation. Pierre and

Maribelle had been wed in the Roman Catholic church at the top of the hill. Everyone within travelling distance had come to the wedding and the two-day celebration that followed.

Maribelle had given birth to seven children and paid the supreme penalty giving birth to the eighth, who succumbed along with his mother. Only four of the children had grown to maturity. Emmanuel, the eldest, had been in charge of the estate before he'd fallen from a precipice in a storm and been drowned in the ocean.

François, another son, was in poor health with an incurable disease. Paul, the youngest boy, was now a wealthy man. He'd become a provisions exporter and importer and was living in Roseau, the capital of the island.

Paul was married and was the father of a little boy, Jean, who stayed with Pierre in Ville Case.

The youngest child, and only girl, Celia, had become Paul's watchdog and the bookkeeper in his business.

Pierre remembered that the specialist in Barbados had not been able to help him. He'd been told that his leg would have to be amputated in order that he might live. He'd visited the priest and discussed the doctor's suggestion.

A few months later, during harvesttime, one of the coffee pickers, a large, middle-aged black woman, had collapsed and been brought to Pierre's home. Pierre had observed the treatment first hand: a boiling hot tub of water, saturated with leaves and berries from assorted trees and a few spoonfuls of powder added to the mixture, and the next day the woman was back picking berries as though nothing had ever happened.

Pierre had decided to find out more about this treatment by the obeah women to see if they would be able to help him. He had gone to see one of the obeah doctors in the village. After going into a long and profound trance, she'd given Pierre an impression of a woman on a dried calabash leaf. She'd handed it to him with these words, "This woman did this to you. I can't do anything for you. It's too late. You'll lose your leg, but it will make no difference; she put the curse on you and your family. If this had happened before you'd had children, perhaps I could have helped. Your seed is in them and it's too late." Pierre's leg had been amputated, and he'd continued to live.

He remembered the land he had purchased adjacent to this estate. This property, together with his half-brother's estate in Macondee, which he also shared, made him an influential man on the island. He called his land Ruleyard. He now had coffee, cocoa, lime, and bananas and had become the benefactor of all the people in the surrounding villages.

Now he was spending what he considered to be his last days on earth and was content, to a certain degree, with the way life had treated him. He had prayed many times to God to grant him time to find out what had happened to the girl in Cayenne, but if this was not to be, then he would try to make restitution so that he would find peace with God.

His grandson, Jean, was his constant companion. This boy, Paul's son, had stayed with Pierre from the time he'd started school. Pierre had also hired tutors to teach him. There was one important reason why Jean was not with Paul, his father, and Pierre dreaded to tell Jean the truth.

Pierre's fortune was enough to take care of himself, and there was enough for his children and his children's children to share after he was gone.

Pierre's only daughter, Celia, worked in her brother's office in Roseau. She was tall, slender, statuesque, and regal. Her eyes were jet black and her silky, long, black hair covered her shoulders and back and stretched almost to her hips. She was haughty, determined, and an independent young woman. She'd been asked to leave the seminary she attended as a young girl when the mother superior had tried to question her about her friendship with a boy in another school. She was supposed to have written a coquettish letter to him, and the contents were about to be read aloud in her class when she'd insulted the headmistress of the school.

After completing her education in a school on the island of Antigua, she'd returned home to assist her brother in the management of his business. She had consulted Paul three different times regarding the aspirations of young men who wanted to marry her, and he had been successful each time in thwarting the ambitions of the young swains.

Celia had other ideas, however, for there was a young man she had met in Antigua who had vowed to visit her as soon as he was able to do so.

All the important events that had occurred in Pierre's lifetime seemed to be confronting him this morning; it was as though he were mentally writing a biography of his life. He could not help but wonder how much longer he would be on this earth.

The sound of little footsteps caused him to turn around. Jean, his grandson, stood beside his wooden leg. *"Bon matin,"* the little fellow murmured.

"Bòn matin, petit fils," Pierre answered and stopped to pick up the little boy in his arms. "Let us *parlez anglais."*

Pierre continued, "Look, my fellow, see that great big ocean," pointing to the distant sea. "Well, far away on the other side there is a big, rich country where everybody makes a lot of money. They become doctors, lawyers, musicians, and a lot of other important things. How would you like to go there?"

"Avec vous?" Jean queried gleefully.

"Non. Parlez anglais. Well, maybe yes, maybe no. You see I am getting old, and perhaps I will not be with you much

longer. Soon you will be big and strong, but for now there is something I must tell you. Come, let us go down to the river."

Pierre's heart was heavy as he trudged along, with little Jean holding his hand. Besides the "clomp, clomp, clomp" of his wooden leg, there was the realization that he was about to talk to his little grandson about a very serious subject.

They reached the mouth of the river Outeau, and Pierre sat down on a rock overlooking the clear, clean water that flowed into the sea. They sat down and Pierre gazed on the pebbles and stones worn smooth by the constant flow of the water.

"Is there something you are going to tell me, Grandpa?"

Pierre just nodded as he continued to stare at the clear water below, just as he'd done so many times before when problems confronted him.

Pierre put his hand on Jean's head and Jean looked up at his grandfather. "Jean, I hope you are going to understand what I am going to tell you."

"Yes, sir," answered Jean, as he knew that his grandfather was becoming serious.

"I feel very sad this morning," Pierre began. Songs in the native patois began drifting down the river as the washwomen, their heads heavily laden with baskets of dirty clothes, began to assemble on the banks to begin their use of the river basin, nature's laundry.

Pierre pointed to the mountain that loomed far above the river. "All that land is ours now; and when I die, Jean, it'll be yours."

Jean nodded his head in acknowledgement.

"Jean, your father made a trip to America once, and when he returned he was a different man. You see he was white over there, but you, his son, are brown. He wants you to stay and grow up here because he thinks if you go to

America you will not be white. I have been there too, Jean, and if you are not white in America it is not so good. You will have to fight. But if you win, you will be respected whether you live or die fighting.

"Jean, I have asked him to send you there after you have had training and after you have grown up a little. I want you to come back here and show him that he is wrong. I have written to a schoolmaster on another island, not far from here, and he will teach you everything. When you are ready, he will send you to America. These are my plans for you."

Jean's head was lowered and as Pierre tucked him under his chin, raising his head, he saw that Jean was crying. "Why does my papa think I am not like him? Look." Jean was pointing to his arm.

Pierre said, "Here you are like him. But over there, if you are not all white, you are all black, even if you are more white than black."

"*Veni, veni,*" was heard in the distance.

"Come, Jean, Antoinette is calling us."

"Grandpa, I thought that all blood was red."

"Yes, boy." Pierre raised his head to the heavens. "But only at certain times; yes, only at certain times."

They started back to the house, but Jean was looking at the ground beneath his feet. He stooped down, picked up a handful of the dirt, and compared it to his cream-colored skin. He carried it with him into the house and put it into a small clay pipe whose stem had long been broken off. He shook his little head as though the problem was too much for him to solve.

Pierre's cook and housekeeper, Antoinette, was waiting for them to have their lunch. Pierre walked to the back of the house and motioned for Jean to follow. As they sat at the table, Antoinette walked over to Pierre, touched his forehead, and asked, "*Voulez-vous?*"

8

Jean looked at Pierre, and asked, "Grandpa, are you all right?"

Pierre put his hand to his forehead and said to Jean, "Son, go to the village and tell the doctor to come."

Jean ran out of the house. Soon the doctor was back with Jean in his buggy. After he examined Pierre, he advised Antoinette to get in touch with the family and ask them to come as soon as possible.

Pierre's condition became worse during the night. The next morning all the members of his family were gathered at his bedside. Pierre asked Celia to stay and motioned for the others to go out of the room.

"Celia, my dear," Pierre began, "I don't think that I have too much time left, but I don't want anyone to feel too badly. I have lived a long time. I have been happy, and I can thank God for the many wonderful things that have happened. If he sees fit to call me, then I am ready to meet him. There is something you must do for me; I want you to promise me one thing before I go."

"Yes, Father, I'll promise, but you're not going to die." Her eyes were full of sadness, and as the tears kept falling, she repeated, "I'll promise."

Slowly and painfully Pierre moved across the bed, reached into a drawer, and pulled out a book. As he turned the pages, a picture dropped on the bed. It was not a photograph, but a crude etching-like sketch of someone who resembled a young girl. He looked at it for a moment, then handed it to Celia.

Celia stared at it, then looked at her father. Her blank, amazed expression caused Pierre to reach out for her face. He whispered softly as he pointed at the girl. "She may be the mother of my child, someone who could be your sister or brother, somewhere in South America. I met her when I visited Cayenne, a long time ago."

Celia kept staring at her father as he confessed to a secret chapter in his life. "The mother put a curse on me and my family when I would not marry her daughter. I want to do what's right. If she did have a child, I want to make amends. If you ever *do* go to America, please try to find her. She might have gone there. Do everything possible for her if you find her. Tell her who you are and try to find out what happened to the child, if she had one."

Pierre seemed to be getting weaker and Celia was anxious to call the other members of the family in. But Pierre kept talking, and she listened. "Take care of Jean; take good care of him. Someday he will be a great man, but he will have trouble, lots of trouble. I know *all* the Mondeaus are doomed. I have a feeling that someone in the family will beat the curse. I hope it will be Jean. Give him a good education, the best, and you'll never regret it. I know he'll come back here to take possession of all his property and maybe to rest his bones with us."

Celia wept and understood what her father meant.

All good things, all good deeds, all good men, and all our needs must end, and so God called Pierre and he answered willingly.

Death—so sure, so cold, so stark, so bold, so tragic—always a grim reminder of the end of existence on earth. Greed, selfishness, lust, contempt, all precursors of that never-failing message, a penalty which we all know we must pay. To some it comes quietly, to others quickly, to some calmly, to others violently.

When a man reaches eighty, death becomes an expectation, a relief from further worries of this world. A quiet, peaceful death is a wondrous thing. At sixty, death is a trademark registered permanently on the thinking brain. At forty, a catastrophe, a sudden halt in the prime of life. Before forty, an accident, or the result of the willful misuse of one's body to insure quick satisfaction characterizing man's failure or cowardice.

To Pierre, death came quietly at the age of sixty-one. He passed away with a smile on his face, his children standing over him, confident he was going to heaven. They all remembered his last words, "Don't feel sad, my children. None of you will ever live to be my age, but God bless you"; and to Jean's father, "Don't go back on your word." Paul knew what Pierre meant, Jean knew also. He was to go to Antigua to be educated.

The day of the mourning arrived. It was raining. The landowners, laborers, and their families from the surrounding estates and those of other parts of the island, from Portsmouth and Roseau, came to pay their respects. All eyes were moist when they saw and left the remains of Pierre Mondeau. His once powerful body, now cold, lifeless, and serene, was bedecked on all sides by gathered flowers, homemade wreaths that came from his dearest friends and most obscure acquaintances. Far into the night the people came to glimpse his remains and to partake in the wake that followed.

In the early hours of the next day, preparations were under way for Pierre's burial. Chimes, weird, sad, and somewhat ominous, tolled from the belfry of the Catholic church that Pierre had attended and where he'd played the organ he had given to the church. From the time the procession left the house in which Pierre had dwelt, the strains of hymns were heard over the village and continued until the body was laid to rest in the cemetery.

As the procession entered the church, the low, moaning chords of the organ began to mourn, and the weeping of those already in the church was indeed solemn. The church itself appeared to be weeping, for it was Holy Week and in

11

the annals of the Catholic church it was the saddest time of the year. The stations of the cross, symbolic of the last journey of Jesus Christ to his crucifixion, were draped in black. All images signifying any glorified or joyful event were in mourning for Holy Week was not a time for rejoicing.

Lit candles stabbed and flickered at the ceiling. From the uppermost stained glass windows high on the wall facing the east, bars of gray light made geometric patterns as the dust twirled and turned and stopped at the boundaries of light, which flickered and found their way towards the windows. Looking down on all the proceedings was the image of the Blessed Mother of our Lord, with the infant Jesus in her arms, as though beseeching all to remember the life of one who lived and had died. A great man in their village.

When the coffin was put down at the foot of the altar and the pallbearers had taken their seats, a soft, shrill, tender female voice suddenly stabbed piercingly through the silence with "Dies Irae, Dies Illae."

A little boy walked slowly up the aisle as an uncanny quiet settled in the church. All eyes followed Jean as he genuflected, made the sign of the cross, and took his seat directly behind the coffin that bore the remains of his grandfather. The funeral services were under way, and soon the procession to the cemetery would take place.

Nature, the almighty God, was weeping also, for the rain kept plummeting down on the sea of umbrellas that covered the heads of the people in the procession. The hearse, a black carriage drawn by six black horses, each covered with black net, trundled and squeaked along the wet gravel and mud in a sloppy but determined fashion. From the church the procession inched slowly up the road, the road Pierre had roamed and knew and lived and loved as he grew up to be a man.

The house from which his body had been taken was now closed. The shutters were barred and the breadfruit tree, whose large branches hung as a canopy over the top of the house, seemed to tremble and shake as the hearse passed. Gusts of wind blew through the leaves and branches, sending a showery blessing of water onto the procession, as though beckoning to the call of the man who had once lived among them.

Two distinguished mourners paid homage that day. Jean's dog bolted from the procession and sat down on the steps of the house. Jean ran after him and brought him back, after much tugging and coaxing. The incessant rain continued to pour down on the people, and the mud underneath made it very difficult for the older people to follow.

The white gates of the cemetery finally loomed before them and the body of Pierre Mondeau would soon go to its final resting place.

The rain stopped suddenly. Pierre was buried as the sun burst through the clouds, sending a glistening sheen upon the wet trees and the ground below. It was as though God was well pleased and was happy to see another soul enter his kingdom.

When Jean passed his grandfather's house, he decided to go down to the river. It was now a swollen torrent, and Jean stayed on the bank and began to cry. He sat down on a wet rock, reached down and squeezed between his fingers a handful of the soft and slippery mud; then he washed his hands in the fast moving water.

Chapter Two

James Turner, a native of Antigua, another of the West Indian islands that lie south of Dominica, was a salesman, employed by a large Canadian firm. He was visiting Dominica on one of his frequent trips.

Celia Mondeau had met James in Antigua at one of the weekly concerts in the public square. James's stay in Roseau had been longer than he'd intended for he had decided to spend more time with Celia. It had taken him quite a while to ask Celia if he could visit her the next time he came to Dominica, for he realized that somehow she was different than he.

James's father was a white man but his mother was a black woman, a descendant from slaves who'd been brought to the island over one hundred years before.

In the West Indies, when an illegitimate child was sired by a white man, the child was usually neglected or disowned and the mother had to take whatever the father decided was right for the child. In the case of James Turner's father, he'd decided that he would see to it that James was educated and brought up as a respectable man since he had no other children. James, therefore, had been educated in the best schools and he'd become a knowledgeable young man.

Celia's brother frowned upon Celia's admiration for James since James was a coloured man. Celia did not share her brother's prejudice. She had argued with him more than

14

once regarding James; finally, she told her brother that she was in love with him.

James had heard and had read a lot about America. He decided to ask Celia to marry him and go to America. He had saved a few hundred pounds and felt that he could stay in Antigua at least another year before leaving for the United States.

James and Celia were strolling in the park one night before he was scheduled to sail back to Antigua when a policeman told them that the barometer was falling and that a storm was expected; everyone was being ordered to go home.

"Come on, Jim. Let's go home. This is one of the reasons why I want to get away. Oh, I have seen storms since I've been a little girl, but the one last year was terrible."

"You know, dear," James said, "there are storms all over these islands; perhaps this one won't be too bad."

The moon, which had been shining so beautifully, was now completely hidden, and thick heavy black clouds were rolling in almost over the rooftops. James and Celia began to run. They reached the small boardinghouse where James was staying; once inside, they felt safer. The realization that this was the first time that Celia had been in James's rooms made her feel a bit awkward, but the thunderous, pounding rain outside occupied her mind more than her environment.

All at once the house shook, not violently, but strong enough to cause Celia to fall to her knees and begin to pray. James came close to her; then a second tremor made her embrace him. James held her close to him as the storm raged outside. Celia looked into the eager eyes of James, "Oh, please, James, take me away from all this. Oh, darling, I am so afraid."

"Dear, calm yourself." *I do hope it's not too bad,* he

15

thought silently, hoping the tremor had not hit Antigua for he was anxious about his relatives.

Torrential rains were falling. Suddenly the house shook heavily as though struck by a powerful object. Celia jumped up, ran to the window, and peered outside. She gasped in horror as she saw that a large coconut palm was resting on the side of the house. James was at her side, trying desperately to calm her. "Darling, you won't be able to go home just now. Perhaps you had better rest awhile."

She turned suddenly, stared at him, but said nothing.

"Suppose it never stops raining, dear? Listen to it; it seems to be getting worse."

"Oh dear, I am so afraid. Yes, I am so afraid of storms." Celia was also afraid of the storm inside of her.

He never let her finish, but turned her around to him and kissed her.

"James, do you know that this is the first time we have been together . . . like this I mean?"

"Yes, my darling. I do. I thought I'd better not mention it."

"Why?" she asked.

"Oh, you might have misunderstood me."

The wind was howling outside and it seemed to whistle right through the cracks. A terrific thud on the roof made Celia put her arms around his shoulders.

"It's only coconuts falling," he remarked softly as he ran his fingers through her long hair, which had now become loose and hung over her shoulders.

She raised her lips to him and he kissed her once more. The storm was really raging inside of Celia. Her calm, determined East Indian blood was fighting that of her French heritage. She began to breathe faster as James kept kissing her.

Then it happened. She pressed her body closer to him

16

and she kissed him passionately, tenderly, and whispered, *"Je vous aime, mon homme."*

"I love you too, Celia. I always have."

"Oui," was all she answered, lowering her head.

"I must go home, my darling. My brother won't know where I am. It's so dangerous being here with you alone. I love you so much."

For hours the wind howled and whistled like screaming banshees. There were only two living people who knew where Celia was during the storm.

There was much anxiety at Celia's brother's house when she did not come home after she left the office. "Diane, where could she be?" asked Paul of his wife. "Suppose she is hurt."

"No, I don't think so. Perhaps she took shelter in the church."

"If it lets up, I'll have to go to look for her."

Jean was sitting up in bed in his little room. He was not afraid because he remembered many, many storms that Grandpa and himself had been through. He had come down to Roseau after his grandfather's death, before he would go to Antigua. He had grown to like his Aunt Celia a great deal, for she was very attentive to him. That is why he was sitting up in bed worrying about her.

The rain appeared to slow up a little and James Turner decided to peep outside once more. What he saw was so terrifying that he uttered loudly, "Good gracious, God in heaven!"

Celia jumped up, "What is it, darling?"

James tried hard to avoid any display of terror, but he was unable to contain himself as he stared at the unusual phenomenon.

"Ashes! Ashes!" He found it hard to keep down his voice, "What can be happening? I'm worried."

"Darling, I was so afraid until you held me in your arms and kissed me and made love to me. No matter what happens, I don't care; no matter if I am to die, I am content. I love you and you love me."

Celia gasped suddenly, "Little Jean, I wonder if he is all right. He is so little and he's the only nephew I have. It's hard to explain to you, James, but his own parents are not too fond of him because he is brown."

A terrific bolt of lightning split the darkness, followed by a loud peal of thunder that seemed to strike the very spot on which they were standing. "James," said Celia, "I have a feeling that something has happened. We must get to the house."

"Darling, we can't go out there."

"We can try," she pleaded.

James opened the door a little. The heavens were red and the ashes were pouring out of the sky. "It looks like the world is on fire."

"James, we're not very far from the house. Come, let's see."

It was no use. The rain was falling and mixing with the ashes; it was impossible to go anywhere. They went back into the house and it seemed that everything was covered with ashes.

"Sweetheart," began Celia, "I love you and I want you to love me. I'm no longer afraid, but we may not live out this storm. We may be doomed, and I want to be in your arms if we do die. In the sight of God we could be married if you want us to be."

James walked across the room, opened the door to the cabinet, and took out a book. It was the Holy Bible.

"Here, darling, put your hand on it and I'll put my hand on yours."

Celia hesitated until James said, "I only want us to become man and wife if anything should happen."

Celia nodded approvingly.

James raised his head, lifted his eyes to God and began, "Dear God in heaven, perhaps this is our last day on earth; only you would know that. Perhaps you are ready to take us. If so, we are ready too, Lord. We love one another ever so much, and we want you to judge us as man and wife. Lord, join us together as man and wife in holy matrimony, we beseech thee."

Celia watched James endearingly as he bowed his head; she did the same.

"Darling, we can't be wrong," and he took a ring from his finger and put it on hers. They knelt down and both were silent. James put his arms around Celia, kissed her, and in the sight of God they were wed.

The storm continued uninhibited. Its force and fury was fierce, and the inhabitants could only pray to God to spare them from danger. The wind howled and whistled through every home, and the pelting rain, mixed with fruits of all kinds that had been torn loose from the trees, gave evidence of the force of the storm.

Tragedy struck the house where Jean lived with his parents. Two large coconut trees had been uprooted by the storm and fell squarely across their home, completely demolishing the room in which Paul and his wife were. They were buried under the debris and became victims of the storm.

It was the next morning when James awoke from a deep sleep. "Celia, I think the storm is over. Suppose we take a look and see what really happened."

"Oh, my darling, oh, I was dreaming . . . or was it . . . " she remarked, a little embarrassed, as she realized her dishevelled condition.

19

"Come, dear, pull yourself together," said James. "We're safe, thank God."

"Yes, I know, but I was thinking of last night and what happened."

Celia was upset. Her clothes were all creased, and her long hair bounced across her neck and shoulders as she shook her head.

James stood over her as she raised herself from a reclining position and propped her head against the right side of the bed. She watched James with earnest devotion as he walked across the room and she suddenly realized that he was the first man ever to enter her body. She wondered if in the sight of God she was *really* his wife.

"Darling," she called to him.

"Yes, dear," he answered.

"I am so happy. I'll never forget last night as long as I live. I'll always love you, dear." She beckoned for him to come to her. He did and they embraced each other longingly and meaningfully.

"Let's see about your family."

"All right," she answered willingly.

There was utter confusion everywhere. As James stepped onto what he remembered to be the street, he gasped at the sight before him. Celia tightened her hold on James as she, too, was astonished.

There was white mud, dirty mud, wet mud, everywhere. "This cannot be," James said, shaking his head. There was an uninterrupted line of vision as far as he could see. There was not a single tree left upright. The tall coconut palms were levelled.

"Darling," whispered Celia, "look at the streets, oranges, bananas, berries, and . . . oh . . . look, those are people! Oh, God, what has happened?"

After much effort they reached the River Blenheim,

which had been a large stream before the storm but now was a swollen torrent. Celia swayed so that James had to strengthen his grip on her to keep her erect.

"Please, dear," she pleaded, "I can't look at this. I want to go home."

"I want to see what has happened, dear. Please."

"All right." She peered at what was once a bridge.

The muddy water was filled with tree trunks, swollen carcasses of dead animals, and torsos of human beings, which had torn loose from the rest of their bodies by sheer force. The pink tint of the mud told the story of the blood that had been a part of these humans and animals. The stench and bloodcurdling sight again got the better of Celia. James moved her back to a spot farther away from the nauseating scene.

James really wanted to see more and so he wandered farther up the bank. He came to a small bridge that had escaped the force of the river, but looking down below, a ghastly spectacle met his eye. Arms, legs, and whole bodies were caught in a narrow inlet that seemed to defy the moving water. As more debris piled higher, James decided that he had seen enough.

He walked back to the place where he had left Celia, who was talking to a group of people, some weeping while others murmured. He learned that on the nearby island of Martinique, less than fifty miles away, a volcano had erupted and wiped out almost half of the island.

He found Celia and they started their trip back to her family.

Celia stopped less than a hundred yards from where she lived at her brother's house. She turned to James, and with her mouth wide open she began to run, pointing her finger as she did. "There," she said, "there." She kept pointing. "There was the place where our home was."

She fell limp into James's arms.

James looked over the debris. He could see nothing but an iron bed sticking out of the mud. Everything else seemed to have completely vanished.

Celia wiped her forehead. She was a bit dizzy. She began to weep when she realized what had happened. "James, this was our house. This is where I lived, and my brother and . . . oh, my God!" She began to run.

"My dear, please," James said. "Where are you going? To the church?"

"Yes, let's see if they are there."

There were many people who had taken refuge in Saint Mary's Church. James and Celia saw the priest and walked towards him.

"Oh, Celia," exclaimed Father Doreau as he recognized her, "we've been looking for you all through the night. Please come with me."

They walked towards the rectory. Little Jean was seated on one of the benches outside the door. When he spied Celia, he jumped up and ran towards her.

"Father, my brother, his wife?"

Father Doreau shook his head slowly. "They were buried under their house. Jean ran away when the house collapsed, and someone brought him here."

"Oh my God!" exclaimed Celia. "James, my brother, is dead! Oh my God! *Mon Dieu!*" she kept repeating.

The family of Pierre Mondeau had now dwindled to two persons. Celia Mondeau, the youngest and only girl, was the only direct descendant. Jean Mondeau, his grandson, the other.

No one but God knew the outcome of the South American romance.

Pierre's half brother was in charge of the estate following Pierre's death, but now at the age of seventy-seven and with no children of his own, decided to sell an interest to a South American millionaire planter. Celia and Jean were given a large sum of money. She decided to leave Dominica and go to the island of Antigua, less than fifty miles to the south.

It took Celia almost three weeks to overcome the tragedy that had enveloped her and, after much persuasion, she finally consented to become the wife of James Turner in a much more legal manner; however, she did so with the understanding that Jean would be taken with them to Antigua, as there was no one else to take care of him.

Pierre was well acquainted with the head schoolmaster of the Antigua Grammar School and had always asked Celia to see that Jean was sent to him to get the education that he knew he could achieve by going to that school if anything happened to Pierre before Jean had grown up.

James had promised to be Jean's guardian while he went to school and agreed to go to America as soon as they were able to do so.

Chapter Three

Mr. and Mrs. James Turner and little Jean boarded a schooner for the island of Antigua one Saturday afternoon. As the boat set sail Celia waved good-bye to the land of her birth, not knowing whether she would ever return. James was at her side as the tears streamed down unashamedly on her face.

Later, the three retired after beseeching God to bless them as they prepared to begin a new life in a new land away from her people and her friends. Celia felt since her immediate family had gone to see their God, she was doing the right thing.

All three awoke before dawn the next morning and little Jean begged to be taken up on deck "to see." As they entered upon the deck, the cool, soft, tropical breeze of the Caribbean Sea wafted lazily across the path of the ship. They stood at the rail of the boat gazing at the magnificent spectacle of God's handiwork above and below.

As the ship plowed onward, all three were silently pondering the outcome of their new adventure.

In James Turner's mind, a great future was in store for him. He would open a store and hoped to become an importer, and an influential and respectable citizen.

To Celia nothing really mattered very much; she would bring up Jean, and perhaps her own children, decently and respectably.

A great many things filled Jean's young mind. He would

go to school like the other boys, play cricket like all those big men he had seen in Roseau, and, when he became a big man, be strong and nice like his grandfather. The picture that seemed to stay with him, however, was the one where he picked up the brown clay on the banks of the Outeau River and compared it to his own skin. He remembered his grandfather's remarks concerning his own son.

As they peered into the semi-darkness the thin veil of night began to gradually disappear. Slowly the distant horizon came into view. They stared as it became apparent that the messenger of God was soon to appear. The borders of the small clouds, which a little while ago were invisible, were now tinged with a bright-orange hue. Presently the rim of that glorious messenger peeped out and a bright ball rose slowly in all its glory. It was a spectacle, majestic in its deliverance and so strong that, at the sight of it, these three bowed their heads. For the battle that was waged between the eyes of men and those of Him was won by Him.

The day had begun, and it being Sunday, James began to pray softly, but loud enough for the others to hear and follow.

As they opened their eyes, they beheld the surface of the water below whose upheaval appeared to engulf the boat at one moment, and in the next to be tossing it into the Heavens. As the glittering, bejewelled spots struck the crest of the waves, they in turn folded over gradually to permit new ones to catch a glimpse of their master and maker.

After having thanked God for his blessing in allowing them to witness the beginning of another day, they walked to the other side of the ship. Straight before them was a triangular piece of land that seemed no larger than a crude hut.

"What's that, Mr. James?" inquired Jean, pointing to the land before them.

"That's where we are going, Jean; that's going to be our home," replied James.

"It really looks small," said Jean.

"Everything looks small from a distance, boy, everything."

They all returned to the other side of the ship and stared at the direction from which they had come.

The island of Antigua was settled by Englishmen and it remained an English-speaking island after many wars with the French.

The present harbor is St. John's, but for many, many years the harbor was English Harbor, about five miles on the other side of the island.

English Harbor was more suitable to accommodate the larger boats but, during the war between the French and the English Lord Nelson, the admiral in charge of the British navy, Nelson ordered a large chain to be put across the bay that prohibited the entrance of large ships into the harbor and to this day the chain still remains.

St. John's became the capital. The entrance to the harbor was very shallow because of a reef that extended from "Goat's Island" to "Rat Island." Large steamers, however, were anchored well beyond the reef and passengers were brought to shore in a launch to the embarkation point or "jetty."

The fort of St. James, at the top of which precautions were taken to protect the island's harbor in the past, was now being used as a picnic ground and the sandy beach surrounding the fort was an enchanting place for bathing.

St. John's was the seat of learning in the Lesser Antilles and the famous Grammar School for boys and high school for girls were proud of their achievements. The Mico was the basic institution for less privileged girls. Mr. Stevens's school, a large public school for boys, was the counterpart of The Mico.

Students who showed unusual ability in their studies were given scholarships that enabled them to continue their studies in the Grammar School or the Girls' High School, which were institutions of higher quality than the public school.

There were quite a number of private schools where the "cane" and "lash" were used often and effectively by the schoolmasters and schoolmistresses, who saw that a student really came to school to learn and not to become a waste of their parents' money. The Grammar School belied its name, as it was the equivalent of a junior college; it produced sportsmen and other professionals of the highest calibre.

Antigua was dependent on the sugarcane industry for its chief means of revenue. The sugarcane plantations were owned by Englishmen who resided in England. They made it their business to visit their estates at least once a year. These estates were managed by coloured men who lived in very large houses on the estate. They had many servants to wait on them and their families. The manager or "overseer" could be easily recognized as he rode on a white horse patrolling the estate. He was attired in white clothes, leggings, and a white helmet, which gave him the appearance of Lord of the Manor.

There were cases, however, where the overseer added additional revenue to his coffers by transferring provisions such as potatoes, sugar, and vegetables to certain merchants in the cities at little or no cost in return for other supplies furnished by the storekeeper, tailor, or other merchant.

On Saturday nights, hucksters travelled many miles to

sell their wares and purchase supplies to take back to their homes, which were little more than huts.

The Protestant Church, or Anglican as it was sometimes called, was the predominant church here in contrast to that of Dominica, which was Catholic.

The Church of England, as it was also called, was a magnificent structure built on high ground, which was situated at the top of the city. It was surrounded by giant date palms and shrubberies of every variety that bordered the cobblestone paths leading up to the four entrances of the church.

After climbing the many steps that led to the southern entrance of the cathedral, one was able to look over most of the city. The large clock in the belfry, which tolled the time at fifteen minute intervals, could be heard over the entire city.

The Archdeacon of this church was the headmaster of the Antigua Grammar School and he demanded that all the Protestant students of the school attend the church services every Sunday.

The Roman Catholic Church, on East Street, was only a short distance from the Anglican Church, and while its congregation numbered much less than that of the Protestant Church, they were more affluent and represented the people of a somewhat higher social scale. The library in the rectory of the Catholic Church was the city's best.

Other churches on Antigua were the Seventh Day Adventist, the Moravian, which housed a seminary for girls, and the Salvation Army.

On Saturday nights the city became alive. Hucksters, shoppers, and vendors of every description concentrated in the market at the waterfront, and many people went walking to the public market either to sell their wares or to purchase necessities.

Others walked towards the jetty, the main landing place for small boats and launches from the big steamers anchored outside the shallow harbor.

The Christmas holidays were somewhat like a barometer that registered the mirth and happiness of the populace. Great masquerades, drills, and dances, with early morning serenades by fife and pipe bands, were great attractions. Crimes in the city were an exception.

A man and a woman of different breeding, traits, customs, habits, and faiths must be well educated and very strong in their beliefs in order to understand their feelings for each other and to be able to love one another forever.

Both attack problems with a different approach and encounter impediments that seem insurmountable but are handled by each in their own individual manner.

Celia was a determined woman. She was young, educated, independent, and religious; a true Catholic, the offspring of a Caucasian and an East Indian.

James was a man who was self-made. He worked hard to achieve his goal. He believed in the freedom of man, but not of women. He was a descendant of a white man and a black woman, an offspring born out of wedlock, as has happened many times in the West Indies.

After a year in Antigua, James had become a big man. He was a merchant; he owned three provision stores. He purchased the first large automobile on the island. It was a Crow El Khart, imported from England.

He played on the island's cricket team, and played billiards with the wealthy Portuguese in a private club. He was invited to the Governor's mansion for certain receptions and was considered to be an important Antiguan.

To be an important Antiguan, however, also meant that he partook in the West Indian custom of having more than one escapade with women other than his wife. Some well-to-do West Indian men had to prove their virility by siring a string of bastards.

Two years had gone by before Celia realized that she had become a victim of this custom.

There was evidence of a rumor that James had sired a boy by one of his women customers in the living quarters behind one of the stores.

Jean had become Celia's joy and pride and she decided to bring him up as her own. There was no marital contact between James and her although for personal appearances they projected a picture of marital bliss.

Celia attended church every Sunday and Jean became an acolyte in the Catholic Church.

Celia had discussed her problems with the parish priest and he had given her advice and counsel whenever she visited him.

Jean was the acolyte at the six o'clock services three times a week and on Sundays he never missed the nine o'clock mass.

On festive occasions he was the incense carrier. He was tutored and trained by Brother McCreery for four months and he knew most of the mass in Latin before he reached the age of six.

On many moonlit evenings Celia and Jean would go for walks to the lower part of town. It was on a Saturday when they walked to the market place, which was open late on that evening. They walked past one of her husband's shops and noticed a light shining through the closed curtains.

Celia walked towards the police station to report it but was told that a policeman had already checked it and found nothing wrong. In fact, the policeman had reported that the owner of the store was there at the time.

They continued to walk towards the jetty and although

Celia was very melancholy she did not want to allow Jean to share her unhappiness.

There was a bright moon and the many sloops and schooners anchored in the harbor were silhouetted against the bright moonlit sky.

Small pin-light dots reflected in the water and a myriad of lights ran towards the shore as someone poured waste material into the water alongside an anchored sloop. Small waves licked alongside the wooden planks, which were green with wear and moss.

Jean did not say much for he sensed that Celia was not very happy.

They arrived home a little before midnight and were asleep a half-hour later.

It was three months later, a very warm night in November, when Celia and Jean went out for a walk.

"How do you like grammar school now, dear?" she asked.

"Swell, Aunt Celia."

"Here, what did I tell you about calling me Aunt?"

"Swell, Mommy, the other boys are fine, but the Archdeacon is very strict. Bobby Hale got a thrashing today just because he didn't do his homework."

"It may seem hard, dear, but you have to learn now, otherwise you won't be anything when you grow up. Remember those men we saw last Saturday pushing those big drays from the wharf?"

"Uh-huh."

"Well, they didn't learn anything when they were like you."

"Oh, I am going to be a big man, Mommy, and when I go to the United States to study some more I will be rich and take care of you." Jean continued, "Mommy, I don't like the way Daddy . . . I mean Mr. Turner, yells at you."

"Oh Jean, you don't understand, you are so little, but he isn't the same, dear. He isn't the same since he's become a big businessman."

As she spoke, her voice was sad and her heart was heavy. It didn't seem possible that James could ever really change to what he had become. As her mind wandered back she remembered the happy night when he told her that he was going to open a provision store, then about a year later he moved to a larger place and began to sell dry goods. His dynamic personality seemed to work miracles, for in a short while he had as his steady customers some of the most influential people on the neighboring islands, but he couldn't stand it. Prosperity seemed to go to his head. Celia remembered the first time he lied to her. He came home one night and, putting about three pounds in his pockets and telling her he was going to "All Saints" to help a friend, jumped on his bicycle and came back very late.

It wasn't long before Celia heard that her husband was going to "All Saints" almost every afternoon. He had hired two other men in the store. Not long afterwards he fired one of the men and hired a woman to work in the store. It was the woman who lived in "All Saints."

Celia and James had agreed when they received from the pope before they got married a special dispensation to bring up their children, if any, in the Catholic faith. Celia had one child who died in infancy and so she had brought up Jean as her own. He had made his first communion and was confirmed and now was an acolyte in the church. The past Sunday morning she had watched him from her pew as he served mass with the other altar boys and she was proud of him. She never treated him or thought of him as her nephew, but as her own son.

Jean, only nine, was a respectable boy, well liked by everybody. He was very quiet and sedate, religious and courteous, and he liked to study. In short he was a good boy. With aid of Celia, Jean mastered his French more thoroughly than his classmates and passed his examinations in French and Latin with honors. He excelled in sports also, and was elected captain of the "Third Eleven," a cricket team comprised of students between the ages of nine and thirteen.

It was during a match between the "Third Eleven" and a team from a public school one Thursday afternoon that Jean's mother came to see him play. It was only four o'clock and Jean was surprised when he went into the pavilion after being bowled out to find her there.

"Hello, Aunt Celia."

"Hello, Jean."

"You came up to see the game?" he inquired.

"Yes, but something else caused me to come up, son. Better get your clothes on. I have already spoken to the schoolmaster, he says you can go."

"Oh, something is wrong. Just a minute, I'll tell the fellows . . . "

"Come on, darling! We must hurry!"

As they stepped into the buggy and sat down, Celia nudged Jean, "Jean, I didn't tell you before, but Daddy is terribly sick and wants us to come and see him."

"Why can't he come to see us? He's stayed away for a while."

"Yes, dear, he has. But I think he is very sick and we are going. Now!"

"All right."

It was almost three hours later that they reached "All Saints".

As they entered the door of the house, strong medical odors caught their breath. Celia had steeled herself for this meeting. She hadn't seen her husband for almost three weeks, but had heard that he was very sick. Pride kept her from going to see him, but she couldn't stay away when she had received his letter asking her to come and bring Jean. Perhaps she would never see him again.

Jean led the way for his aunt. It was only one large room and they could see him lying on the bed in the far corner. He turned his head and, as he recognized Celia, his head dropped. Jean hesitated, but went on as Celia pushed him a little.

This meeting between Celia and James was like the master of a sinking ship sighting a vessel in the distance. Gone was the pretense, the boastfulness, and the "I don't care" attitude of James. A doomed man, he looked into the eyes of the woman he swore with God as his only witness to love and protect always, as he lay in another woman's house.

"Celia," he mumbled, "please come closer, I can't believe it's you. Something went wrong, dear. I'll never know, but I think somebody did this to us." Tears were pouring from his eyes as he continued. "Night after night, I lie here wondering why. Was I crazy or was it really me?

"Celia, I am going to die soon. The doctor says it won't be too long. They don't seem to know exactly what it is."

Celia uttered not a word, her quivering lips spoke for her.

"Before I go, dear, I want to beg your forgiveness, just a little. I know I've been cruel, cowardly, but I still believe I was tricked. Anyway it is too late, dear. The most important thing is this, I know you can't live here after I am gone. I know you'd be too ashamed, but here, put this in your purse." He handed Celia two letters.

"It may sound incredible but it's true . . . what I wrote in them, I mean. Under no circumstances must you let anybody know about it. If God keeps me longer than expected, I'll write to you. If he doesn't, then God bless you both."

"Go now please, before I collapse. I am a beaten man."

Celia and Jean arrived home well into the morning, and tired as Celia was, she opened the letters as soon as she struck a light to the gas lamp. She read one addressed to her:

My one and only Wife,
I loved you with all my heart, but my wildness got the best of me. I have nothing left but this. Please take it and go to America with Jean. I have written someone already. She will write you. Give Jean an education and teach him the right way and be good yourself.

J.T.

Celia counted the money in the envelope and repeated aloud, "Fourteen hundred pounds. A year ago he was worth over four thousand pounds. Good God!"

Chapter Four

The three long blasts of the steamer whistle were the signal for its departure. On board were Mrs. James Turner and Jean Mondeau, bound for the United States of America. The ship stopped at the island of St. Kitts for three hours, then at St. Croix and St. Thomas, and then, after two days without sight of land, they encountered a comparatively calm stretch of water in the midst of the ocean, the Gulf Stream.

At last the first sight of land—the land of golden opportunity where "money grew out of trees and each one could pick to his heart's content." Landing in New York with fifteen hundred dollars in one's pocket was very unusual for a West Indian before the war. Celia and Jean were admitted into the country in the custody of Mrs. Erskine, a friend of Mr. Turner.

It was the first Saturday in June that Celia and Jean went downtown with Mrs. Erskine to go shopping. The next day Celia and Jean were taken to the rectory of the Catholic church on 53rd Street after Mass to meet the parish priest. They lived on the next street in a somewhat respectable house, but their neighbors were rather vulgar, it seemed to Celia. The next day Mrs. Erskine took them to the movies. They really had a good time. Every evening they came home tired and by the fourth night they were exhausted.

Celia and Jean talked about a lot of things with Mrs. Erskine, except for one thing. Celia agreed with Jean to ask her about it that evening.

"Listen, Eva, I don't seem to see any colored people here selling in the stores or in any businesses here. They all seem to be doing menial work, well, not all of them. White men are even sweeping the streets and driving garbage wagons."

Eva looked at her slyly. "No, and you never will. I hope you two don't expect to stay in America too long. I don't think you'll like it. You see, they call it a white man's country."

"Oh, yes, but we thought we could work a little and save some money. Actually I would work while Jean is going to finish school. Where do you suggest sending him?"

"There are a lot of well known Colored colleges further south, but I think he'd be better off in Howard University in Washington, D.C. But, he'll have to graduate from high school first."

In the ensuing two weeks, Eva's husband had showed Jean around much to Jean's displeasure. He really did not like the type of people that were his friends. It was one of these nights when Jean was out with Mr. Erskine that the door bell rang, and after Eva had opened it, two men came in. Celia was sitting in the living room and as she looked toward the door she saw Eva kiss one of the men. Then she heard her voice. "Darling, come on in, but not for long. He may be back real soon."

As they entered, Celia saw that they were young, much younger than Eva, and the one whom she had kissed could have passed for her son.

"Rest your things," Eva told them, "and, oh, meet a friend of mine."

"Mrs. Turner, meet Mr. Stewart and Mr. Johnson."

Celia bowed without rising. She had been aware of a flirting stare from Mr. Stewart, but smiled rather distastefully.

"Oh say," Eva inquired, "Mr. Johnson, wouldn't you care to go for a little ride?"

"I really wouldn't mind. It's too stuffy in here." Turning to Celia he asked, "How about you, Celia?"

"Oh, no thanks, I expect my nephew home very soon and I am very tired."

Eva nodded her head disgustedly and walked towards the window. "Well, you wouldn't mind staying alone for a few minutes till they come back? I am going over to a friend's to play whist. If George comes before I get back, just say I went over to Betty's and we'll be back soon."

Celia noticed she emphasized the words "just to Betty's" as though she wanted her to say nothing more. She did not answer.

The next day Celia and Eva were talking. "And what were you saying about work? What kind of work could you do here, Celia? Perhaps you could wash dishes in a restaurant, or take care of somebody's rich child. Then again," Eva stared at her, "you could pass for Spanish but you can't speak it."

"Pass. What do you mean?"

"Oh. Well, just forget it."

That night Celia told Jean everything about what Eva had said.

"Guess she is right, dear. I think we'd better go back home," she added.

Little did she know that fate had different plans from those which she had made.

The next morning when Eva opened the mailbox there were two letters, one addressed to her and the other to Mrs. Turner. The B.W.I. stamp from Antigua told her from whence they had come, but not the whole story. She hurried back in and handed the letter to Celia. Celia opened it.

Dear Celia,
I am sitting up once again and I am taking this opportu-

nity to write to you. First of all I want to know how you are. I hope you arrived in America safely. I know you will be surprised when you read this letter for the doctors did not believe I would be alive today.

Celia, I prayed to God with all my heart to spare my life to see you once again. If only to look at you, whether you wanted me to or not. God in Heaven knows, I know and everybody knows, I have been most unkind to you. I know how much I have made you suffer. It really was not until I lay on my bed that I realized the worries I caused you. All the bad things came back to haunt me. I begged God day and night to forgive me, to let me live to prove that I really loved you and that I am really not a bad man.

Celia, I know if I was in your place what I would do, or rather what I should do, and that is to forget that I ever lived. Perhaps you even prayed for me to die. But please, Celia, I beg of you, give me another chance. I sent to Barbados for a well known doctor and he has come. With the help of God I will be up in a month and around. The doctor says I should go away as the sea air would be good for me. And so I am planning to come to America. Please, dear, even if you don't want me as a husband anymore, please give me another chance to show that I care and could be worth something to you.

In any case, please answer me and tell me the truth from your heart and soul, if I can see you only once again.

My best regards to Jean
Goodbye till I hear from you,
James

Fear, doubt, surprise, and exultation registered on Celia's face. She was unable to understand how all this was happening to her.

Eva kept looking at Celia, who appeared to be on the verge of hysteria.

Celia kept muttering, "James is well again."

"What are you going to do?" asked Eva.

"I don't know, honest I don't. I'll have to think it over."

Celia staggered to her room and threw herself across the bed.

Eva followed Celia and tried to console her but nothing she said seemed to make any difference.

Celia knew in her heart that she wanted James. She was going to be happy again.

"James is well, James is better," she kept repeating again and again.

Jean wandered into the room and Celia hugged him and told him what had happened.

"What are you going to do?" he asked.

Celia just shook her head.

Jean left the room and Celia motioned for Eva to close the door.

"I'll be all right," she said, "I'll see you later." Celia turned away and went to bed.

Chapter Five

There were five passengers on the launch that chugged the way from the jetty at the foot of Long Street. It passed the anchored schooner in the shallow water of the harbour through the bay between Rat Island and Goat Island on towards the large steamer that anchored in deep water beyond the reef at the entrance of the harbour of St. John's.

As the launch drew alongside the 15,000-ton ship and maneuvered its way to the platform at the base of the ladder down the side of the ship, a rope thrown by a member of the crew was caught by his counterpart on the launch and soon the launch was secured to the ship.

Huge jellyfish slapped and cavorted alongside the ship and other fish could be seen in the blue-green water battling this huge intruder of their natural abode.

A long loud blast from the steamer's whistle signalled its readiness to begin its voyage to another section of God's handiwork. Papers in the purser's office had to be signed after the passengers had settled in their respective cabins.

James Turner, with a reprieve from death by God for mending his evil ways, entered his cabin and closed the door behind him. He walked towards the porthole, stared through the glass at the disappearing land he knew so well.

He had memories of an earlier voyage aboard a two-masted schooner that brought him from Dominica to the island from which he was now leaving.

The similarity ended there, however, for at that time

there was his ambition for creating a new life and to trust in the Divine God to aid him in establishing a new chapter in the lives of three people. He remembered the promises he had made then, when the three were together in the early hours of that glorious day many years ago.

He was now travelling alone after a battle with the evils of the world that had almost ended disastrously.

The change in his life was prophetic as he remembered the words of the Bible: "There is more joy in heaven for one sinner doing penance than for ninety-nine just ones."

The next island on the itinerary was St. Kitts, which James had visited many times before, then to St. Thomas, St. Croix, where the ship would anchor for three days taking on sugar, and then five days on the Atlantic Ocean to the Land of Golden Opportunity—America, the United States.

Rough weather was encountered after leaving St. Croix. Passengers were not allowed on deck as the ship plowed through twenty-to-twenty-five-foot swells and many passengers became seasick.

The sun came out on the third day and many passengers took advantage of the clear, calm weather to sun themselves on the deck in comfortable deck chairs.

A passenger seated next to James was going to America to visit relatives for the third time in the last five years and they both discussed the advantages and disadvantages of the land of opportunity.

Two more days and nights of calm, cool weather, followed, then, suddenly, on the morning of the eighth day of the voyage from Antigua, a long stretch of land appeared.

James's acquaintance was on deck in the early morning and was pointing out the circles and the towers of Coney Island. The Statue of Liberty was seen in the distance and the ferryboats, tugboats, barges, and other water conveyances traveled in the harbour of New York.

Two tugboats finally guided the steamer *Parima* into its dock in Brooklyn. After the paperwork was completed, James was permitted to go to the waiting room to meet his family.

In the room was Celia, whom he had not seen for many years, and Jean, her nephew.

Slowly they came together. Hugs and tears followed, as his wife embraced him. He picked up his two bags and followed her as she led the way to the nearest subway station.

They rode to 59th Street where they changed for a Lexington Avenue local—their destination 135th Street. The uniformed doorman and the men whom he had seen from the deck of the ship as it docked were all white men and he asked Celia about this with curiosity, for all the laborers and workmen he had seen in the West Indian islands were black.

Celia reminded him that this was not the West Indies.

The three got off the train at 135th Street and, after a struggle with the two bags up the subway steps, went to their temporary living quarters in a five-story tenement house.

They were on the fifth floor.

James was disappointed at the sight of the place.

In Antigua they had lived in a large house with six rooms. In their yard were many fruit trees—pomegranate, sour-sop, guinip, banana, lime, a tall tamarind—and a small garden and a "stone heap."

They had two servants including a housekeeper, and an errand boy. Once a week Mrs. Holiday, the seamstress, came.

As he looked at the front room, he saw that it was separated by a curtain. Farther back was a kitchen with an iron coal stove. The bathroom was in the hallway. There was no hot water. There were a table and four chairs in the kitchen. In the other room was a cot, a dresser, and wardrobe.

James stared at the surroundings and realized that he was hungry and tired and decided to delay further discussions until he had eaten.

"There's a grocery store on the first floor and I'll send Jean down for something."

An hour later they were seated in the kitchen having sandwiches and coffee. After unpacking his bags James decided to rest, so all three went to bed early on James's first day in Harlem, New York.

James and Celia awoke early the next day and James voiced his suspicions that this new land was not what he had imagined and decided to wait a while before making up his mind as to the feasibility of staying in the United States.

He had brought almost 300 pounds (U.S., almost 1,500 dollars).

His wife decided to introduce him to their neighbor who, after a frank talk, told James to forget the possibility of opening a grocery store in Harlem—there were A & P, James Butler, Daniel Reeves, and no coloured ownership of any grocery store—and that if he was going to stay he'd better get a job downtown.

There were openings for porters, elevator operators, and chauffeurs and jobs for couples as butler and housekeeper in the homes of Germans and Jews in Long Island's five towns.

James listened and for the next two weeks decided to look around.

Two weeks passed and James decided to go to an employment agency on 59th street on San Juan Hill. The jobs offered to him were for a couple in Woodmere, L.I. They had to sleep in and there was a three-year-old to take care of, but they could not accommodate Jean. They turned it down.

The salary was 100 dollars per month and living quarters were included.

Their neighbors invited them to a party on Saturday night and James and Celia decided to go.

The small crowd was very noisy and James and Celia did not stay long. Celia remarked to James later that they were not her idea of respectable people.

As time usually heals disappointments, James finally accepted a job as a superintendent for a six-story, 58-apartment building in the Bronx.

He was given a five-room apartment for his family and a janitor who would take care of the dirty work and handyman duties.

Jean would be able to go to school and get an education and, with the pay of 150 dollars per month, would be able to save a few dollars.

The following year was one that James thanked God for His blessings. The owner of the building increased James's salary to 175 dollars and advised the tenants that their month's rent would be collected by James on the first of the month, which would amount to over 3,000 dollars per month.

Loneliness began to overcome James in the ensuing months and he invited over the couple with whom his wife had stayed when she came to the United States a year before. This led to weekend drinking and James began to show signs of weakness for hard liquor.

He accused his male guest of flirting with his wife and this led to a near altercation on one Saturday night, which ended James's invitations to his friend's visits.

The old bugaboo that haunted Celia in the West Indies began to show up again in New York. James began to visit the nearest bar and soon became a regular visitor.

Love and liquor did not mix and Celia realized that Jean,

growing up without a fatherly role model in the house, might become unmanageable.

Arguments in the family became regular and Celia decided that some changes had to be made. She decided to visit an employment agency and apply for a job.

The realization that Celia was on the verge of leaving him caused James to drink even more and many Saturday nights Celia did not see James until early Sunday morning.

One Saturday night James went out with one of his drinking buddies and did not show up at all. At seven A.M. Celia decided to go out and look for him. She took Jean with her and began asking questions from tenants in the apartment house. She finally decided to visit the police station and learned that a man answering James's description was taken to the hospital at four A.M.

They took her to the hospital, but it was too late. James had been fatally stabbed and all hope was gone for his recovery. He died in the hospital an hour later without recognizing her.

Chapter Six

One Sunday evening about eight o'clock, Mrs. Turner was sewing a pair of torn pantaloons. A little boy of five was in the next room. She could tell by the conspicuous silence that he was up to some mischief.

"Toddy, what are you doing?"

There was no answer.

"Toddy," she called again, laying her sewing kit on the chair and going towards the room.

"Oh!" she gasped. "When did you come in?"

"Just now," answered the man whom she addressed "and I brought a new toy for the youngster. Just watch him, he is having the time of his life."

The little boy did not even appear to notice his mother. He kept right on pushing the toy train back and forth.

"Come now, Toddy, it's time to go to bed."

"Aw, Mom. I ain't sleepy."

"Oh yes you are, my little man. You'll have plenty of time to play with that tomorrow." She reached down and lifted him from the floor. He kicked a little, pouted, and finally gave up with a "good night" to the gentleman.

"Good night, little fellow," he replied, and turning to Celia, he remarked, "I think I'll run along too. I didn't really intend on staying. I'll see you tomorrow."

"All right, Harry, but you don't have to hurry."

A half an hour later Celia was back at her sewing after putting Toddy to bed. But somehow she couldn't sew.

Memories began to filter through her mind. A review of her life seemed to be in order. She laid down her kit and walked to the mirror. She stood there staring at her face. She played with the flesh on her cheek, pushing it up, and letting it drop back to where it was. Then her fingers found their way through her hair. It was coarse, dry, almost brittle. It had suffered along with her during the past few years.

The day when James landed. How he pleaded with her to take him back. He appeared so sincere, and she was lonely. She did weaken and accepted him once more. They were happy then. They lived in contentment and peace for a time. James got a job as a superintendent of a large apartment house and Jean made their life complete. She was happy once again and life meant so much to her.

It was not long, however, before James began to find excuses for going out nights. First, one Saturday he stayed out till three in the morning. He was only going to be gone for a few minutes he had said. He was drunk when he returned home. She forgave him for she realized that he needed to go out with some of his friends.

A few nights later, however, he went out and didn't come home until daybreak. This time he smelled of perfume. She remembered the argument that ensued. Jean criticized James and he had struck Jean, who moved away after that altercation.

Celia did not know many people but she had gained the sympathy of some of the other tenants in the apartment house.

James became worse. He was finally fired from his job and Celia was forced to accept the hospitality of one of the tenants who offered her a place to stay, for she was big with child and unable to work even if she had wanted to.

James had gone out the evening before Celia was

scheduled to go to the hospital for the delivery of her child and he did not return home the day after.

Celia gave birth to a boy and when she did come home there was only Jean to look after her.

Tragedy struck the family of Celia once again. James Turner was killed in a fight with another man in a bar in Harlem the same night he had become a father.

Three weeks later Mrs. Celia Turner was to move to a furnished room with her son and her nephew and to begin a new life.

She had a few hundred dollars left after she buried James and had contemplated going back to the West Indies.

Little James Turner II was a year old when Celia finally made up her mind to stay in New York and bring up her son and nephew as good American citizens. She had become acquainted with a woman who operated an employment agency.

Celia had been in charge of her brother's business in the island of Dominica in the West Indies, but when she discussed her qualifications with Mrs. Forrest, the owner of the employment agency, she learned that there was a difference in the hiring procedures of a company in the United States as compared to one in the far-off land of Dominica.

It seemed that companies in the U.S.A. were not yet ready to give a woman of colour an office job, whether she was qualified to do the job or not.

She finally accepted a job as a chambermaid in a hotel and made arrangements for her landlady to take care of her little son while she went to work.

For two years she sweated and saved her money in order to give her son an education.

While working in the hotel she met Harry Manning. He was a butler and valet for a very wealthy man. Harry appeared to be a decent and respectable man, but Celia was hesitant before accepting any men friends in view of what had happened with her late husband.

She had confided her troubles to Harry and he seemed attentive. She finally allowed him to visit her.

He was very kind and generous to her little boy. She was very lonely and when Harry made advances to her she disregarded convention and returned his affections.

She became very fond of him but refused to marry again.

Here was a girl, brought up in the most respectable homes, reared in a decent and honorable environment, where the necessity of discussing morality was never needed. She was now living in an apartment partially paid for by a man, not caring about herself, just sacrificing herself for the benefit of her child, whom she loved more than anything on earth.

Chapter Seven

Jean Mondeau was going to school at night. He wanted to be a lawyer. The money that his grandfather had left to him was gradually diminishing and Jean realized that sooner or later he would have to get a job. He had left Celia's house because of an argument he had had with James and was staying at the YMCA. He had always kept in touch with his Aunt Celia and visited her and her son, Toddy, regularly.

A series of events in the past few years had caused Jean to doubt the philosophy of his grandfather. He had on many occasions thought back to that narrow stream in Ville Case so many years ago.

Radio was a new invention and the newspapers were full of advertisements concerning this new field. Jean was looking through the advertisements one evening when he saw the following ad:

Wanted, College men, capable, intelligent. Young men who want to learn Radio from the beginning. Many positions open to those who qualify. Apply Radio, Inc., 485 Fifth Ave., NY

Jean applied at the address but was told that they wanted "white." There were other concerns to which he applied and the best position he was offered was that of a porter. From place to place he went seeking a responsible position but was unsuccessful. Finally, he enrolled in an auto school and after almost fifty dollars for a course in driving and auto mechanics he began to learn the "automobile industry"—he thought. He finally received his driver's licence, but could not qualify as an auto mechanic.

It was during the summer that he joined an athletic club comprised of college men of his own race. They played other school teams and went through an entire season without being defeated. Jean saw the possibilities of making some money and they began challenging professional teams throughout the country. The success of the team made an impression on a wealthy man who became interested enough to invest some money in it. Jean played for a while, but later he acquired a position with a Negro law concern and abandoned active participation in order to have more time for study. He continued, however, to act as social manager and instructor and became one of the chief factors in establishing the popularity of the club.

Jean filed his application for citizenship in the United States and continued to keep in close contact with Celia.

Toddy was becoming a big boy. He liked to tinker with musical instruments. The phonograph, which his mother had bought, became sort of an idol to him. He would sit and listen to the piano solos on some of the records and would actually tap with his fingers on any object nearby, in time with the music. His mother noticed this and more than once hinted to Harry about getting a secondhand piano and letting Toddy take piano lessons.

One afternoon, when Celia returned from her shopping, Toddy was extremely fidgety.

"Toddy, what is the matter?" she asked.

"Oh, nothing." But Celia discerned in his answer an expression of disgust.

"Now come on, darling, tell Mama what is the matter?"

"Mom," he said wistfully, "I want to study piano lessons."

"Well, darling, we'll have to see what can be done about it. Don't worry, son. I was thinking about the very same thing."

"Yeah?" and he clapped his hands, for he was happy.

Later that night, Celia sat on the sofa reading the paper after she had finished supper. She was reading another chapter in a serial in the paper when a sequence of events reminded her of her own youth.

There were many times when memories of her youth flashed across her mind and, comparing it with her present life, she knew she could not continue to live this way. Of course she liked Harry, but she was afraid to marry again; however, her son was growing and she knew she could not depend on Harry to support him unless she was married to him.

True, she had worked and worked very had when Toddy was a baby, and she remembered how confining it was. How much she had to do when she did come home. Now it would be worse. Toddy would be running around the streets like the other boys in the neighborhood and she would be worried to death about him when he came home from school in the afternoons.

An unexpected knock at the door frightened her a little.

"Come in," she called out.

The door opened and Harry entered.

"Hello," they greeted one another.

"Hungry?" questioned Celia.

"Well, a little."

"Yes, I know what that means. It means you are hungry."

"Mommy," came a voice from the bedroom.

"Excuse me, Harry. What is it, Toddy?"

"Could I say hello to Mr. Manning?"

"All right. All right, come along. Harry, Toddy wants to

say good night to you." The little fellow came bounding across the floor.

"Hello there, my little man."

"Hello," came the reply.

"Please make it short, Harry. You know he'll keep you up all night, and it's time for him to go to bed."

Harry had picked him up and Toddy began to play with his tie. "Mom says I am going to get a piano."

"Well, that's fine."

"All right, Harry. Come on, young man, let's go."

"Good night, Mr. Manning."

"Good night, Toddy."

Toddy went back to bed.

Seated in the parlor again, Harry put his arms about Celia and kissed her on the cheek. Celia never turned her head.

"Why don't you marry me, darling, and let us make a home together? You know I love you an awful lot."

"You know why. I've told you so many times. I am afraid. Only today I was thinking . . . "

"Thinking what?"

"Well, er, I was thinking about going to work."

"Well," he interjected, "what sudden ambition brought this on?" He arose and walked to the door.

"Yes, I know, Harry. I realize what you have done for Toddy and myself, but I think it's best."

"But why?" he asked in a tone of despair.

"Because, Harry," she was wringing her hands, a bit confused, "oh, I don't want to marry. I don't want Toddy to become so used to you, and I want to be more independent. Do you understand what I mean?"

"No! I don't understand. I can't see why you absolutely refuse to let me take care of you and Toddy. I have no one but myself and I would gladly love to be happy with you for the rest of my life."

"Harry, maybe it would be better if you didn't bring him so many things when you come. He is getting used to it."

"But, Celia, don't you see the boy likes me and I am crazy about him?"

"That's beside the point. I just don't think you should be so fatherly to him."

"But, dear, I think he does need a father. He needs a person who can teach him things and make him learn to respect other men. Why, he'll grow up to be carefree, won't take orders from anyone. Perhaps a great indecision may wreck his whole life. Now perhaps if he had someone to guide him in the ways of the world. Oh, I don't mean just living, about knowing right and wrong, about every person or persons whom he will eventually come in contact with."

"Oh please, that makes no difference. When I met you, if you can remember, you used to ask me why I had such a worried expression and when I told you, you seemed to understand. But now you have forgotten the promise that you made to me. No, Harry, I meant what I said then and I mean what I am about to say now. I am afraid of marriage, and I never want to be married again."

"Now, now. I didn't intend to make you angry," he answered consolingly, "only mark my words, someday you'll wish he had someone to be a father to him."

He then got up and after a sharp "Good night" left.

Celia remained silent; her chin trembled and quivered and she buried her head in her hands, uncontrollable tears moistening their palms.

"Oh God," she murmured, "sometimes I wish I wasn't so determined. Perhaps I am just a darned fool."

She prepared for bed and a few minutes later lay down to sleep. Those miserable months she spent with James were stamped on her brain. "No, no," she had said, "I won't ever marry again."

Celia did get a job, in a factory, a dress factory. She was a presser. The same routine was repeated all over again as before she had met Harry. The janitress of the house had a boy of five and Celia asked her if she would take care of Toddy when he came home from school. She agreed, for the sum of three dollars a week. It was not very much; in fact, Celia considered herself very lucky and she appreciated it to no end.

Celia worked a half a day on Saturdays and was thankful for the opportunity to rest a while in the mid afternoon before doing her shopping and preparing for Sundays.

It was on one of these Saturday afternoons when Celia, coming home from the humdrum and monotony of the work in the shop, saw a small crowd in front of the house in which she lived. As she came closer, she looked from face to face, trying to grasp the substance of the murmurs from those who were standing around.

Toddy, who usually was looking out of the window at about this time, was not there. Eagerly she hastened through the front door, and then, a cold shudder overwhelmed her. A few persons were in front of the janitress's apartment. Some were on tiptoes peering over the others' heads into the open door. Celia, a bit inquisitive herself, tried to peep also. She did, then her sudden scream caused a mass of heads to turn around as she bored through them into the room. There, on the bed, lay her son.

"Mom," he wailed when he saw her.

"What is the matter?" she cried hysterically.

"Are you his mother?" inquired a man who appeared to be a doctor, for he was bandaging Toddy's knees.

"Yes, Yes. What is the matter?" she repeated.

"It's not very serious," he replied.

"What happened, darling? Tell Mommy."

"I wouldn't talk to him now," put in the doctor, "he is more frightened than anything else."

"All right, yes. But why won't somebody tell me what happened, please?" She looked at the others in the room.

"Mrs. Turner," began the janitress calmly, "he was settin' near de winder, lookin' for yer, Ah guess, when all of a sudden he jumps up an' fore Ah cud stop 'im, he made fer de door and ran on out. I thought sho' nuff 'twas you he seed, so I didn't go after 'im, but a sudden yell made me run tuh de winder and I mos' broke mah neck gettin' out de do'. Den I felt awful weak an I musta fainted. Somebody musta knowed him 'cause when I come to I was a settin' in here and the cop was a pushin' ever'body out the hall. They done brung 'im here too and I jes' was settin' dere as nervous as a needle near tuh a magnet. And," she whispered in Celia's ear, "Ah peed mah clothes."

Celia could not help but smile a little at the remark in the midst of near tragedy.

"But, I still don't see why he ran out of the house so suddenly."

"Das what surprise me too, but 'e musta seed somun he knowed." She stopped talking suddenly, snapped her fingers and excitedly blurted out, "Now I kin remember, yes'm. Mr. Manning was here afore you came in."

Celia looked around the room. She thought a while, then she said, "It's all right. I think I understand," and she walked towards the opened door.

"Is he hurt bad?" someone asked.

"No, thank God," she answered.

She walked across the hall and knocked once, and then again. There was no answer. She tried the door but it was locked. She went back to where her child lay. Toddy was

57

asleep and the doctor told her it would be best to let him lay there for a while.

She turned and went back out the door and upstairs to her apartment. As she opened the door, she faced Harry. Half dazed, half surprised, almost exhausted, she fell into his outstretched arms. He helped her to her room. As he closed the door behind them, he raised her head and kissed her. "I am so glad that he was not seriously hurt."

Two weeks later Toddy was able to walk again—there were no broken bones to be healed—the bruises had healed completely and he was good as new.

A week later he went back to school and studied diligently at night to make up for the two lost weeks because of the injury.

James "Toddy" Turner graduated from public school and entered high school in the spring of 1920. He had learned to play the piano very well; however, with a more prolonged study period confronting him, he decided to delay his music studies for about another year.

He wanted to be a doctor, and was pleased when his mother approved of this desire.

Vacation arrived and Toddy found that it was not easy to study. Having met new friends in high school, he was kept very busy socialising in the summer months.

The realisation that his mother had been working to keep him in school played upon his mind, and, having talked with other boys who were in the same predicament, he decided that he would try to get a job and to continue his studies at night.

Three days after school opened, Toddy went to the principal's office and inquired about the possibility of acquiring working papers. He was told to bring his report card the next day.

The next day Toddy wasted no time going to the principal's office with his report card.

The young lady in the office looked at it, got up from her chair, and motioned for him to follow her.

The principal was not in and she told him to have a seat.

"How old are you, Turner?"

"Almost thirteen," he answered.

"Don't you know it's impossible to get working papers at your age?" she asked. "Tell me, why do you want to leave school?"

"Well, I think I am wasting my time here. I am studying the piano and I think I should give it more attention."

"That may be true, but you don't seem to understand. It's against the law to leave school before you reach a certain age."

The principal walked past them and sat at his desk. At a nod from Miss Randolph, Toddy went to the principal's desk.

"Well, Dr. Emerick," began Miss Randolph, "what do you think of a young man with this record wanting to leave school?" She handed the principal the report card.

The principal scanned the report card, then, looking up at Toddy, said, "You will have to bring your father, young man. You are too young . . . "

Toddy interrupted him. "My father?" he said looking straight at the principal, "I am sorry, sir, but they are both dead."

The principal turned to Miss Randolph and they both cleared their throats simultaneously.

"Both?" inquired Dr. Emerick. "What do you mean?"

"My real father was killed in a fight a long time ago, and my stepfather was killed in the war."

"And your mother? Is she living?"

"Yes, sir, she is, but it won't be possible for her to come, sir. She is working on Long Island and only comes in the city every other week."

"Whom do you live with?"

"Some very nice people, sir."

"Yes, yes, I should have known you do."

Toddy squirmed a little as Dr. Emerick removed his glasses.

"Have a seat, er, Turner" said the principal, looking once more at the report card for the pupil's name.

Glancing at Miss Randolph, he nodded to her and she left the office.

"Now, my boy, even if it were possible for you to leave school, I can't see why you would want to do so."

Toddy parted his lips as if to speak and the principal raised his hand, "No, let me finish please."

"Excuse me, sir."

The telephone rang and the doctor lifted the receiver.

"Excuse me, will you, a minute. I have to run upstairs. I'll be down in a moment. Wait a few minutes, will you?"

"Yes, sir."

The principal went out of the office and Toddy was left alone. He turned his head and looked at the pictures on the wall. The bust of George Washington adorned the wall over which the principal sat. Directly in front of it was a painting by a famous artist. To the right was the founder of the school etched on white paper. Smaller pictures of graduates of the school were scattered around the room.

Toddy admired the teachings of these men. Why even his history book was written by one of the former students of this high school. "Wonder if they felt like I did when they were thirteen?" he said to himself. "No, I guess not."

He walked over to the window and looked out. A man with a lemonade and hot dog stand was doing business. He looked at the man. He was old and appeared to be badly in need of some clothes. "Wonder if he wanted . . . " The same question seemed to come to him again. There were some kids across the street running up and down the sidewalk. They were having fun. "Older people are so funny. Don't they think that a boy wants to have fun? Don't they know that we are human too? Shucks, seems like everybody is always telling me what I should do and what I shouldn't do. I am smart. I've had enough education. I want to go out and make some money, like the other fellows."

The door opened and the principal walked in. "Hello there, sorry I kept you waiting so long. Come over here and sit down."

Toddy walked back to the chair and did as the principal said.

"Now let's see where we were. Oh, yes. You wanted to leave school. As I was saying, according to your report card you are an intelligent fellow. I wish I got marks like that when I was your age. You're smarter now than I was then, yes, but I went on. I didn't quit. I was lucky enough to get ahead. You can do the same thing."

Toddy again tried to interrupt but the principal refused to be stopped.

"Now," continued Dr. Emerick, "you have passed in all your subjects, and I see no reason why you should not continue your schooling. There are many boys and girls like you that want to leave school early and somehow they wind up as failures.

"Ten years from now you will see your friends whom you went to school with in many fields of endeavor. The majority of them will be doctors, teachers, artists, lawyers, and others may represent the people in the government as congressmen, senators, or other representatives. You will begin to realize your mistake. It may be too late then. You will forever blaming yourself when you are denied jobs because you will not have the necessary education to fill the position.

"You won't know the suffering that great men had to go through because you would never have acquired the knowledge necessary to fight. You would not have had anything to fall back on when your ambition appears to be thwarted.

"Here, in high school, you get to learn a little of everything, to prepare you for a college education, and that helps you to make up your mind as to what you want to be.

"You have not had enough of anything as yet. I am going to suggest that you go home and think it over. Read some autobiographies of great men, and there are some whom you must have admired, I am sure. Come back tomorrow and I will personally bring you some books that I have at home."

Toddy's determination to leave school seemed to have vanished after he saw Dr. Emerick. He found himself admiring the doctor for being so convincing.

The following Saturday, Toddy decided to visit his mother, who was employed as a governess for a very wealthy family in one of the "Five Towns": Woodmere, Long Island.

As he gazed at the homes going by the train, he made up his mind that someday he would purchase a home for his mother.

There were many things that happened in his young life and he could not help but go back to the misfortunes that had taken place.

The death of his father when he was very small, the death of his stepfather a few years later. He wondered why his mother never talked about her life in the West Indies.

Why didn't she go back home? His grandfather had had a very large estate at one time and her brother's son Jean must be a rich man. If he could only see his cousin. Perhaps he would ask his mother if he could go to visit him.

Chapter Eight

On Toddy's fourteenth birthday he began to be cognizant of the fact that he was too dependent on his mother. The lines in her face were becoming more and more prominent. There were other times when she would hint that she would be unable to keep him in school much longer.

His friends had begun to invite him to parties and dances. He had started to go out with other boys and he found that it was impossible for him to be popular without any money. He decided to get a job. He began to trudge the avenue every day after school. He would go into drugstores, delicatessens, and luncheonettes. Finally the proprietor of a drugstore gave him a job running errands after school. He was given four dollars a week to start and to him it was a great deal of money. He was growing considerably and really looked a great deal older than he actually was.

He had also begun to acquire the friendship of girls much older than himself. One of these girls was Ginger Martindale. She was almost eighteen years old. It was during the summer vacation that he thought himself quite a man. He had definitely made up his mind to quit school and go to work for more money.

Three days after school reopened in September Toddy applied for his working papers. There was no talking him out of it this time.

He found out that it was no easy matter for a boy of fourteen to go out and find a full-time job. There was a law that stipulated that if any boy or girl left school before they had reached their sixteenth birthday, they would have to go to continuation school.

Toddy would hunt through the papers in the morning and if he did not succeed he would go to work in the drug store in the afternoons. Toddy "chased paper" all week with no success.

On Saturday morning he received an invitation to a party given by some friends of Ginger's in Mt. Vernon. He was supposed to bring her along. It was to be given a week from Sunday.

Toddy went to see his mother the next day as he had to work very late Saturday night. His mother was not feeling very well. She had been in bed for a few days due to a cold but her employers did not think it was important enough to worry Toddy about it, knowing that he would be there at the end of the week.

"But, Mom, they should have let me know that you were sick and I would've come over last night no matter how late."

"It wasn't that bad, son. Besides, they only told me not to work because they hate to hear me sniffling. I'll be all right soon."

"I hope so, Mom."

"I am invited to a party up at some friends' home in Mt. Vernon next Sunday. You have heard me speak of Ginger. Well, her folks are very nice people and her friends have invited us to a party. It's all right to go, isn't it?"

"Seems to me that you waited an awful long time to tell me about this party. I mean about the . . . er . . . niceness of your . . . er . . . young lady."

"No kidding, Mom. She is, really."

"All right, I guess she is. So I won't see you next week then?"

65

"Oh yes. I will be out on Saturday. I'll ask the man to let me off early. I'll stay all day Sunday. I mean until time for the party."

"How in the world are you going to get from here to Mt. Vernon on a Sunday?"

"Oh gee . . . I never thought about that."

"Well, I'll tell you what. Suppose I come to New York next week and then you won't have to come all the way over here."

"That would be fine, Mom, honest, but do you think they will let you off?"

"Oh, sure."

"That's swell."

"Guess I can go to bed now."

"Yes, I think you can. Good night."

"Good night, Mom."

The party at Ginger's friends' house was a terrific success. Everyone played "Post Office," "Spin the Bottle," and told jokes, and Ginger played the piano with Toddy. They ate three cakes, drank up almost ten cases of soda, and to hear the host tell it, she didn't know where the fifteen quarts of ice cream went.

Toddy met Mr. Poole and, after talking to him about his difficulty in getting a job due to his having to attend continuation school, he was given an address to go to on Monday morning.

All in all, the party was a terrific success.

Toddy received the job he learned about at the party. He became a messenger for an auditing concern on Wall Street. He was earning the stupendous sum of twelve dollars a week. He had to open mail and carry papers from one office to another in the same building and was to dress neatly at all times. It was his first real position and he was exceedingly nervous. After he was given his preliminary instruction, he was put on his own. When the buzzer for his first assignment rang he rushed to the office as fast as he could, only to find that he had gone to the wrong office.

By noon, he was more at ease and by nightfall he had conquered the more "intricate steps" as he called it. Mr. Poole called and asked how he was getting along.

When Toddy arrived home that night, he was surprised to find his mother there. She had bid him good-bye in the morning and she had planned to go back to Woodmere. She explained that she felt a wee bit worse and called up her employer, who told her to stay in the city for another day or so.

Toddy was alarmed for he saw that his mother looked ill. Her eyes were starry and she was constantly coughing.

"Don't you want me to get a doctor?"

"No, son, I'll be all right in the morning."

He did not want to go to work the next day, but his mother told him that she would be all right and that she would call him up if she felt any worse. All throughout the day he was anxious to hear from her, but when she did not call he felt better for she had said she would call only if she was worse. He lost no time in getting home, however. His mother was no better and, on the pretense of going to the drugstore, he called Doctor Nichols, the family physician.

The next thirty minutes seemed like ages to him. His mother became very hot and Toddy actually forced her to go to bed.

The door bell rang and Toddy rushed to open it. Mrs. Turner was very much surprised to see the doctor.

After examining his mother, the doctor told Toddy, "It's a lucky thing that you did call, my boy. Your mother has pneumonia. She has to go to the hospital right away."

Toddy looked at the doctor in blank amazement. The words that he was saying did not make sense. Slowly, it dawned on him that the doctor had said his mother had pneumonia. He had said she would have to go to the hospital right away.

"Hurry, son," the doctor was saying, "go downstairs and find a policeman and tell him. He'll know what to do."

Toddy obeyed hesitantly. All this was so sudden to him. He had never thought of this happening to him, to his mother. "What is happening?" he asked himself as he reached the street.

"Did you find one, son?" asked the Doctor on Toddy's return from the street.

"Yes, sir. He said he'll be right up."

He went to the bedside of his mother. She tried to speak, but the doctor persuaded her not to. He kept looking at his watch and Toddy knew by his expression that his mother was really ill and needed immediate attention.

Toddy turned to his mother. "It's all right, Mom; it will be better you know. You'll have all the nurses to look after you."

"But who'll look after you, Toddy?"

"Oh," he turned to the doctor, his eyes watery, but with a forced smile on his face, "look, Doctor, she's worrying about me and she's the one that's sick."

The doctor shook his head in approval.

They both knew that these were not the words he wanted to say. He really wanted to throw himself across the bed and dare anyone to remove his mother to any hospital. But he was fighting hard to remain calm.

The clanging of an ambulance bell outside took away his courage, however. He felt himself slipping, that lump in his throat; he was on the verge of bursting. He jumped up, ran to the door, and opened it.

Thirty minutes later Toddy's mother was in the hospital.

Toddy stood beside her. The nurse told him he couldn't stay any longer and he left and went home.

As he opened the door, a sickening feeling overcame him. *Perhaps it was the emptiness of the place*, he thought to himself. No, it wasn't that. He had been alone before and he didn't feel the same way. It was something else, some unexplainable feeling, different. He walked slowly to the room that she had left. He felt very weak as he entered it. He came out and went to his room, threw his hat on the chair, looked in the small mirror that hung on the wall, and said, "Suppose . . . oh, no, no, no, no! no! no!" he kept repeating and shaking his head. The tempest broke. The torrent of tears that he had fought so hard to keep from falling before poured down his face.

The lump in his throat was not there anymore and he was crying loudly and unafraid as to who might hear him. He threw himself across the bed.

Gloom, loneliness, and fear seemed to be all about him. "Suppose . . . ?" He kept the thought out of his mind. But somehow it always returned. He had never thought of his mother being this sick. He couldn't imagine her dying before he grew to be a man. He had already lost all those others before her.

"No, no." He was actually afraid.

"Oh God, please let her get better," he prayed.

He then really knew how it felt to carry a man's burden. He had no one to turn to but his cousin Jean and he would not have been able to get here before the next day. He would have to send him a telegram right away.

It was three in the morning when sleep finally came to Toddy.

A loud whistle from some nearby factory awakened him. He jumped up and looked at the clock. Swiftly the events of the night before crept back and he hastened to get his clothes on. The drug store on the corner was open all night and he could telephone from there.

"The patient's condition is serious, but not worse," he was told.

"Thank you very much," he replied and went back to his home.

After washing up and making up his bed, which had not been ruffled much, he again went out. This time to get to work.

There was a commotion in the street as he turned the corner. A lot of people were running to what seemed like a fight. Toddy also ran. A policeman was also on the run and when Toddy saw him reach for his pistol, he slowed up. The crowd had divided and from where he stood he could see one of the men lunge at the policeman with a knife in his hand. The crowd took to their heels as the policeman levelled at the man and blazed away. The man spat blood from his mouth as the bullet must have landed in his throat. He went sprawling on his face with a splashing, sickening thud. The policeman then slammed the other fighter across the face. The second man was unarmed.

A woman in the crowd screamed and fell over the body of the man whom the officer had sent to either God or the devil.

By this time, several other policemen had arrived and Toddy was close enough to hear the first officer at the scene remark, "I think he's gone, Joe."

"Yeah, the crazy fool . . . " answered another officer.

The officer turned him over and as Toddy beheld the face he let out a gasp that caused the nearest person to him to inquire if he knew the man.

"I have seen his face somewhere," replied Toddy, not even knowing who had asked the question.

"Dat's Jarge Jahnson," remarked an old man standing nearby, "It's Eva's ole bwoy fren' down in nummer terty."

Toddy knew at once this was West Indian speech.

Then Toddy remembered. That picture on his dresser with his father. He was the man his mother always told him was responsible for the death of his father. His mother had showed him the picture. Those were the people with whom Jean and she had lived when they came to America, many years ago.

Toddy arrived at his job at ten minutes after eight. After telling the boss the reason for his lateness, he went across the street and ate some breakfast.

From the moment he returned, everything seemed to go wrong. First the letter opener could not be found; he had to run upstairs to get another. On his way down he tripped on the stairs. He seemed to forget what was told to him. Every time the phone rang, he became panicky.

He was on the third floor at eleven o'clock, when he heard his name called. The ten steps on a landing were made in almost one jump. It was the telephone girl who was calling him.

"For me?" he asked.

"Take it in there," she said, pointing to the reception room.

"Oh . . . thank you."

Consternation gripped him as he picked up the receiver.

"Yes?" he answered, almost in a whisper. His voice trembled a little. "Oh, all right. I will try to be there as soon as I can."

"Please, ma'am," he told the telephone girl, "it's from the hospital. My mother is worse and I've got to go to the hospital. Will you tell the boss for me, please?"

"All right," she answered.

That ride on the subway was the longest that Toddy ever took. He was at her beside in three quarters of an hour. There was his mother, yes, but what a change. Her once full jaws that clearly showed her Indian heritage were now almost sunken. There was little flesh on her face. Overnight she had aged more than ten years.

The flesh that once rounded her cheeks was now sunken. Her soft, alluring eyes were now protruding glassily. She was lying there on the bed dressed in a white gown. The nurse led him closer to the bed. His mother now stared at him. As he returned her look he could not imagine that a person could change so much in such a short time. Only the night before she had been looking as fine as ever. Now, as she continued to look at him, the thought that came to him that night again crossed his mind.

She tried to raise her head. "Toddy," she whispered, "my son."

"Oh Mom," he said consolingly, "what is the matter?" He could not control the tears that tumbled down his cheeks.

"My son," she answered, "I don't want you to cry. Please. I really think I am going to leave you, Toddy."

He tried his best to stop crying, but found it impossible. He really felt like screaming out loud.

"Toddy," she went on, "I am going away and there is something I want to tell you. You remember when you were a little boy and one day you came running into the house, and you saw me writing and asked me what I was doing?"

"Yes, Mother, I do remember."

"Well, when you go home I want you to look under the last picture in the top drawer of my table, you know, my sewing table, and you'll see a large envelope there. Open it and read it."

"Yes, Mom, I will."

"Now, Toddy, we've spent quite a while together, haven't we?" She paused for a moment as if to catch her breath, "And now perhaps I may have to leave you.

"Somehow, Toddy, I, er, do know that you will be a good boy."

Toddy kept staring at her. She wasn't speaking like a dying woman, but a little lump in his throat kept him from saying a word. He felt that something terrible was about to happen. He had never seen anyone in this condition before, and the realisation that it was his mother lying there on the bed, helpless, had not fully dawned on him. It was happening so suddenly. Only the night before she had been at home—a little ill, yes—but what a change. He had never thought that working as she did to take care of him would make her so weak in body.

His thoughts wandered back for a moment. He saw his mother four, five, ten years back. He remembered when Mr. Manning used to put him on his knees. He remembered how he had to break up wood on the sidewalk in the winter to make heat for the little flat that they had once lived in. He also remembered the scoldings he had received; yes, they did hurt but he could see the necessity for those whippings. She had taught him to be decent, clean, mannerly, and respectable.

He was thankful for all this, but why shouldn't she live to see the fruits of her labor? Why couldn't she stay to see him grow up to be a man, a big man? He wanted her to be so proud of him. He wanted to show his gratitude and here she was deathly sick before his very eyes.

"Mom," he cried, "please don't die! Please, Mom!" The tears were almost blinding his eyes, making her face almost indiscernible. But she lay there quite still, ever so still.

He put his right hand on her forehead, his head shaking from incessant sobbing. His fingers rested on her cheek. He bent over and kissed her but there was no life to her lips. Her face was set in a stoic smile. Toddy knelt down, prayed aloud, laid her hands across her breast, and then in an uncontrollable fit of sorrow, he screamed. A nurse who was not very far away came running. She looked at the bed, put her hand on Toddy's shoulder, and led him away. Peering over his shoulder as he walked away slowly, he saw another nurse open a screen and place it around the bed. Then he realized what had happened. He couldn't believe it but it had happened. His mother was gone and he was alone, all alone. All he could think was *Why? Why? Why? Why did Mom have to go now?*

This world as we know it is one of variety. Sadness and joy are in full view of each other. As Toddy passed another bed, he saw a large bouquet of roses adorning another patient's bed. There were two people seated, laughing, happy. This patient was going to be well.

Outside, there were people standing in the streets; men and women, children, and even dogs lined the sidewalks. Music was in the air. A parade was in progress but Toddy pushed through the crowd silently, sadly, and walked home.

There was nothing but emptiness all around him. He wanted nothing better than to take care of his mother for as long as she lived. Now she was gone; what would he do?

Of course, Jean would be coming to New York to take charge of the arrangements for the funeral and Toddy would discuss his future in America. He knew that Jean would want him to come and live with him.

There was one more thing to be taken care of, the letter. He found it in the place his mother had said. He opened it and read:

A letter to my son. Dear son, this picture was given to

74

me by your grandfather many years ago. It's a picture of a girl he met years ago in South America.

You remember the story I told you once of the "Obeah" woman in Dominica and of the man who went to Cayenne and how he found out later that he was a father. That man was my father, and he made me promise on his death bed to try and find his daughter.

It makes no difference what you think, she is still your aunt, my sister. If you ever do meet her, remember, she is your mother's sister.

Chapter Nine

Four years later James Turner was employed as a soda clerk in a drugstore. He did not stay at his position as errand boy on Wall Street more than three months after his mother's death. The firm had merged with another company and they had let him go. He was living in a furnished room, for which he paid four dollars a week.

Toddy's cousin had wanted him to come and live with him after his mother's death and he did stay with him for about two years, but he wanted to be on his own. He decided to get a job for himself back in New York. His cousin knew the people and the four dollars that he paid included one meal, his supper. He worked long hours and his salary was eighteen dollars a week. He had returned to night school about a year earlier, but had had to curtail one subject due to his inability to get to school before seven fifteen. For this reason he had decided to look for a better position in order to take the maximum amount of subjects that he could.

It was Sunday and the rest of the people in the apartment had gone to church. Toddy did not go, but stayed at home to do his homework. On Saturday night he attended music school.

After he had finished his homework he looked through the wanted columns. The following advertisement attracted his attention: "Young man to work in shipping department of wholesale drapery firm.

"Salary to start, eighteen dollars a week." The advertisement included an address.

"It doesn't say white or coloured," he commented aloud.

He wrote an answer to the ad, and went out to mail the letter.

The following Tuesday, on his return from work, he found a letter on his dresser.

Please call at our office on Wednesday or Thursday morning regarding your answer to our Ad in the paper of last Sunday.

He went back into the street and called up the drugstore. He told them he would not be able to come to work the next day. He was told if he couldn't come in, not to worry about coming in anymore. Toddy thanked them and decided to gamble on his getting the job downtown.

Toddy arrived downtown the next morning at a quarter of nine. The elevator man told him that the firm did not open until nine. He waited in the lobby of the building and in a few minutes the elevator operator beckoned to him that the firm had opened. He went upstairs and met a rather gruff-looking individual who told him that he would have to wait for Mr. Dyer.

"Thank you very much," said Toddy.

"I am the manager," the man said, "Mr. Drake is my name. If you happen to get the position, er, that's what you want to see the boss about, isn't it?"

"Yes, sir," replied Toddy.

"Well, as I was saying, if you get the position, I will be your boss."

Toddy did not know whether he was in luck meeting the boss before seeing the manager, but he decided to find out what the boss thought of him.

"Do you know anything about shipping?" the man asked.

Toddy decided to make a favorable impression. "Well, not exactly," he answered. They were inside the office and Toddy, seeing the mail, stooped and picked it up. "But, I can learn very quickly. I am sure you'll be satisfied with me if I get the position," he continued.

"You seem to be all right. Anyway, wait here."

The door behind him opened almost immediately and in walked a distinguished-looking individual who Toddy surmised at once was the boss.

"Good morning."

"Morning," the man answered. "Oh, yes, you are Turner, I suppose."

"Yes, sir."

"Come in."

Toddy followed him into the office.

The interview lasted about fifteen minutes and Toddy walked out of the building smiling. He got the job. He had to start the next day.

Within one week Toddy liked his job very much. He always left the house at a quarter of eight every morning and carried his briefcase with him. He usually sat in the last car of the train to summarize his homework, and, with the half hour of his lunch period that he utilized for more study, he was well prepared for school every evening.

Toddy rested on the cold iron of the fire escape during his lunch hour and the surrounding quiet caused him on many a day to contemplate his future. It was on one of these days, while studying a passage in his Latin book, that he came across a section that dealt with brotherly love.

Suddenly he wished he had a brother. Memories came to haunt him as always when he was alone. His mind wandered back to his early days in school. He remembered the many sleepless nights after his mother's death. One thing that he was thankful for was that his cousin had taken charge of her funeral and had deposited the balance of her insurance money, three hundred dollars, in the bank.

Looking at his watch he saw that he had overstayed his time by five minutes. He went back to work.

Toddy began to feel lonely. True, he had met some very nice boys in school, but he realized that he would not be able to go out with them. Up to that time, he had declined any invitations to go to parties with them; however, the monotony of his duties had begun to irk him, so when a schoolmate, Thomas Johnstone, asked him to go to the Savoy that Saturday night, he told him he would let him know before he went home.

By the time school was over, Toddy had decided not to go.

"Oh, come on, man. Buck up, don't you ever go any-where? Good heavens, you are a young fellow. What's the matter? Come on, you will have a nice time." Thomas finally convinced him to go.

He looked fine in his new suit, shirt, and tie on that Saturday night. He rode up on the Seventh Avenue bus to 140th Street and walked east to Lenox Avenue. As he reached the corner, he looked at his watch. It was eleven o'clock. Two girls passed him, turned, and looked back at him. Toddy thought he caught the words "student prince."

Toddy looked up the avenue. The big sign two blocks away blinked "Cotton Club." To his left, up one flight, was the world famous chop suey rendevous. Strains of music struck his ear and whistling gaily he crossed the avenue.

At the entrance of the Savoy, he stood, hesitant. Thomas had promised to meet him there. He waited about ten minutes, then began to grow impatient. The music from the

Savoy became clearer and Toddy found himself tapping his foot to the tempo.

Surveying the crowds going in he began to scrutinize them. Pretty girls with their escorts, and some girls not so pretty passed him. Young "sheiks" with their coats belted high in the back passed. A young white girl alit from a cab alone. A hatless, very dark young man with his hair plastered to his head joined the line at the window. Taxis kept emptying their fares and the doorman appeared to be doing a rushing business. The low moaning of the saxophone caused Toddy's face to break into a smile. He reached into his pocket and took out a coin. "Heads I go in, tails I don't." He looked at the coin. It was heads.

A few minutes later Toddy stood at the rail upstairs that surrounded the dance floor. The place was not as crowded as he had expected and he was glad.

It was the end of a number and many of the dancers were leaving the floor. Toddy felt rather awkward for he did not know the latest steps. He really did not care. He had no intention of asking any young, frivolous-looking girl to dance.

One hour passed and Toddy thought he saw a girl dancing in a manner that he admired. She had been on the floor for the past three numbers and each time with a different partner. She did not seem to be in any particular group, nor did she seem to have any escort. The peculiarity of it all was that neither she nor her partners seemed to dance to suit each other.

Her partners, it seemed, wanted to get off in a big way and this appeared to bore her very much. He also took notice that she had not danced with the same partner more than once.

Toddy decided to ask her for a dance. If she refused, he would go home.

The number was finished and as she approached the exit, he said, rather shyly, "May I have the next dance?"

She was very close to him and the sudden realization that she was a great deal prettier than she had appeared to be from a distance sent an unexplainable feeling through his body.

Her eyes were brown, and her black hair looked darker as the soft light from the wall above them shone directly on her. She was the color of the maple chair in his room. Her makeup was a bit on the heavy side.

In the seconds while he waited for her to decide, she stared at him rather searchingly and when the orchestra started to play the next number, she put her hand in his arm and he walked her onto the dance floor.

She did not utter a word. As they started to dance, he became a bit uneasy. His right hand had found her back and her right hand was clasped within his left.

He bit his lip and looked at her as she raised her head to his face. She only smiled. She was almost as tall as he was; he didn't even have to bend to look into her eyes.

The orchestra was playing a waltz, and for the first time the young lady spoke, "This is the first waltz they have played all night. Do you like to waltz?"

He nodded affirmatively and they danced. After a few steps he felt a certain amount of freedom as they moved together. It was as though they had danced together before. Her left arm, which had just touched his right shoulder, eased slowly upwards and her fingertips half circled his neck.

She nestled closer to him, so much so that her cheek touched his; neither made any effort to move away.

A surge of passion enveloped his body as they became closer and closer. Then the music stopped. Neither made a move to break away until they realized, by the giggling of nearby couples, that they were the only ones embracing each other on the floor.

They finally separated and he hesitated before saying anything, for he had not forgotten her silence when he had spoken previously. She had made no effort to leave the floor as she had done with her previous partners and evidently he was not a pest, as the others had appeared to be.

Her lips parted and she said, "Er, you waltz very well."

"And so do you," he answered smilingly, "I . . . "

She interrupted him. "I guess you must think I am a bit foolish, but sweet music does something to me. I am a sort of a dreamer and just now I seemed to be dancing on clouds."

She closed her eyes, encased her own cheeks with the palms of her hands, opened her eyes slowly, and stared at him. He returned her endearing look.

"Forgive me for staring, but you are rather a good-looking young man."

"Oh, please," was all Toddy could say.

She reached for his hand and led him off the floor. Finding a place to stand, they looked at each other once again.

"You are very beautiful. Would it be possible to know your name?"

"It certainly would be possible," she retorted, "why don't you ask me?"

He felt rather stupid at her answer and he smiled. "You are right. Now I am asking."

"Stella."

"Mine's James, James Turner."

"Jackson is my last name," she answered.

"I am very happy to know you, Stella."

"So am I, James."

The orchestra was playing again and their hands found each other. They walked to the floor and danced once more.

"You know," she began, "when you first asked me to dance, I was wondering, and at the same time hoping, that you didn't do that crazy dance. I was dancing with a couple of fellows before and they wanted to hop, skip, and jump like leap frogs. I really shouldn't tell you this."

"Why not?"

"I began to get disgusted. I was really going home. I was on my way when I saw you. Please don't think I am fresh, but I really saw you before you asked me to dance."

"You did?"

"It's true, really. I saw you standing at the rail." Her head nodded to the exact spot where he had been standing.

"Well, can you beat that?" he sighed.

She seemed perplexed. Toddy continued, "Two people with the same thought. That happens quite often but sometimes they never meet."

"You don't come up here very often?" she asked. Their eyes met once again and she whispered, "Please don't look at me like that. You go right through me."

"No," he answered, "to tell the truth, I have never been here before."

"Your first time?" she asked, surprised.

"Yes." He felt her body snuggle closer to him. "By the way, how about you?"

"What do you mean?"

"Do you come here often?"

"Well, I, er, used to. Every Saturday, but I missed the last two."

"You like it so much, here?"

"Well to tell the truth, I like dancing better than I like the place. But tell me, if you don't go out much, where did you learn to dance?"

83

"Oh, I really can't dance. I only try to do what the others do."

"Stop. That's nonsense. You're kidding me."

"No, I am not. That's the truth."

"You know, somehow I believe you. You don't look like a liar."

"Thanks."

There was a pause; then Toddy asked, "Are you alone?"

She perked up a little. "Why?" she snapped.

"Just inquisitive."

Her lips were so close to his and yet they appeared to be a mile away. It would have been so easy to kiss her, but what of her reaction? Perhaps she would slap him. It was a crowded place and no one would know that they were strangers and had met each other tonight for the first time.

The spell was broken when Stella said, "Pardon me, Mr. Turner, but I really must be going."

"Home?" He was really surprised.

She laughed.

"Why?" he stammered, "It's still early. Well, I guess it is late for a lone girl to be out by herself."

"Girl?" she answered back. "I would not have called you a boy."

"Oh, I am terribly sorry. Please forgive me."

"That isn't necessary, you see I am only going to the corner." She pointed to the far corner of the hall in the direction of the ladies' lounge.

"Oh, yes," he replied, "I was hoping that I would have a chance to talk to you a little while longer."

"Certainly," she said. "Why not? I will be glad to. Tell you what, suppose you wait for me, right there, under the light." She pointed to the light under which they had first held hands when he had asked her to dance.

So they parted. Again he was alone, only this time he was not contemplating going home just yet.

Toddy walked towards the other end of the hall and, after a few moments, he returned to the designated spot, but Stella was not there. He waited. Five minutes passed, then ten, still she was nowhere in sight. He looked on the dance floor to see if she was dancing.

"Did you give me up?" a voice whispered in his ear.

He turned around and their eyes met once again.

"No, I really didn't," he answered.

"I wouldn't lie either. It was just a little crowded."

"Would you care to have some ice cream?"

"No thanks. Are you tired of dancing?"

"No, not at all. I would like to ask you something."

"Can't you ask me here?"

"No. I would like to sit and look at you."

"Oh, I see," she said as she narrowed her eyes. "Well? Would you care to sit for a while then?"

"All right."

Gently he put his arm around her. He led her through the crowd to an empty table at the far end of the dance hall.

A waiter appeared and Toddy ordered some ice cream for two. Stella looked at him, surprised, but said nothing.

While they waited, Toddy began to put his thoughts into words. "Do you live in New York, Miss Jackson?"

"Yes," she said abruptly, "do you want the address?"

"Oh, you seem to be expecting that question."

"Yes. Only I thought that you would have asked that before now. They usually ask during the first dance."

"They?"

"Sure, all you men. Next you'll wonder if we haven't met somewhere before or something like that."

"I am very sorry, extremely sorry, that you think I am that way."

The waiter brought their order and Toddy ate without saying anything.

"What's the matter?" she asked. "Have I offended you?"

"Oh, no. Only I hate to think that you consider me the same as all the others you have met here."

"Oh, I don't know. Perhaps I was wrong. I do hope you are not. I didn't really mean to offend you. I am really sorry."

"It's perfectly all right. Do you care to dance anymore?"

"No. It's too late, I prefer to sit and talk."

"Sure. So do I, but what should we talk about? You seem to know all the questions I am about to ask."

"Well, that shows how smart I am. See?" And she laughed. "No, I was really only kidding. Do say something, please? If you don't, you will make me feel that I have spoiled your entire evening."

"What do you think of the leader of the band?"

"Oh," she appeared surprised, "he has got a lovely voice. He'll be going places. Of course, if he was white, he'd be there already."

"Maybe, just something new, a new kind of yelling, but he has got a lovely voice. I heard he was studying law and gave it up to lead a band. His sister is the real musician, I hear."

"Do you go to the movies?" she asked suddenly.

"Well, you see I really haven't got much time. You see, I er . . . " He hesitated. He thought it better not to divulge the fact that he was going to school, so he lied. "I have to work a little late some evenings, but, er, there is that coloured picture to be shown at the Lafayette Theatre next Wednesday evening. Would you care to go?"

"I don't mind."

"Fine. I will call for you. Oh, you haven't told me your address yet."

"I'll give you my telephone number. You can call me."

"Oh, that wouldn't do."

"Why?"

"I don't want you to change your mind. You know girls usually do that. I have heard that it is their privilege."

"So, you are comparing me to the other girls that you have met."

"Ha. Ha. That does sound familiar. Giving me some of my own medicine?"

"Oh, yes. I always like to get even. Well, not always."

"Come on, tell me where you live."

"One-hundred-and-thirty-ninth Street."

"That's not so far from here, is it?"

"No, just about three blocks."

Toddy reached for a pencil and wrote down the address and her name. "Now you can give me your phone number."

"Clever boy indeed, and suppose I don't want to now."

"I can find out, can't I, providing that you gave me the right address?"

"Oh well, to save you the trouble, it is Endicott 4432."

"Now, I'll never lose you, I am sure. Thanks very much. I will call you on Tuesday and let you know if I am able to get the tickets."

"So I won't see or hear from you until Tuesday?"

He reached and found her hand under the table. She just nodded her head and squeezed his hand a little.

Toddy was sure that the girl liked him and he realized that he liked her too.

They looked into each other's eyes for a minute and Toddy asked, "Do you care to dance anymore?"

"Just one more, James," she said softly, almost a whisper.

She arose and walked to the dance floor with his arm around her.

The dance finished. Stella looked at her watch and

remarked, "I think it's time to go home now. Look, it's almost two o'clock."

"That is late," he answered, "and as you don't live so very far and I am going in the same direction, couldn't I go part of the way with you?"

"You mean you want to see me home?"

"Yes," he confessed.

"No, I don't think so."

"Now, why should you go home alone? It isn't right, you know."

"I have always been going home alone, since I have been coming up here."

"My, that's good to hear you say that."

"What do you mean?" she asked.

"I'll tell you some other time."

"I must say goodnight then, until Tuesday."

"Well, I think I am going home, too. I guess I can see you downstairs, anyway. By the way, how do you usually go home?"

"How?"

"I mean, do you usually ride or walk?"

"I always take a cab, but tonight I think I will walk."

"Why?"

"Oh, I can't tell you everything at once."

"Well, do you mind very much if I were to walk, too?"

She eyed him coyly. "The streets are free you know. I can't stop you from walking."

Half an hour later they were standing on the stoop of her home.

"Good night. Stella."

She extended her right hand and he grasped it.

"Thanks for the most enjoyable evening I have spent in quite a while."

"You are certainly nice, Stella."

"Good night," she said, softly.

Toddy waited until she had opened the door and gone in. He turned towards Seventh Avenue and walked home.

Toddy did not awaken, until eleven o'clock that morning. There was no one at the house. "They must be at church," he concluded.

After taking a bath, he dressed and went out. He was not hungry and so he strolled across the street to the park. He sat down on a bench and looked around.

Had the day been a summer day there would have been very many people sitting around, but it seemed that coloured people did not like the cold very much. The air was brisk and sharp. A few feet in front of him a young girl slowly pushed a baby carriage past him. As it passed him he followed it with his eyes. Then he turned away his gaze for a moment and looked into the heavens. He closed his eyes and smiled a little. "I wonder if she is a nice girl."

It was ten o'clock that same morning when Stella awoke. The sun was up in the heavens and the glare of daylight burned her eyes. She squeezed her eyelids and turned her head towards the room. Squinting at the clock she pulled the cover over her head and went back to sleep.

A sharp knock on the door awoke her the second time and after a long stretch she asked, yawning, "Who is it?"

"Mildred," came the reply.

Stella jumped from the bed and opened the door. "Come in; have a seat."

"Well, goodness gracious, you certainly must have had a party last night. What time did you come in?"

"Oh, not so late," answered Stella, and started whistling.

"My, you look happy, even if you do look a little beat. What . . . ?"

"Sh. It's a secret, can't tell you."

"Well, when do I meet him?"

89

"Oh, Mildred, you wouldn't understand. He is an awfully nice fellow."

"Go on, tell me more. Please, tell me more."

"Well, you'll see him yourself, he'll be here Tuesday or Wednesday. He must be a foreigner or a 'homeboy' or something. Anyway, he is nice, too nice. Can you imagine, he came home with me this morning and didn't even try to get fresh."

"Where did you meet him?"

"Can't tell you that either. You wouldn't understand."

"God, he must be the cat's. I must see him."

"Okay. You can come up, don't stay too long."

"Aha, dirty work?"

"No, but . . . "

"But suppose he bumps into Dev . . . "

"Oh, that guy is scrambled now."

"Yeah, but don't be too sure."

Tuesday evening came and Toddy was standing in line in front of the Lafayette Theatre. For the first time since he returned to school, he missed class. He decided to only miss the first period, however.

He thought he heard his named called. Someone behind him was talking. "I wonder if the picture is any good?"

"Ought to be," someone else answered, "the amount of money they are charging for seats."

Toddy turned around and said, "Why, hello, Scotty, you skipping class, too?"

"Oh, I thought that was you. I called you but you didn't answer. Oh, I don't think there is much doing at that English class tonight."

"Nope. But it's my first absence."

"When are you going?" asked Scotty.

"Tomorrow, in the evening. I think it is the best time."

"Well from what I hear, there are no tickets for the evening shows. Only midnight-show tickets."

"Goodness, I had no idea," Toddy replied.

"Say, I am going to that midnight show, also. Why don't you come along with me?"

"No, Scotty, I can't. You know the girl I told you I met at the dance Saturday?"

"Girl?"

"Sure. She's nice, too. I am taking her to the show."

"Oh, I thought the boys in school said that you didn't go out with girls. They said you didn't even go out on dates."

"Well perhaps they were right, but it's never too late to get started."

"You've got something there."

"You are next," came a voice from the window.

"Oh yes, two tickets please, orchestra, not too far back."

"Only for the midnight show."

"Yes, I just learnt that."

"All right, how about the eleventh?"

"That'll be fine."

"Three fifty, please."

"Will see you later, Scotty," said James, looking back at Scotty.

"Okay, boy, have a nice time."

"Thanks, you do the same."

Toddy hurried towards Lenox Avenue and caught the trolley. In ten minutes he was in the class. As he sat down he decided he would call up Stella as soon as school was over.

Two hours later, he was in the telephone booth across the street.

"Hello, Stella."

"Oh, er, hello, darling," came the answer, "how are you?"

91

"I am fine. And you?"

"Fair. Are you going tomorrow night?"

"Oh, yes, I bought the tickets tonight, but there is only one thing. We'll have to go the midnight show. All the tickets were sold for the earlier one."

"I guess it is all right. Why did you wait so long to call me?"

"I started to," he lied.

"I thought you were coming up tonight. I had some friends here and they wanted to meet you."

"I didn't know."

"All right, I'll see you tomorrow night then, huh?"

"Yes, I'll be up about eleven-thirty."

"Why so late?"

"I'll tell you tomorrow."

"So. A secret, huh?"

"All right. Bye."

"So long."

On Wednesday night Toddy left school at ten-fifteen and walked west to Seventh Avenue. He asked Thomas to take his books home for him and boarded a bus going uptown. He rang the bell ten minutes later.

"Is Miss Jackson in?" he inquired of an elderly lady who opened the door.

"Yes, I believe she is. You can go right up."

Toddy looked at the woman, a little surprised. Had she mistaken him for somebody else? She had never seen him before. "Oh, I am sorry. What floor is she on?" he asked as he tried to hide his astonishment.

"Top floor, to the rear."

"Thank you," he answered, and he started up the stairs. Calling back to the woman, he asked, "Well, er, are you sure she is in?"

"Sure she is, less'n she forgot to turn off the lights."

Thanking her once more he continued on.

Looking around him as he reached the second floor, he noticed it was a private rooming house. Walking very softly on the carpeted floor he climbed the second flight. He became puzzled for there were two doors to the rear. He put his ear to one and could hear nothing. Doing the same thing to the other, he could hear someone walking back and forth. He decided that he would knock. If it was the wrong one he would try the other.

"Who is it?" a feminine voice answered his knock.

"Is this Miss Jackson's apartment?"

The door opened and Stella faced him. "I am sorry I didn't tell you what door to knock on when you called up. Come on in."

"Oh, it's all right. I found the place."

"Here let me take your hat and coat."

Taking them off he looked at her rather admiringly and she smiled in return.

"You look lovely," he remarked, as he looked at the dressing gown that she wore.

"Thank you. So do you," she replied. "Sit down while I get ready. You are a little early, you know, it's not eleven yet. I won't be long."

Toddy had never expected to see such a lovely girl without makeup. She was very pretty; however, she seemed a bit masculine in her walk. His eyes followed her to the door to what appeared to be another room. As she opened the door a pair of gold drapes hid what lay beyond. She turned her head and smiled before she disappeared behind them.

The room in which he was seated was very richly furnished. A medium-sized bed sat in the very middle of it and nearer the door was a large sofa that seemed to be very expensive.

On the bed were two long-legged fancy dolls, and

around the room were an assortment of parlor chairs, each upholstered in a different but harmonizing color.

A magnificent, walnut chest of drawers, with a glass top, and decorated with glass ornaments of different colors that reflected the light, sat on the other side of the bed. On the right side of the room, facing him, was a dressing table to match, loaded with an assortment of perfume bottles and gay-colored cream jars.

There were tables with table lamps and one bridge lamp overhanging each lounge chair. A floor lamp stood at the corner of the sofa on which he was sitting. A large Chinese rug covered the entire floor. The room was very rich indeed.

His eyes wandered to a picture decorating the dresser and, curious, he got up and walked towards it. It was a picture of what appeared to be Stella in a bathing suit standing close to a young man. She had a lovely figure. The young man was homely. He looked closer and there was a resemblance, but it was not Stella. It took him all of ten minutes to notice everything in the room, for Stella was constantly interrupting with questions.

"What have you been doing since Sunday, Toddy?"

"I've been working every day."

"No, I mean at night."

For the time being Toddy did not want to let her know about his going to night school. For some reason he wanted her to think him a man of the world and he thought she might think him a sissy for going to school.

"Staying at home," he answered.

"Live near here?" she asked.

"No, I am down on Morningside Avenue, near One-hundred-and-nineteenth Street. Nice, clean, and quiet down there. Only I haven't got as nice a place as you seem to have here."

"I like nice things," she answered.

The portieres opened and Stella walked slowly into the room. She was dressed in a lovely black dress. Toddy's pulse quickened as she walked toward him. He just stared at her. "That's why I like you," she added.

Toddy stood and they were face to face. "Do you really?" he asked.

She smiled and nodded. "You know," she said in a whisper, "you are the first young man to bring me home the first night I met him."

"Stella, I like you too."

He wanted to take her in his arms, but he just reached out and held her hand, squeezing it a little.

"Are we ready to go?" he whispered.

"Yes, dear," she replied very softly, "in a few minutes."

She walked over to the dressing table and applied her makeup, then a dash of perfume, and then she walked to the closet and took out her coat and his.

Toddy laid his on the back of a chair and helped her with hers. As she put both arms through the sleeves she suddenly turned around and kissed him on the side of his face.

His heart thumping, he put his arm around her and since she made no effort to free herself, he tucked his left hand under her chin, raised her head, and kissed her longingly and meaningfully.

She struggled a wee bit, then her arm went about his neck and she returned his embrace.

"We better go," she whispered.

Slowly he loosened his hold on her and then put on his coat. Taking a handkerchief from his pocket, he mopped his forehead.

"Oh, er, yes, I forgot to tell you. A couple of friends on the next floor are coming along. I just mentioned it to them today and they wanted to go. They are just going down with us. I don't even think they have tickets. Oh, look at your lips."

He wiped his lips, then looked at the red smear on the handkerchief. "That's okay, but I don't think they are going to get seats," he said.

"That's what I told the fellow, but he is very stubborn. West Indian, I think. They think they know everything. Oh, pardon me. I don't know whether you are one or not."

"Well, I was born here but my parents are, so I guess I am one."

"Oh, I am sorry I said that. Really, I didn't mean any harm. Most of those that I have met seem to know everything. Well, let's not worry about it, there are some that are not so clever, I guess."

Toddy let the matter drop.

"These are my keys, put them in your pocket. I don't want to lose them. I am not taking my pocketbook, just this little bag with my compact."

They went out the door after Stella turned out the lights.

Reaching the second floor, Stella knocked on the door directly below her room. A voice answered, "Come in."

"It's just me, Irene. Are you ready?"

"Yes."

The door opened and a girl accompanied by a young man came out.

Irene turned to lock the door behind them.

"We were waiting for you."

"Miss Roberts, meet Mr. Turner."

Toddy bowed. "Delighted," he greeted her.

"And Mr. Gray, Mr. Turner."

They shook hands. "Glad to meet you," said Toddy.

"Same here," responded Mr. Gray.

"George and James," added Stella.

Irene walked with Stella and George and Toddy followed.

As they reached Seventh Avenue, Toddy stood at the curb as though waiting for a cab.

"Let's walk," George said. "It's only a few blocks."

"Do you call seven blocks only a few?" asked Toddy. "It is a little late and we might miss something."

"Miss what? 'Tain't nothin' to miss."

Toddy felt that he was not going to like this fellow. He just whistled for a cab.

"Well," he said turning to George as the cab drew up, "we are riding. Are you going to walk?"

Irene said nothing, but stepping into the cab she murmured something that sounded like, "Oh, they make me sick." Toddy knew who she meant by "they."

George appeared not to hear it. In a little while they were at the theatre.

"My, what a line!" exclaimed George.

"That's right. You still have to buy tickets, don't you?" put in Toddy.

"Oh," George drawled, "there'll be plenty of seats. Ain't nobody goin' to pay all that money they asking for orchestra seats."

"I hope you are right," said Toddy, sarcastically, "but I don't think you are going to get any seats."

"Well, we'll see," said George. He walked past the line and asked the girl, "Any orchestra seats left?"

She shook her head negatively.

He strolled back to where they were standing. "Well, ol' boy, I guess you are right. Only upstairs seats left. Can you imagine? Oh, it's just as good. Besides, the picture won't be so hot, I've got a hunch," he said, and went back to the end of the line.

"We'll see you after the show."

"Okay."

Toddy and Stella both shook their heads as they passed the ticket taker. Stella turned around, saw Irene standing with George a little disgusted, and went in with Toddy. An usher took them to their seats.

"Did you like it?" asked Toddy, when they met outside after the show.

"Oh, er, I er, think it was swell," Irene answered, "but, George didn't think it was so good."

"Why, George?" Toddy asked, turning to him.

"I don't like that religious stuff, I guess. And that moaning and singing, phew, I could pass I guess. Did you care for it?"

"I did. Really. Perhaps because it was so true to life. In fact, I would not be a bit surprised if some of our own didn't care for it because it was too true. You remember the scene where the body of the murdered boy is brought home to his mother. She had a premonition of danger, just like most mothers do."

"So what's so exciting about that?"

"Nothing. Only I looked at Stella and she was actually crying."

"Nonsense."

"No. She really was. I didn't think it would affect her so much."

Toddy turned and looked at Stella, whose eyes were still red.

"Well, I don't know. The tears just came that's all. Didn't anything ever affect you so that you forget everything else and just think of that moment?"

Returning her stare, Toddy answered, "Yes, sometimes."

George just shrugged his shoulders and Irene cleared her throat.

"Are you folks hungry?" asked Toddy. "I could eat a little something."

"No thanks," put in George. "I am terribly sleepy and, besides, I have to work tomorrow.

"Well, so have I," returned Toddy.

"No, I think I'll go right home."

"All right."

"Good night," said George.

"Good night," replied Toddy.

"So long," put in Irene.

"Glad to have met you both," answered Toddy. "I do hope we'll meet again."

"Funny fellow," remarked Toddy, as they sauntered across the street to a restaurant.

"Yes, he is," answered Stella.

An hour later Toddy and Stella were standing in front of her house. "Well," Toddy said, "I really had a wonderful time. Didn't you?"

"I most certainly did. You will not think I am bold when I say this, but you are a very nice person to go out with."

"I try to be pleasant," he said, smiling.

"You don't have to try," she answered, "you are."

"It's almost four o'clock, my dear. I think I'll leave and call you tomorrow or rather today."

"What time?"

"About six."

"All right, dear." Stella started up the stairs and opened her bag while Toddy stood there.

"Oh, my. I don't think I've got my key," she said excitedly.

Toddy just smiled. "Looks like you'll have to ring the bell."

"Oh, what will I do?"

"Listen, Stella, didn't you introduce me to George and Irene last night?"

"Yes, but what's that got to do with . . . "

"You remember that, don't you?"

"Yes," she answered, smiling, puzzled.

"But, you don't remember giving me the keys before we came out."

"Oh, Mr. James, I really ought to shoot you," she said indignantly, "making me wait here all this time. Well?"

"Well what?"

"The key please."

"Oh, yes, the key. Well, that'll cost you just two kisses. One for the key and the other for forgetting."

"Is that nice?"

"Maybe it's not but it's the only way you are going to get the key."

"All right, Mr. Smarty. I'll get even. And besides, it's a pleasure."

She came down the stairs and as she reached him she closed her eyes and puckered her lips in the darkened entrance.

Toddy just looked at her, however, and taking the keys from his pocket he put them in her hands, which were clasped in front of her. He made no attempt to kiss her.

Stella suddenly ran up the steps, hurriedly opened the door, and went in without looking back.

Toddy came down the steps and went home.

He wondered what she thought of him as he lay in bed for a few hours sleep.

The alarm clock woke him and for the first time that he could remember his eyes were burning him. After washing up, however, he felt better.

That evening before entering school he called up Stella.

"So that's the way you treat girls," she asked, sounding peeved.

"No, dear, please don't be like that. I really meant no harm. I don't usually kiss girls in the streets, that's all."

"But you suggested it."

"Maybe I was experimenting, am I forgiven?"

"Yes, this time."

"Thank you."

"Going any place tonight?" she asked.

"No. I think I'll stay in."

"Sleepy?"

"A little. How about you?"

"Oh, I didn't get up till after twelve."

"Oh. Don't you have to go . . . " He decided not to finish the question.

"Don't I have to what?" she asked.

"Oh, er, nothing," he replied. His somewhat happy countenance gradually grew stoic. The realisation that she had never mentioned anything about going to work hit him. Perhaps she did not work. Maybe she was not such a nice girl after all. The lovely furnished room she had, and she did not have any occupation? Her voice interrupted his thoughts.

"Well, er, darling, will you be up on Saturday evening?"

"Yes. Yes, sure. What time will you be home?"

"About nine."

"Well, so long till then, darling."

"Good-bye."

"Bye."

Toddy hung up the receiver very slowly and stood staring at the telephone. He bit his nails a little, a habit he had when he was perplexed.

Saturday finally came. It was eight o'clock that night

when Toddy phoned Stella. "Where are we going tonight?" he asked her.

"Oh, you'll be surprised."

"I would? Why?"

"Well, Irene is going home next week and her friends are giving her a party. It's to be at her sister's house."

"What time are you going?"

"Well, it'll be around ten-thirty."

"I don't mind going, but do you know many of the guests?"

"Sure I do. Darling, you don't think I'd take you anywhere that was bad?"

"All right, what time shall I call for you?"

"You won't have to, dear. It's down your way. If you don't mind I'll ring your bell about a quarter past ten."

"Why not come up? It's only one flight. Here, wait a minute, I'll give you the address."

"Toddy, are you sure that it will be right? I don't think I should. It doesn't look very nice."

"Why, it's nothing. There are decent people at the house. Besides, the folks I live with have gone away for a week."

"Yes, but, er."

"All right, have it your way. I'll be downstairs till you come."

"All right."

As he hung up the receiver, he murmured, "She's pretty decent after all. Oh, well, I guess I'll have to solve this riddle pretty soon or give it up altogether."

Toddy was downstairs at ten minutes after ten.

"My goodness," he exclaimed, as he saw her at the door, "I swore you'd be late."

"No, dear, I didn't want to keep you waiting."

"How long have you been here?" he asked, as they walked away.

"Not long."

"How far is the place?"

"Not far. Just around the corner."

"On the avenue?"

"Yes, you might even know them."

"No, I don't know many people."

In a few minutes they were at the party. It was already in progress and after introducing Toddy to everyone, Stella asked to be excused.

The men at the party were much older than Toddy. In fact, he felt a bit awkward. It was nearly twelve o'clock when the other guests began to show the effects of the liquor. Up to then, Toddy had been offered drinks many times but had politely refused them. He felt peculiar, thinking that they may have thought him a snob.

They all went into the kitchen. Toddy followed. As he walked behind them he thought that if he did drink it would be his first time and that he was nearly eighteen years old. He wouldn't touch any more that evening and it might make him appear more sociable. The other guests had poured their drinks into their glasses and were waiting for him to do likewise. As he poured, however, he felt a bit dazed, but attributed it to the close atmosphere of the room.

Everyone lifted their glasses and as Toddy did likewise, Stella, who seemed to have come from nowhere, rushed over and grabbed his left hand. "Let me have yours, darling, and you take mine," she said.

The sudden jerk sent his glass into the air and Toddy stood there more stupefied than those around him.

"Oh, I am sorry, darling," she wailed. "Here, take another."

Toddy did not answer but led Stella back to the front

room, implying to the other guests that he thought she was intoxicated.

"Come on. Let's dance then, dear," he whispered.

Puzzled, she put her arm around his shoulders and stared at him. "What's the matter, sweet?" she asked.

"Eh?"

"I said what's the matter. You look as though you were drunk, but I know you had nothing to drink."

"Just a little dizzy, I guess."

To everyone else it seemed an accident, but to Toddy, well, he thought it very uncanny. All night long he had refused to drink and now for the first time, when he had agreed to do so, the glass was knocked right out of his hand.

The party broke up about half-past-two, and, after seeing Stella home, Toddy returned to his house.

As he stood undressing before the mirror he began talking to himself. "Well, Mom, I can't help thinking that you had something to do with that. I am sorry I ever attempted it, but no other time until I get old enough to know what I am doing. Just like you said in the letter."

He was referring to the letter that his mother had written to him before her death, in which she begged him not to drink until he was of age and sure that he knew what he was doing.

It was almost two o'clock the next afternoon when Toddy decided to make a surprise visit to Stella's house.

"Is Miss Jackson in?" he inquired of the old lady who opened the door.

"Yes, I think she is. You can go right up."

"Thank you."

As Toddy reached the floor on which she lived, he heard voices, men's voices, emanating from her room. *Probably some friends*, he thought, as he knocked upon her door.

"Come in," Stella answered.

He pushed the door and saw that there were quite a few people in the room. As he entered he thought he detected a sudden uneasiness in Stella, but she seemed to erase it just as suddenly.

In the room were Stella, and two other girls whom he did not recognize at first, but a second glance he remembered their faces from the party the previous evening. There were also two others whom he had never seen before.

"Hello, James. Have a seat; meet some friends," said Stella.

The words seemed to come all at once. Toddy believed that she was embarrassed about something.

"Mr. Johnson, Mr. Turner."

Both shook hands. "Glad to meet you," said Toddy.

"How are you?" Mr. Johnson replied.

"Mr. Devon, Mr. Turner," continued Stella.

Mr. Devon rose to extend his hand, but Toddy perceived a slight stiffness in his attitude.

"The others you have met before," continued Stella.

"Oh, yes," he replied, "glad to see you again."

The others returned his greeting.

As Toddy looked around him, he realized he was the only odd one in the group and he felt a little uncomfortable.

His entrance seemed to have interrupted a sort of discussion and he felt that they were opposed to his staying. He was conscious of a certain situation, and the idea came to him suddenly that one of these men was more than a friend of Stella's.

He suddenly jumped up. All eyes turned towards him. "I just dropped in to say hello. Guess I'll be running along."

"Oh, no, please," Stella put in, "what do you mean 'running along'? You know you promised to take me to the Savoy this evening."

Toddy flinched a little. He had no appointment with

Stella for this evening, but he was quick to realize that she wanted an excuse for something.

"Well, er, I think I, er, didn't think I'd be able to make it."

"Oh, come on, stop kidding, we are almost ready."

"What do you mean 'stop kidding'?" he said a little peeved. "You are going with friends, aren't you? Looks like an even team to me."

"Oh, please, Toddy, Mr. Devon just came along with Mr. Johnson" she said, and Toddy detected a sarcastic scowl in her tone as she turned towards Mr. Devon, who arose immediately.

"That's right," he replied, a bit sullenly, "I am not going," and he took his coat and hat from a nearby rack. Walking towards the door he exclaimed, "I hope you all have a lovely time." Turning to Toddy, he concluded, "Glad to have met you, Mr. Turner."

Toddy knew that his tone was far from sincere and he knew he did have strong competition for Stella's affections.

Before Toddy could answer, Mr. Devon closed the door. Looking at the faces of the others in the room, he felt that they knew more about the obvious connection between Stella and Mr. Devon than he did.

"Well, are we ready?" asked Stella, who obviously seemed relieved.

The rest reached for their hats and coats.

"Don't forget your key," reminded Toddy.

"No, I won't. Thank you," she answered, a little embarrassed, as the others looked on rather significantly. "Besides, I am spending the night with Sybyl, Irene's sister."

"Oh, I see," said Toddy. He was thinking of Devon's actions a few minutes earlier.

As he walked along with Stella, he began to solve the somewhat mysterious affair in his mind.

It occurred to him that Devon had been, or still was, her boyfriend. He had appeared rather prosperous-looking. Stella did not seem to have any job and Devon didn't seem to have approved of her friends. Toddy decided to act very nicely for the rest of the evening and write a her nice letter the next day. After all, he felt foolish for not already thinking that a nice-looking girl like Stella might have a boyfriend or perhaps a husband. *That's it*, he thought. *Perhaps he was her husband. They might have been separated and he was taking care of her. Otherwise, where would she get such nice things?* Anyway he was glad that the affair with him had not gone any further.

Toddy danced with Stella the first three dances. As they were leaving the floor, George was waiting and asked her for the next dance. She looked at Toddy as if asking permission. He bowed, nodded, and walked towards the lounge seats. He felt slight pressure on his arm and turned to see one of the other girls in his party.

"You are Sybyl, aren't you?" he asked her.

"Yes."

"I knew I saw you at the party, but I had completely forgotten your name. You will forgive me, won't you?"

"That's quite all right."

They were near two empty seats and Sybyl sat down first.

"Do you mind?" said Toddy, politely, and sat next to her.

They looked at each other.

"Well, I can tell that you want to tell me something. You look awfully worried."

"Well, Mr. Turner . . . " She sighed, tragically.

"Just call me James," he interrupted.

"Well, James, evidently you don't know that Stella is my cousin and I shouldn't really be doing this, but, you seem to be a very nice and decent fellow."

"Go ahead," said Toddy, anxiously.

"Stella is crazy about you. She wanted all of us to meet you and you should know how much she talked about you. But . . . "

"But what?"

"You have got to watch your step."

"What do you mean?"

"That man, the fellow you met tonight, Mr. Devon, he is very jealous, and he carries a gun."

Toddy shrugged his shoulders, leaned closer to Sybyl, and whispered, "My dear, I have done nothing to Mr. Devon. Why should I worry about him?"

"I know you don't know what you have done but Stella has done something."

"What?"

"She has given him up for you. You figure it out."

"Well, is he her husband?"

"Oh, you'll have to ask Stella that."

"You mean you don't know whether she is married or not?"

"That's right. No one knows. But I really don't think so."

They were interrupted by Stella and George.

Toddy couldn't help but notice the fierce look that Stella gave her cousin. Toddy got up, looked around, said "Excuse me" to Sybyl, and walked to the dance floor with Stella.

As he stood at the rail, he surveyed the giggling, sophisticated young men and women, older ones, too, who were cavorting to the fantastic tunes of the orchestra. Further on, he noticed a couple attracting considerable attention by their vulgar dancing. It didn't last long, however, for one of the bouncers saw them and asked them to dance properly or get off the floor.

As the music stopped, Toddy turned towards Stella,

who seemed to be eyeing him with every ounce of admiration.

"What is the matter, Toddy?" she asked, pleadingly.

"I am not feeling so well. I hate to break up your party, but I think I'd better be going."

He was lying and he knew that she knew he was lying.

"I thought so. Somebody has been saying something to you. If you wanted to know anything, why didn't you ask me?"

"As a matter of fact, I didn't ask. I was told."

"Oh, whatever you heard, you are going to tell me tonight. I am going with you, and I am going now. Please take me home, James."

"All right, don't get excited. I thought you were going to spend the night with your cousin."

"Maybe I've changed my mind. And how I've changed it! Will you wait here a minute please?"

Toddy took out his handkerchief and mopped his brow. "Phew!" he said to himself. "Is she angry!"

It seemed less than a minute later that he saw the whole party coming towards him.

As they stood around him, Stella began, "I am sorry but Mr. Turner wants to leave and as you are not all ready to go, we are saying good night. Come on, Toddy."

"Well, I like that," said Sybyl, as they walked away.

Toddy was amazed at Stella's frankness and he followed her.

"Let's take a cab tonight, darling, I am in a awful hurry. There is something I must tell you."

"Fine," he answered, "we both have something to say to each other."

In less than five minutes they were in front of Stella's house. They got out and Toddy paid the driver.

"Come on up."

"It's rather late, Stella, isn't it? Won't the old lady complain about you having company so late?"

"Maybe," she answered dryly.

"Am I going to get hurt or something? I don't like the way you said maybe."

They had reached Stella's floor and after unlocking the door she pushed it.

As they walked in, Stella snapped a switch. A dark-red glow swept across the room. The furniture appeared tinged with the tint of sunset. The reflection of the pink haze shone through the many mirrors and the room seemed a bewitching haven such as Toddy had never seen before.

"Pardon me, darling," she said, and went into the adjoining room. "Rest your things," she added, as the door closed behind her.

After removing his hat and coat, he sat down. The atmosphere had created an unexplainable feeling of deviltry in his mind. He was a little uneasy but not afraid.

In a few minutes Stella returned. The silken robe of what appeared to be white that covered her body shimmered in the glow of the room. Even her feet were covered by a silken pair of slippers that glistened with every movement of her legs.

Stella came towards him, sat down next to him, and ran her hand through her hair; her face seemed like a brown opal in this atmosphere of ecstasy.

She broke the silence with one word. "Smoke?" she asked.

"Yes. I'll try one."

She arose, pulled one of the drawers from a small table, and took out a cigarette case. She extracted two, handing him one and putting the other to her lips. She held the lighter to his and looked into his eyes, at the same time putting her warm hand across his forehead.

110

Toddy's pulse quickened at her touch. He took hold of the lighter, laid it down and held both her hands, putting them behind her back. Their eyes met.

The unlit cigarette dropped from her lips and he made no effort to retrieve it.

"Stella, you've got me guessing. I wonder if you really like me."

"Toddy, I can't make you believe me if you don't want to, but the truth is, you are the first fellow I have met that I've felt this way about. You seem to be so different."

Toddy's heart was beating fast, he couldn't explain it either.

She turned her head as she continued, "I have slept on this bed many, many nights and dreamed of someone like you. I have wanted to meet a nice, clean fellow that I could love with all my heart. When you treated me like a lady the first time I met you, you did something to me. I love you, Toddy, but I am afraid of you. I might love you too much. Darling, all I want is a chance to prove it."

She leaned towards him and kissed him. Something inside of him seemed to burst, he was hurting and his desire was uncontrollable. He could feel the thumping of her heart.

They embraced each other. Her eyes were closed as she continued to smother him with kisses, and then became limp in his arms.

Her body was soft against his and he laid her across the bed.

Her hand touched his manhood as he lay next to her and she whispered to him, "Toddy, please don't make a fool out of me," then she reached across him and switched out the light.

She whispered in his ear, "Honey, put your things over there."

It was bright daylight when Toddy awoke. He was sur-

111

prised, a little dazed, and bewildered as his eyes searched the room.

Everything was strange to him. He sat upright in the bed and rubbed his eyes. Slowly it dawned on him, he was not at his home. The furniture around him brought the realization that he was at Stella's. Someone was coming towards him; it was Stella.

"Do you like your eggs straight up or scrambled?"

Toddy blinked a little, then stared and rested his chin on his hand. He smiled dazedly and answered, "Any way at all, any way."

Stella kissed him and left, mumbling over her shoulder, "There is a clean washcloth and towel in the bathroom."

One hour later Toddy was on the subway on his way home. He grabbed his books and continued on his way to his job.

All day Stella was before him. He smiled as he remembered the night before. He was a man and Stella had made him prove that. The first girl he had ever been with. He could not wait until that night to see her again.

Twelve o'clock came and Toddy went to lunch. He could not eat and decided to call up his girl.

"May I speak with Miss Jackson please?" he inquired from the lady who answered the phone, recognizing the voice as that of the landlady.

In a few minutes he would hear the voice of the first girl he had ever loved. What would he say? What would she say? Those eyes, that voice, those lips he had kissed so often and so tenderly, and that feeling of supreme ecstasy that he had experienced.

"Hello," said a voice on the other end.

"Yes," answered Toddy, "hello."

"Sorry, Miss Jackson can't speak to nobody her husband said before he went out."

"Her what?" Toddy almost screamed, as the click told him that someone had hung up.

Another nickel, another answer. "Please," pleaded Toddy, "just a minute. You said her husband left that message before he left?"

"Yes, sir, he sho' did."

"Oh, all right. Thank you," said Toddy, and he hung up very slowly.

Stella would not do that, it must be some mistake. He was at a loss to understand. Stella never mentioned anything about being married. He remembered Sybyl's remarks of the past night.

The afternoon never seemed to end, but finally he was on the subway. He had to go home to see if any messages had been sent to him as he had not been home since the night before.

There were no messages and fifteen minutes after he had arrived home, he was on his way uptown to Stella's house.

As he turned the corner he saw her. She was seated on the stoop. His pace quickened and as he reached her she appeared to look a little different.

"I tried to get you on the telephone today but somebody said something about your husband."

Stella walked into the building motioning for him to follow. She opened the door and waited for him to come in.

What a difference a few hours had made. Earlier that same day he had been in Heaven, now he seemed to be entering a maze, not knowing what the outcome would be or where it would lead to.

"What's it all about, Stella? I don't understand."

"I was going to tell you a little story last night but you know what happened instead. We didn't get a chance a talk."

"Yes, we both forgot, didn't we?"

"Yes, we really did," Stella replied.

Suddenly he remembered Sybyl's remarks at the dance and said to Stella, "Did Devon have anything to do with this?"

"Yes. But, Toddy, I will have to tell you everything. I don't care what happens. I've got your love, if I don't keep it, then . . . " She began to cry. "You are going to hear everything."

She stood up and walked to the mirror, and then Toddy realized why she looked different. Her face was a little puffed and there was a bruise on her forehead.

"Toddy, you'll always love me, won't you?" she asked, without looking at him.

"You don't even have to ask that," he retorted.

"Darling, it hurts to even begin to tell you how it all started."

"Well, I did not even know that you were married, but I had an idea there was someone who was helping you."

"You knew that when you took me home last night?"

"Well, not exactly, but I had an idea. Sybyl said something to me that made me think you were mixed up with Devon, in more ways than one."

"So now that you do know, what's going to happen?" she asked.

"Don't you remember when I told you that I had something to say to you?"

"You mean when we arrived home after the dance?"

"Yes, but after I kissed you and held you in my arms, I forgot everything else."

"I was about fifteen when a fellow from New York came to visit his folks who lived in my hometown. He had been away a long time, and I was the only girl in my group that he liked. I didn't like him, in fact, I really didn't know whether I liked him or not. He kept coming to my house, almost every night. Finally I went riding with him."

"He had a car?"

"Yes, he did. Well, one Sunday, he took me all the way to Philadelphia. I was real stupid, or maybe I was all excited. I thought that the other girls would be jealous. They were older than I was and they were always kidding me about the fun I was missing."

Tears were falling as she turned her head away from Toddy. "Don't tell me if you don't want to," he said.

"I want you to know everything." She turned and faced him once again. "If you don't want me after I tell you, then I won't have anything to be ashamed of."

Toddy leaned over and kissed her on her cheek.

"He took me to some swell people. They were really nice and they treated me real nice. We went to a movie and I stayed with him that night."

Stella stared into space as though she were reliving the incident.

"Yes?" Toddy prodded her.

"Somehow I didn't realize that I had done such a terrible thing." She wrung her hands in despair. She kept shaking her head from side to side. "Oh, Toddy, you'll never know what I went through after that." She stood up and walked over to the window.

Toddy waited for her to continue.

"I had to tell my mother why I stayed away from home. She told him that he'd have to marry me or they would put him in jail. I was underage and they would have really put him away for a long time. He sat right there and told my mother that he couldn't marry me because he was already married. Everybody called me names. They all said that I was a bad girl. The friends I thought I had suddenly became strangers to me. I took it as long as I could and then I decided to go away. My mother took me to a doctor and he examined me and said he could not tell if I was going to have a baby.

I went to Raleigh and stayed a couple of months, but I finally was told that I was pregnant.

"I really caught the devil for the next few months. God must have been very sorry for me, anyway; whatever He did, the baby was born dead. I went back home and they really treated me rotten around the house. My father was nothing but a rummy and he cursed almost every day. It became so bad I couldn't stand it and I ran away again, this time to New York City. I guess a lot of people, especially girls, take a chance coming to a big city like New York, and I just did the same thing."

"Did you know anyone there?" he asked.

"Well, I did know a couple of people, but I went to the Y.W.C.A. on 138th Street in Harlem. They were very nice. I only had thirteen dollars in my pocket, but a lady in the office asked me if I was interested in getting a job. I said I was. After a lot of questions, she told me to come in the next morning at nine.

"They asked me if I would be interested in working on Long Island. I agreed to take a job for a Jewish family and they were very wealthy. I started to send money to my mother every month. Although they treated me pretty bad when I was home after what happened, I still couldn't desert them.

"A little further down the drive there was a chauffeur named Slim, who asked me to go out with him to the movies. At first I hesitated, remembering what had happened in the South, but he seemed to be a nice fellow and I was getting a little lonesome.

"He talked to me like a father; he was much older than I was. He used to warn me about going out with boys. I respected him more than I liked him. I told him all about my parents and I mentioned about what had happened to me.

"About a month later I received a letter from Pop telling

116

me about Mom being sick. I showed Slim the letter. A week later I received a letter from Pop thanking me for the seventy-five dollars, which I had not sent. I realised Slim had sent the money."

"Was this fellow Devon?" he asked.

"Yes," she admitted. "Well, I was thankful for what he did, but later, when I found out he was married and had three children, I decided to quit him.

"Every month I mailed him fifteen dollars until I paid him back the money he sent to my father, but he was awful persistent. He wouldn't leave me alone, so the only thing I could do was to quit the job. I stayed on long enough to pay him the rest of the money, then I came to New York.

"I was lucky enough to get a job right away, a few days after I got back to New York. It was with a theatrical woman. She was very famous and she paid me good wages. She also gave me a lot of nice things. I saved a couple of hundred dollars in two years. Then I ran into Devon. He had come to New York, went into the numbers racket, and had become a big shot.

"In those two years, by working for this woman and seeing more than I had ever seen before, I got wise to a lot of things. When I met him, I just told him that I didn't want to be bothered. He trailed me, found out where I was staying, and called on me anyway. This was one month before I met you.

"That night I met you I was really running away from him. He tells everybody that I am his wife, even the landlady in the house where I live. Toddy, I am really afraid of him. This morning he must have seen you go out and he came up later and called me all kinds of names.

"He said, 'So you slept with him last night, huh?' and then he slapped me. I slapped him back, told him that he had no right to hit me, that I wasn't anything to him. He slapped me again and I fell against the bed and bruised my hands. I went out and had him arrested."

"That's what I was going to suggest," put in Toddy.

"He won't bother me anymore."

"Somehow though . . . " Toddy began to think out loud.

"Yes, I know. I am afraid to go back up there. He has a few very tough friends."

"Yeah. But, what are you going to do?"

"I am going to get a small apartment and I thought you could help me look for one, a nice one in a decent neighborhood."

"I was thinking . . . ," said Toddy.

"What?" asked Stella, jumping in.

"You could stay with me. The people I live with won't be back for another seven weeks. I will write them and tell them. We are going to be married anyway, so it'll be all right. Oh, I forgot. You might not want me."

Stella's mouth was wide opened. She couldn't believe what she had just heard. "Darling, you want to marry me? After what I just told you?"

"Of course. Only there is a little secret I must tell you. I should have before but . . . "

"What is it?"

He showed her his books. "See these. Well, I am going to school at night. I am studying to be a doctor."

"Oh, darling, that's wonderful."

"I only have a few months before I graduate from high school, then I intend to enter college."

"That's lovely. You'll be a big man some day."

"Stella, there is something on my mind. I might as well ask you now. Those lovely things in your room, how did you get them?"

"Oh dear. I knew you were going to ask me that. I stay with a girl who dances. She's on tour now and I guess I did act as though her things belong to me. You can go and see for yourself, or ask the landlady."

"It was worrying me a little; now I feel a lot better."

"Now you know everything."

"You can stay with me tonight, Stella, and tomorrow we can talk things over."

Toddy did not go to school that night. He went down on the subway and rode. For almost three hours Toddy changed from one express train to another, thinking, wondering.

He came home about eleven o'clock.

"How was school tonight?" Stella greeted him.

"All right," he lied.

"What's wrong? You look a bit worried. I can stay at a hotel if you don't want me here. You know it's not right for me to do this."

"I am not exactly worried, but come over here. I want to talk to you seriously."

They sat close together on the side of the sofa.

"Darling, I am ready to hear what you have to say," she said.

"Listen, I am going to try to help you and I want you to help me. Right now I am very much in love with you, but I have not been with many girls. I didn't think you would want to marry me right away. It's too sudden. It will spoil everything. You say that you love me. As soon as I get my diploma we can be married. In the meantime we could stay here as brother and sister, if you wish to. After all, we have only known each other three weeks. You know nothing about me at all."

"Don't say that, I mean about me not knowing anything of you. I know everything about you, sweetheart. I think you are right about one thing though, about us not getting married so soon. I have never been married, dear. In fact, I've never been this close to a man before."

Chapter Ten

It was just one week later when Toddy received a letter from Jean. It read:

Dear Toddy,

I was very happy to hear from you. I am fine and well. I have a surprise for you Toddy. I am married. I am really happy now and would like very much if you would come and spend a few days with us. Bring Stella with you and we'll talk the whole thing over.

If you are coming, send me a telegram and let me know what train you will be on, as I will meet you at the station.

Lots of luck,
From the Missus and Myself,
Your Cousin, Jean

Toddy was glad to hear from Jean. He had aided him so many times. Toddy was actually proud of Jean. He had always wanted to be like him when he became a man.

"Gee," he said to himself, "bet he is a big fellow in Detroit by now."

Toddy would answer that night and try to go to Detroit to see Jean the next week. The main reason that Toddy was anxious to see his cousin, however, was that he wanted to seek advice in his romantic adventure and he knew of no one else better equipped to give him such advice than Jean. Toddy thought that he was doing the right thing regarding Stella, but he was not exactly sure.

Toddy arrived home from work that night and Stella was sitting on the edge of the bed crying. In her hand was a telegram, which she handed to Toddy. He read, "Your mother is very sick. Please come at once."

"Darling, I am so sorry and I just had a surprise for you too. We were going to Detroit to see my cousin," he said.

"Well, dear, you go ahead. I think I will leave in the morning."

"Why can't we go tonight?"

"We?"

"Sure, you don't think I would let you go alone, do you?"

"I must go by myself. You wouldn't understand."

"All right. How long will you stay?"

"About a week if she isn't worse."

"Well, I will go to Detroit then, and in case you need me you will let me know."

"Yes, dear."

"Fairville," bellowed the conductor.

Stella hastily grabbed her bag and walked to the platform.

"So long, beautiful," muttered one of the porters, as she stepped off the train.

"So long, freshie," she answered back.

"Now where is Ted Jenkins?" she murmured, as she scanned the platform for the sight of that never to be forgotten faithful friend, who, as far as she could remember back, had always told her he wanted to marry her, despite the large difference in their ages.

Finally, she saw him hobbling towards her.

"Hello, Ted."

"My Miss Stella, yo sho looks good. But," he said, as his face became sad, " 'tis bad news, awful bad."

"Ted . . . is Mom d . . . ?"

"Yas'm, yo' maw done gone tuh de Lawd las' night."

"Oh, god! It can't be, Ted. It can't be. Why didn't some-one let me know sooner?" cried Stella. "I so wanted to see her before she died."

"She want sick long. She jes' took in las' week. Doc said she wa'nt so sick, but las' night she got ver' po'ly and soon's we tried tuh git ol' Doc she was long gone."

"And my father, you mentioned about him."

"Well, tuh tell de trute, Mis' Stell', I would'n know much 'bout 'im. Yuh see, doan no body know much 'bout him or even care 'bout him lately. 'E's in a very bad fix, ma'am, very bad."

"Go on, Ted, please tell me."

"Well, ye 'nowed 'e usta drink his licca, but lately fer 'bout de pas' tree months he dun drunk hisself sick. An', Lawd, ever' day the sun shine he's drunk. 'E lives all by hisself in a ol' shack up ne'r the ben' in the railroad track wid Pepper, 'is ol' dawg. An' doan no body pay any tenshun tuh 'im."

"Ted, take me there first, please?"

"Oh, Mis' Stell', please doan axe me tuh do nuffin' like dat. Ah knowed it, ah knowed it, I shoulda kep' mah big mouf shut . . . "

"Ted, please take me there?"

"Yuh would'n wan' tuh see him, Ah nose yuh would'n."

Stella did not answer and Ted knew she was a very determined person. "Aw'right, I'll take yuh to 'im."

They entered an outmoded Model T Ford that Ted had parked quite a distance from the depot.

They soon came upon familiar ground. The once-beau-tiful place where she used to roam as a little girl had become a dilapidated piece of land. It seemed that the place had been neglected for years. The house that she had once called home seemed to be leaning to one side. The roof was almost off and even the trees resembled straight stacks of wood. A few leaves sprouted from branches that seemed to have been cut by storms and died through neglect.

Ted stopped the jalopy in front of what seemed to be an entrance. Stella looked at Ted and stared at the house in front of her.

"Home?" she whispered softly. "Home," she again repeated. "Oh, Ted, this isn't where I used to live?"

"Ya'as 'm, but the house is old and no mo'good. Yer pappy is staying in the ol' shack way in back o' de house. I'll pull round teh de back."

The car started and the bumpy road caused Stella to stammer as she spoke. "The rose bushes, Ted, the shrubberies. Ted, they are all dead."

"Ya'as ma'am, dey bin daid."

The tears that were dropping from her eyes obliterated the rest of the scene.

Ted brought the car to another stop and it leaned so much to one side that Stella almost fell getting out.

There was no one in sight. The house itself was deserted. The front had almost collapsed. The roof, which had appeared from the other side of the house to be almost off, was even worse from this side. As she pushed in the door, it squeaked back at her. There were no curtains at the windows and all the shutters were broken.

"My home, Ted. Imagine, I was born here and grew up here. Could anything in this world change so much? I can't believe it."

"I knowed it. I tole yuh not to come, I tole yuh."

"But, where is my father?"

Ted walked towards the back of the house and Stella followed. As they approached the shack the low grumbling of a dog greeted them. Then, wagging its dirty tail, whining, the dog came slowly towards them, then it stopped, as

123

though wondering who these people were. Then it walked slowly towards Ted.

"Go la down, Pepper, go la down." He motioned to Stella to follow him as he reached the shack.

Stella remembered it. It was the old barn, but it was moved nearer to the railroad tracks. She followed Ted. Soon he had reached the door and opened it. Stella walked hesitantly into the room. Directly in front of them lay a mattress, dirty and torn, on the bare floor and on it was stretched the body of a man.

Slowly, Stella walked towards it and then she saw the body of what was once a powerful and strong human being. She stood motionless, staring at the almost unrecognisable features of her father.

He lay there, a human derelict, drunk, of this Stella was sure. The room was full of the stench of newly cooked liquor. On the floor lay a bottle whose mouth had deposited its last drop.

His clothes were a patched up pair of pants and a dirty, ragged shirt that seemed to be the haven of at least a hundred flies, which buzzed and hummed as Stella and Ted stealthily approached this stinking, slimy creature.

Stella felt like turning back but the fight waging in her body seemed to convey the message that it was her father lying there as she walked towards the door.

"Wait for me outside," she said to Ted.

"Aw'right, ma'am," he answered, with a sigh, and shaking his head he turned and walked towards the door.

Stella went back to her father and, as she stood there, her childhood days flashed across her mind.

"Pop," she called weakly. She repeated the word again, "Pawp."

Tears, large tears, rolled down her cheeks, blurring her

features and she made no effort to stop them. "Paw, Paw," she called once more, this time shaking him.

Jim Jackson grunted once, twice, three times, then his huge body heaved to one side, and he rolled off the bed onto the floor, panting. As he lay there the flies followed him. Again Stella shook him and slowly his eyes opened.

Stella knelt next to him and his large hairy arm raised up and found haven on her shoulder as he made an effort to rise. He sat up on the floor, his chest heaving violently as he continued to make an effort to stand up.

As Stella looked at the broad shoulders, now covered by rags, she remembered the many times he had used those shoulders to ward off slaps that her mother took to her when she did something wrong.

She fought to keep him erect.

"You. Who are yuh? Talk! Who are yuh?" he cried.

Stella was afraid. His voice was sore and raspy and he sounded very ill.

"Who are you?" he growled between his slobbering lips, his red eyes blinking constantly.

Stella realized he was trying hard to keep them open.

"It's Stella," she finally answered, "your Stella. Remember me, Pa, remember me?" she pleaded.

Jim Jackson's eyelids parted as he shook his head from side to side. He raised his hands up to his eyes and almost lost his balance. He stretched out his right hand towards her face and as his rough fingers scratched her she winced a little, but said nothing.

As her father's body straightened and his eyes found her face, she felt that she was being recognized.

"Stell . . . my gal Stella . . . what run away . . . is that you?"

"Yes," she answered, "it's me, Pa. I am here home with you."

"Sho' yoh're hare. Yah . . . sho'. Cause yo' ma's daid. Yuh'd nebber be hare for no udder reason."

"No, Pop, I didn't know how things were, honest I didn't."

"It's all right, gal, it's all right, but who tole yuh? How did yuh git down here? Who sent and tole yuh?"

"I got a telegram from you, Pop."

"From me? I ain't never send yuh no tel'gram, gal." He stared at her. "I ain't been outta here for over a week. 'Twas your ma, gal, but now she's gone. Honest, I feel mo' safer."

Stella took this rather hard; her father wasn't even sorry that her mother had passed on.

"Say, who brung yer to this 'ere place anyway?"

"I asked Ted Jenkins to take me to you."

"Oh, po' Ted. He was here 'bout three days ago and tole me 'bout yer maw. Ted is mighty ol', but he sure got some funny ideas. He don' want me to drink no licca. But I gits it jes' the same. Bet he's the one that sen' yuh that dere tel'gram."

"Yes, but what's the difference, Pop? Please come on, and get up and straighten yourself out. You are going with me."

"Now listen, chile, there's a heap what you don' know. But all I got tuh say is, I don' evah wan tuh see yo' maw daid or 'live. Now go 'long 'bout yo' bidness."

Stella only stared at her father.

He pointed his finger at her. "Yo' married, ain't cha?"

"Yes, Pop," she lied, "and soon I am going to make up to you."

"Got any young'uns?"

She lied again, if only to get him to go with her. "Yes, Pop, a boy. He looks just like you."

"Jes' lak me?" he muttered, his body heaving. "Jes' lak

me," he repeated, and he looked at his clothes; then his eyes wandered over the room.

When he turned to face her his eyes were red. He sauntered towards the bed and plopped down on it.

Stella knew at once that she had made him feel ashamed and she walked over to him.

He waved her away. "Jes' lak me. Chile' yo' don' mean that. Effen he was lak me, he would be nuffin'. Look, baby. Yo' pa, me, when you was born everything was going good wid me. But yo' maw, she done went and turned out to be no good."

"Pa, please don't speak that way about Ma, she's dead and gone."

"Yes, but yo' mus' know the truth, chile. Yo' ma, she . . . yo' jes' wait till you find what it is tuh have sombody roun' yer what ain't no good." Jim Jackson stood up. "That's what I said, gal. Now git goin' before I do sumpin' real bad."

Stella was surprised at the sudden change in her father.

He appeared to go mad suddenly. He reached down and picked up the mattress. He seemed to be possessed with the devil. He was cursing loudly. He flung the mattress across the room and the wall shook as he continued cursing. "Gawd damn 'em!" he swore, "they done it to me," and he fell on the floor, exhausted.

Stella ran from the room and called to Ted, who was waiting just outside the door.

Ted came running. "Miss Stella, you ought to ah knowed by now, but ef you don't know, your father is crazy. Them fits come on every now and then. You'd better come on now, he'll be all right."

"Gimme a drink," cried Jim Jackson. He struggled to his feet and before they realised what was happening he ran past them right out the open door, and kept on running.

127

Reeling from side to side, he stumbled, fell, arose, and kept running.

Stella and Ted were running behind him and kept calling to him, but Jim Jackson continued running and yelling, "Gimme a drink, I want a drink!"

He reached the railroad track.

Ted could only hobble along behind Stella, who was still trying to catch up with her father.

"Oh Lord, Miss Stell'," he cried, "I hope he ain't gonna run on dat dere track. Number 44 'bout due."

Stella was still screaming at the top of her voice, "Oh, Pop, please come back!"

But Jim Jackson kept running. He staggered to the bend in the track, now less than fifty yards before him, with Stella in pursuit. But they were unable to catch him. The man was running as though possessed with the devil.

"Oh, Mr. Jackson, puhleese," Ted sang pleadingly, but he never turned around.

Stella began to tire and stopped running at the curve in the track. The whistle of the number 44 blew, long, long, short, and long.

Ted knew that whistle. He had heard it so many times before, but it had never sounded like this. Again it blew. Jim Jackson was on the railroad track and Ted was about fifty yards behind him.

A few more steps and Jim Jackson was on the trestle above Winding Creek.

The hum of the train was running right up Ted's legs. He looked ahead of Jim and saw the train coming directly at them. The trestle was about forty yards long and fifty feet below was nothing but 200 feet of dirty water.

Ted had reached the trestle when he knew that Jim Jackson was doomed. Even if he had seen the train, it still would have been too late.

The cowcatcher on the locomotive hit Jim Jackson and threw him straight up in the air; he cleared the trestle and went tumbling below to certain death.

Ted seemed doomed to die the same way. He climbed quickly through the opening in the tracks, caught one of the beams, and held on with both hands.

The engineer had applied the brakes when the train hit Jim, but it kept going, grinding and blowing steam at a fast pace. The engine passed over Ted and the soot and grime shot at him with a wind that almost tore his arms apart. Ted squeezed his eyes shut, bit his lower lip, and prayed.

The trestle trembled as the train came to a stop.

Ted was still unable to move. The whole train was above him. He could hear the people mumbling excitedly above him. He summoned all his strength and yelled, "Git this train moving 'fore I fall in this 'ere river!"

An answer came from what sounded like the conductor. "We just killed a man. You know anything about it?"

"I sho do, but ef you don' git this train off me, I ain't gwine to be able to tell you all nothin'."

"Okay, boy."

Ted felt his strength leaving him as the train started. The two cars passed and the train stopped. There was daylight above him once more.

Then a pair of hands pulled him up. He could see Stella at the far end of the trestle and knew what had happened, for everyone was looking down into the river below where the remains of Jim Jackson lay.

Ted remembered standing on the trestle with people looking at him from the back of the train when everything before him went black.

When he opened his eyes again, he was in his sister's

bed and Stella was standing above him with a wet towel, which she applied to his forehead.

"Ted," she said, "I saw it all happen and I thought you were gone too."

Chapter Eleven

Many miles farther north another train arrived in Detroit, Michigan, one Sunday morning.

"Well, well, young man, you certainly have grown," greeted Jean. His cousin, James "Toddy" Turner, had alighted from the train, looking like a big football player.

"You are even taller than I am," continued Jean; he seemed to be waiting for Toddy's young lady.

"Yes, sir," was all Toddy could say.

"Where is that young lady you wrote us about?"

"Oh, Stella couldn't make it, sir. She had bad news from her home. Her mother is very ill and she thought she would go there."

"Oh, that is too bad. I am awfully sorry to hear that."

"I started to go with her but she wanted to go alone, and, if her mother was not too bad, she would get in touch with me here and perhaps join me later."

"Well, I do hope she can make it."

"Yes, sir, I do also."

"Come, let's go to my house," said Jean, he took Toddy's bag and Toddy followed.

"I was surprised when you told me that you were married, sir."

"Oh, James, let's stop that sir business. You are my first cousin. Oh, yes, about Marie, my wife. Yes, we have been married about six months. I thought I would keep it for an Easter surprise."

Jean stopped in front of a car and motioned for Toddy to get in as he opened the door.

"Yours?" asked Toddy, a little surprised.

"Yes, I got it a couple of weeks ago."

"Sure is a beauty."

"Hope you like Detroit, young fella. It's not as boisterous as New York, but we will try to show you a nice time."

Fifteen minutes later, the car stopped in front of a beautiful brick house, in a suburban area, on a well manicured lawn.

"Here we are," remarked Jean.

"You are doing all right, to live in a neighborhood like this, I mean," Toddy commented.

"I am not doing too badly," Jean retorted.

They walked across a stone path and soon Jean was opening the door. Toddy looked behind him and admired the entire scene. The path was bordered with well-trimmed green shrubbery and the entrance to the house seemed rather palatial. Toddy wondered what his cousin's income was to have such a beautiful home.

Jean opened the door and again Toddy was awed by the magnificent beauty of the room they had entered. In the far corner was a piano, which attracted his attention.

He was still admiring his cousin's home when feminine footsteps caused him to turn towards the sound.

They were coming down the stairs. Jean had walked into the adjoining room, evidently a dining room, and had taken Toddy's coat with him. He then reentered the room.

Seeing his wife, Jean said, "Hello, dear, see what I have brought you?"

James "Toddy" Turner had not heard anything that his cousin had said. He was staring at the girl who stood at the foot of the stairs. It was as though someone had cast a spell upon him and he was enveloped in a strange web of gossamer that was slowly beckoning him to enter a rapturous world from which he would never want to escape.

Never before, in his young life, had he stood face to face with a woman so beautiful. She was very young. Then a hand on his shoulder startled him and he turned to see his cousin looking at him.

"James, or rather Toddy, this is my wife, Marie."

The room seemed to be in a complete silence, and then the dream came to life. She walked towards him. He looked into her eyes for a moment. They were changeable green for a moment then grey the next. He had seen her before, but where? She extended her hand and he took it. The softness was bewitching and he said, "How are you, Mrs. Mondeau?"

Her skin was like clean sand on an ocean beach and as smooth as satin. Her hair was jet black. She was tall, a trifle shorter than he was, but taller than her husband. She stood erect; her bosom was the resting place for two well-rounded breasts that stood out like ripe pomegranates from their young branches. Her face was long, but not thin, and was separated by a long thin nose that dominated a pair of full well-rounded lips. Again her eyes met his, and he said to himself, "Cat eyes."

All this he had to take in in only a few seconds, for her lips were parting and words came. "I am quite well, zank you, and very happy to know you." She seemed to have a slight French accent.

She turned towards the dining room and said, "Come in and see our house."

He followed, with Jean bringing up the rear.

"Jean told me you were a good looking boy, but I never thought you'd be such a pretty young man," said Marie. She smiled and their eyes met again.

As she walked before him, it occurred to him that she

did not fit into the role of Jean's wife. Her accent reminded him of his French teacher of many years ago. The close-fitting long maroon gown she wore swept the floor as she walked. As she swayed her hips the perfume she wore played havoc with Toddy's senses.

She turned suddenly and Toddy felt that she was aware of his admiration. Her eyebrows narrowed a little and she smiled dryly.

Jean broke the spell. "You want to wash up, don't you, Toddy?"

Turning to Marie, Toddy said, dramatically. "Pardon me?"

"Certainly. Jean, show him where the bathroom is."

"Sure. Come along."

An hour later Toddy went back downstairs. Mrs. Mondeau was seated at the piano looking at sheet music.

She whirled and faced him. All he could think of saying was, "Where's Jean?"

"Oh, my," she commented, "you look, 'er, so—what must I say—chic."

He did not reply.

"Ah, yes. Jean, he drove to the corner to get something. He'll be right back."

"Thank you."

"You may sit down. Make yourself comfortable. I'll be right back."

She made no effort to go anywhere and he knew that she was looking at him.

He walked over to a magazine rack, took out a copy of "The Musician," and sat down in a large club chair across the room. He cast a glance in her direction and their eyes met. Toddy remarked, rather quickly, "Lovely place you have here," while looking around the room.

"Thank you, I am glad that you like it. By the way, how's

New York? I have some friends up on Edgecombe Avenue and I may be running up to see them very soon. Mr. and Mrs. Milton. You don't happen to know them, do you?"

"No, I don't. In fact, I don't go out very much. You see, I don't know too many people in New York."

She did not answer. She got up, walked over to the window nearest to him, and adjusted the shades; then she turned, looked at him, and then walked towards him.

As she stood over him, her face became flushed for a moment. She said, "Why did you stare at me like that today? You know, I mean when you first saw me at the foot of the stairs." Her eyes grew smaller as she continued. "You seemed to go right through me, as though you were . . . undressing me."

Where had he heard those words before? Oh, yes, Stella had said the same thing to him on the dance floor in the Savoy Ballroom not so long ago. Was it the way he looked at girls? Did his eyes cast a spell over them?

"I am terribly sorry, I meant no harm," he remarked, as he looked up at her. "You see," he hesitated, "I have never seen a beautiful girl before."

The door opened, suddenly, and Jean walked in with a large paper bag. "Ice cream for dessert," he said.

Toddy realized that his cousin must have seen the embarrassment in the faces of both Marie and himself, but Jean did not act accordingly.

"I am crazy about ice cream, are you, James?"

"Sure," he answered.

Jean walked to the dining room and they followed.

After supper, Jean and Toddy went into the drawing room and Marie went upstairs.

"Smoke these?" inquired Jean, offering him a cigar.

"No thanks, they are too strong for me."

"You are not missing anything. How about a little wine, or do you prefer something stronger?"

"No thanks, oh well, just wee bit of the wine would be all right."

"Marie," called Jean.

"Coming," she answered, as she came down the stairs.

"Oh, I didn't know you were going out," said Jean, as Marie was dressed to go out.

"Not anywhere special, I was just going to take a run up to Mrs. Vincent's, but if you prefer me to stay . . . I won't be long, really."

"All right, but bring in a bottle of wine before you go."

"Certainly," answered Marie, and Toddy detected a bit of anger in her tone.

"Where do you get it?" Toddy asked Jean, as Marie went out the door.

"I do know some people," Jean replied.

"That's what I always say, it pays to know the right people. You know, I really came here mainly to ask your advice about something very important to me. You are successful, I can see that, and I am hoping that you can help me to make up my mind."

"Go on, what's it all about?"

"Well, take you, for instance. When you first met Marie, how did you feel? I mean, how did you know that she would be the girl you'd want to marry? Did you love her right away, or did it take a little time to find out?"

"I see. You are in love."

"Well . . . " drawled Toddy, "that's it, I don't know. I think so, but I am not so sure."

"You are worried about getting married?"

"I . . . er . . . "

"You are not in any trouble?"

"Oh, no, No. But, it's a rather long story."

Toddy told Jean the story of his meeting with Stella and of their relationship up to the time she had left to visit her sick mother.

"All right, old boy. For a young person like you, this is a little odd. You say this is the first girl you ever went with? I mean, the very first?"

"Yes, sir, that's the truth."

"Well now, perhaps I can tell you my story."

Jean opened the bottle of wine and poured a half of a glass for himself. "Help yourself," he said to Toddy.

Toddy hesitated.

"Go ahead," Jean urged him.

Toddy did not want to divulge the fact that his mother had asked him on her dying bed not to drink, or rather, had written to him asking him not to. And, he remembered when he did try to, at that party in New York, what had happened. But perhaps this was a bit different. After all, Jean was his mother's nephew, and she wouldn't have minded.

He poured some wine in a glass; Jean was waiting for him and toasted. They raised their glasses together and Jean said, "Here's luck."

"To you too, sir," said Toddy and almost choked on the first swallow.

"You don't drink, you don't smoke. You know what the saying is about those that do neither of those things."

"Yes, sir, but . . . "

"Oh, you do know, well . . . "

They both smiled, took another swallow and put down their glasses.

Jean relit his cigar and drew his chair closer to Toddy as though he were afraid someone would be listening.

"Toddy, you are only here a few hours and if you were here for many, many days, you'd think that I am the happiest man in the world. But let me tell you something. I lied to you

137

when I wrote you that letter. I live in a fine home, I have a new car every two years, and I make a pretty good living . . . and that's all."

"I don't understand, what do you mean that's all?"

"Oh, I haven't finished. I made a big mistake in my life, and I'll never be able to rectify it as long as I live."

He paused, poured out another drink, and continued. "James, about ten years ago I could have married a girl that knew everything, she knew the world. She knew the pitfalls of life. She was not an angel but she was honest. This may sound incredible, but there's one thing you'll have to look for in a woman: if a girl comes from a good family. I don't mean a rich one. Oh, there are good families that are also rich, but what I mean is, if she has a background. Take you, for instance, or even me. We were brought up to be decent, to be honest. We know when we are doing wrong. Are you following me? When you have that certain thing to fall back on, you have a certain amount of self-protection when a crisis develops.

"If things went bad for us we'd prefer to beg rather than to steal because we were brought up to die rather than to disgrace our name.

"Now, if a girl knows everything and has done everything and decides to be good or to fall in love with someone who she feels is her saviour, providing she wants to be good, wants to be saved, she will make a better wife than one who has to be told to be a good wife.

"Woe to a man who picks a maiden and decides to try to conform her to his will. It doesn't work, and I know," Jean said, banging his hand on the arm of the chair, "I really do know, believe me."

Toddy kept silent while Jean was discussing his problem, something that Toddy was not aware of, but how could he help him? He continued to listen as Jean continued his story.

"I am going upstairs for a moment. I'll be back with something to show you."

Jean returned with an album. He opened it, turned over a few pages, and placed it before Toddy. "Do you recognize them?"

"Yes, it's Marie, isn't it?"

"Yes, but that picture was taken while she was in a convent up in Canada. She is seated beside a nun. Look at her, doesn't she look like the most pious person you have ever seen? I met her shortly after that picture was taken. She had left the convent. She was so chaste and pure, and I was rather frivolous."

Jean closed his eyes while recalling the events of his younger life. "She was very bashful when I tried to speak to her. I took her to a dance and it was a long while before she'd let me hold her. You know the way we danced. I took her to our baseball games. Of course, she is much younger than I am and I guess that had something to do with the way she acted. But as time passed she said that it made no difference.

"It wasn't easy to pick between her and the other girl I knew and liked very much. Dora was the other girl. She thought it would be much better that I, then a college student, should marry a girl like Marie. She said it would be better for me socially and educationally but, Lord knows, I have regretted that decision I made many, many times.

"Marie, she was sweet and innocent, a clean girl, a virgin. She lost her mother and father early, she said. That was a long time ago.

"A few weeks after we were married, something happened. That sweet disposition she had suddenly disappeared. She became wild, uncontrollable, and abnormally love crazy. She wanted to make love every night. Are you following me? I couldn't satisfy her in any way. Then one night she told me, 'You are too old for me, you only make me crave excitement and affection from other men.' I didn't want to lose her. I really loved her. She was my inspiration. Every successful thing I did depended on her. So after weeks of torture we decided on her plan.

"She could do what she wanted, go wherever she wanted, but we would continue to live together as man and wife. Sooner or later I will be completely out of my mind and she'll be the reason, or perhaps she won't be. I'll probably kill myself after I kill her."

For the first time Toddy spoke. "Well, Jean, I don't think that would solve any problem."

Footsteps coming up the porch put an end to the conversation. The door opened and Marie came in with some friends.

"Hello," greeted Marie. "See, darling, I didn't stay long."

He smiled and got up and greeted the guests.

Marie turned towards Toddy and said, "Meet some friends, James. Mrs. Vincent, Mr. Vincent, meet Mr. Turner from New York, Jean's cousin."

Toddy acknowledged the introduction.

"And Miss Lee, Mr. Turner."

Again Toddy bowed.

"Excuse us, gentlemen," said Marie, and the three ladies went upstairs.

"Well, Bob," asked Jean of Mr. Vincent, "how is everything?"

"Not bad, old man," came the reply.

Toddy detected a sort of derision in the emphasis on "old" as he saw that Mr. Vincent was at least fifteen years younger than Jean.

"Nice looking fellow, your cousin," remarked Mr. Lee.

Toddy was a bit embarrassed. Why did they all say he was good-looking, or why did they *have* to say it? After all, he was no baby.

Mr. Vincent begged to be excused and went upstairs. Mr. Lee followed, so Jean and Toddy were left together again.

"You see," Jean went on, as though he had never been interrupted, "she's always out. Parties, friends, day, night, no let up. She's constantly running. But now to get back to our discussion.

"You met a girl who knows more of the world than you do. Don't let it worry you. If she loves you, and you'll be able to tell that, you know, she'll stick to you regardless, whether you are rich or poor, or whether you have to fight to live.

"One thing every man wants is to become a success, to amount to something. And get this, there are many more that are happy in our race than are successful."

"I started out to be a doctor, but it didn't work out that way. I am not sorry, I have made good in other fields. In these United States, if you fail at one thing you can always try another. Sure, you'll meet some tough times, but you'll have to make the best of it, especially if you have someone on your side who has faith in you and is willing to go all the way.

"A woman is always the inspiration behind the man, you know. Stella may be yours, and believe me, it won't take you long to find out if she's the one. Stella may be yours. Get married if you really love her.

"Sometimes I wish that the law would permit people to try what you are contemplating. You know, to find out things before it's too late. I am sure there would not be half the divorces and separations as there are in the world today. I don't believe that people should use living together just for a thrill. But people who really intend to get married, they would learn what responsibility means and they would be

educated about the subject before going into it wholeheart-
edly."

Toddy kept shaking his head in agreement all through
Jean's talk and he was impressed. It was what he wanted
to hear, especially from one who had not made a success
of his domestic life, contrary to what he had believed. He
respected his cousin more than ever. Instead of discourag-
ing him, he had actually told him not to be swayed by his
failures.

It was nine o'clock that evening when guests began to
arrive at the Mondeaus' home. To Toddy, they seemed a
rather distinguished-looking lot. At least three were doctors
and the others were black men and women of a higher
social set than many people whom he had had the oppor-
tunity of meeting before. There was a very anemic-looking
character, however, who by his suspicious nature seemed
to stand out above the others.

This particular individual was constantly in the com-
pany of Mrs. Mondeau. Toddy could see that his cousin was
not very pleased, but he cloaked his displeasure very well
by mixing with everyone, especially the other male guests
who "lived" in the kitchen, where the drinks were. As Jean
passed him to go to the kitchen, he decided to join him. He
was only in there a few minutes when Mrs. Mondeau came
in. She was followed by some of the other ladies. As she
passed him, their eyes met and as always a cold shudder
ran through Toddy's whole body. Suddenly he found himself
wondering if his cousin was telling him the truth about his
wife.

She was really very attractive and Toddy was somewhat
ashamed at himself for convicting her on his cousin's words.
Perhaps there was some truth to his story. After all, this girl
was young and beautiful and perhaps his cousin could not

give her the affection she craved. All these thoughts ran through his mind as she stood close to him, watching him.

She took three steps toward him and Toddy then realised that she appeared to be getting a little drunk.

"Won't you have a drink?" she asked.

He meant to be abrupt, but somehow he could not be rude to her. "Well, er, I don't think I will, at least not just now."

"Not even a little wine? You had some this afternoon. They say once you stick to one thing, in drinking, you'll never get sick."

Toddy realized that to displease her would probably cause her to act rather stupidly, so he agreed to take just one.

"It is really crowded in here, don't you think? Let's go on the porch. Oh, that's right, you've never seen the back porch. Come, I'll show it to you and you can tell me what you think of it."

Toddy, a little frightened and embarrassed, followed. They were now at the back of the house and the wall seemed to stop the noise from the rest of the house, so much so, that he could not imagine he was on the porch of the same house.

"Here, sit here. It is a little cool but I don't think you'll freeze," she said, and a swift turn of her head again brought that peculiar feeling over him. "We were interrupted today. Do you care to talk any more about why you look at me so seriously?"

"Oh, please, let's not discuss it. I told you that I was sorry if I offended you . . . "

"But you haven't offended me. I just never had anyone go through me the way you do when you look at me like that."

The blood seemed to rush to Toddy's head, and he stood up. "I think we'd better go inside . . . "

"I hear you have a lovely girlfriend in New York. Why couldn't you send for her and stay a little while longer?"

"Oh no, I couldn't do that," he answered.

"Gee, that's too bad," she remarked, and crossed her legs.

He felt like rushing inside to where the other guests were, but something held him back. He couldn't explain it himself.

"Have you ever played football?" she asked, and took hold of his hands. She then said, "Please sit down. You have such large strong hands."

Toddy obeyed.

"You look so big and strong," she continued.

"No, I have never played football," he answered, curtly.

"I admire big men. They seem so forceful."

"Is that the reason you married Jean, my cousin?"

She did not answer. "Oh," she gasped, suddenly, "my shoe is off. Do you mind?"

Toddy quickly reached for the shoe and hastily put it back on her foot.

"My, you seem awful nervous. Is it my legs that make you . . . "

"Please, Mrs. Mondeau."

"Why can't you call me Marie? After all, I am your cousin, you know." Toddy just stared at her. Then Marie said, "I don't know why I am going to do it, but tomorrow I am going to tell you something very important."

"All right then. Tomorrow," replied Toddy.

She got up and Toddy finally drank his wine and went inside with her. *I've seen her somewhere*, he thought to himself. *There is something about her, something familiar.*

They joined the other groups in the dining room. A crowd of men rushed over to Marie and for the next few minutes she was the center of attention for a very lively group of young and old men.

Just at that moment Jean came in and his wife, on seeing him, left the men. Marie put her arm through his and the couple then walked to the porch from whence she had just come.

Toddy, under the pretense of going into the kitchen, followed and stayed close to the window. He overheard their conversation.

"Well, Jean, what do you think of him?"

"Fine, handsome, but a bit shy, you know, for a boy from New York."

"His mother brought him up that way. He is going to be here a week, so try and be decent."

"Decent? I am going to be very decent."

To Toddy it was all a mystery. That afternoon his cousin had been telling him a lot of things about Marie, and now they were talking about *him.*

"Good morning, James," greeted Jean the next morning, as they met in the hall about nine-thirty, "didn't think you'd be up so soon."

"Good morning," answered Toddy.

"Sleep well?"

"Yes, sir, I did, very well," he lied.

"I have to go to Chicago today, on business. I received a letter from a friend there. He is in some sort of a jam and I am going to see what I can do for him."

"You won't be long, will you, sir?"

"No. I'll be back tomorrow morning. While I am gone Marie will show you around. Hope you don't get fed up on her parties. She certainly throws them. Have a nice time. I'll see you in the morning."

"Oh, don't you think I could go along with you? I'd like

to be in court to see how you work. You know maybe I'll be a lawyer, too, some day."

"No, boy. This is strictly business. Besides, you are here on a vacation. Marie is going to Mrs. Bruce's today. A lovely place, I know you will have a nice time."

"Yes, sir, I know I will."

"We have an invitation for a frolic Thursday night at some exclusive place. So you have that to look forward to. Boy, you're sure going to have a whale of a time while you are here."

Toddy went back to the bathroom as he heard the door slam and knew that Jean had left. He was still dressing in his room when he heard a knock on the door.

"Who?"

"It's me, Toddy," answered Marie, "I just wanted to know if you are coming down for breakfast. It's almost ready."

"Er, yes, good morning. I'll be down in a few minutes."

"Excuse me, good morning. Please hurry."

"All right."

They had breakfast about ten-thirty, and all through the meal Marie purposely ignored Toddy. But he was indeed happy, for he had been afraid that she would begin something, knowing that her husband was away.

Suddenly, the telephone rang.

Marie jumped to answer it.

Presently Toddy heard her voice: "Hello, Bruce, how are you? Yes, I was coming over, but I've changed my mind. Yes. I don't think I'll see you all before this evening."

Toddy thought, *I wonder what she is up to now. Jean said that she was going over to visit this Bruce.*

She walked back to the table. She looked at Toddy very calmly and said, "That place just called, Bruce's. They have a very exclusive club. We are going there this evening. Did Mr. Mondeau tell you?"

"Well, he did in a way. What he really said was that we were going there tonight."

"Well, he meant in the evening."

"Oh, I see."

"That's right," she said, with a snap of her fingers. "Jean did tell me that you could play the piano. You wouldn't mind playing me a piece later, would you?"

"Isn't there something you said that you had to tell me today? I am very anxious to hear it."

"Later," she said, almost in a whisper.

They finished the dishes and Marie led the way to the drawing room. She had brought along two glasses.

"Is it necessary for you to drink so much?" asked Toddy.

Her eyes glared at him, "No, it's not necessary," she replied, "but it helps me to forget a lot of things."

"Forget? First you have to do something to remember in order to have something to forget," remarked Toddy.

"You think I have never done anything?"

"You are too young to have done anything. What you are doing now is something that you will want to forget later."

"One will not hurt you, I am sure. Please do not make me feel so terribly bad."

She poured out the liquor and then the seltzer. She handed it to him and he drank it. The warmth of the room bothered him a little and he loosened his collar just a trifle.

"You may remove your coat, if you want to," suggested Marie.

"Thank you," said Toddy, and he removed his coat.

They walked over to the piano and Toddy sat down. First, he ran up and down the keys and as he tried to remember something to play, she asked, "Do you know 'The Song of India'?"

"I think so."

He started to play it slowly. He closed his eyes and the notes seemed to come to him so easily. He went back many years to the time when he had thought that music was the greatest thing on earth. She sat near to him while he played, and soon she was playing the higher notes.

As the final note of the song was played, he turned and once more their eyes met. Her eyes were playing havoc with him. First, he looked into one, then the other. Her face was closer to him. His head was in a whirl. There was a peculiar look in her eyes. Even Stella had never looked this way to him. No woman ever had. Closer she came. He felt her breath on his cheek, then something inside of him suddenly burst.

Her eyes were afire, her lips were parted, and she kissed him. A passionate warm kiss, that burned his very soul it seemed. Her lips were warm, burning, and he returned her kiss. The world was lost to him and he was lost to the world.

She whispered in his ear, "Darling, I wanted to do that since the first minute I laid eyes on you."

Slowly the revelation came to him. He shook his head as though suddenly waking from a dream. "What have I done?" he asked himself. "Good God, Marie, what have we done?"

"Oh, please don't feel that way. I know how you should feel, but maybe after you hear what I have to say you won't feel the way you do now."

"Are you mad?" he asked her, slowly pushing her away from him.

"Mad? Yes, mad with feeling that at last I have found someone who can make me feel like a woman."

148

"Tell me," he asked, "how did it ever happen? I mean, you marrying Jean."

"Oh, you would not understand. Maybe, if you want to listen, I could try to make you understand."

"Yes. Yes. Go on. What were you going to say?" urged Toddy.

"I was wondering, perhaps you will repeat what I am about to tell you. After all you are his cousin."

"No. I wouldn't do that. You can depend on that."

"Don't look at me like that!" she almost yelled. "I can't stand it. You go right through me."

"I am sorry. I thought maybe that you would feel a little ashamed."

"Ashamed? Why? Should I be ashamed to say that at last I've found someone who I know could make me very happy?"

"Oh, please don't talk like that. You do not know what you are saying."

Again those eyes befuddled him. He found himself looking into them once more. His eyes roamed over her body and he could see that she was breathing very fast. Faster still as she looked at him without saying a word. She kissed him again; this time she cupped his face in her hands and lavished him with kisses. He squeezed her to him and returned her affections.

Gone was the thought that this was his cousin's wife. Gone was the thought that Stella was in the South, soon to be near him. Everything in this world was forgotten.

"You are young and strong," she whispered in his ear, and blew softly into it.

The ticklish sensation made him more vibrant and he kissed her again and again. Then all at once he pushed her from him and ran upstairs to his room.

Panting, he sat on the edge of his bed. He felt really

149

ashamed, but somehow he didn't care. He knew that he'd never be able to explain it to anyone. He stood up and walked towards the door. He opened it slowly and there she was, framed in the doorway. He felt weaker than ever now, and he reached out and took her hand. She came willingly.

Slowly, she closed the door behind them.

James Turner opened his eyes and peered at the ceiling above him. A feeling of fear and suspense crept over him. For a few moments he lay blinking. Then, rubbing his eyes, over and over again, he stared at the open window. The cool breeze was blowing the curtains into the room. Suddenly, he sat bolt upright in bed.

Doubtful, he slapped his own face. "Was it a dream?" he asked himself. "Dream?" *Oh sure*, he thought. His eyelids narrowed. A lady's watch was on the dresser. It was no dream. He jumped up, walked over to the mirror and looked into it. Then he walked back to the bed and sat on it.

"Lord, God in Heaven, it couldn't be, it couldn't be," he kept murmuring.

Again he walked towards the mirror. Again he stared at himself. His hands found their way up to his face and he hid his face from himself. Bursting into tears, he threw himself on the bed once more. The place was so quiet, so guiltily silent that his sobs sounded like thunder. It was like a prison. He wanted to open the door, but dared not. There was someone there, outside the door. Of this, he was sure.

"Who is it?" he bellowed.

"It's me," came the reply.

He turned the doorknob slowly. It seemed to him that he had done this same thing once before. He turned the knob again and there she was, Marie, standing in the doorway. *Repetition*, he thought, *no, it did happen before, this same thing*. He had turned the knob before, and there she had stood, framed just as she was now. Marie. His cousin's wife. The wife of the man to whom he had come for advice.

"Good morning," she said smiling.

Now was really the time he wanted to "go through her" as she had always said he did when he looked at her. He stared long and hard at her. She held her head high in defiance, but not for too long. He could see her lips begin to quiver and her eyes reddened. Then tears began to seep through the corners of her eyes. He answered in a challenging voice: "Good morning. . . . You, here, in this room . . . " He wrung his hands over and over and lamented, "Oh, why did I ever come here? Why?" He turned to her again and said, "Don't you think you have a bit too much nerve? Please get out."

But she only walked past him into the room and sat on the bed. His temper flared up and he ran after her.

"You didn't ask me to leave . . . last night."

He lost all control of himself and walked menacingly towards her. Then he stopped, turned around, and walked out of the room.

He returned in a few minutes, but the room was empty. He dressed, put on his hat, and started for the door with his packed bag.

He heard the door close downstairs and then he heard Jean's voice. "Hello, hello, where is everybody?"

"Oh, hello, dear. There you are. You look as if you have been crying."

"I got something in my eye and I was rubbing it, I guess."

"Where is Toddy?"

"Upstairs, I guess."

Toddy realized that he could not go out now with his bag. Slowly he walked back into the room and closed the door.

He heard Jean coming up the stairs. Toddy quickly

pushed the bag under the bed, donned his coat and hat, and walked over to the dresser. He picked up a comb and was combing his hair when the door opened.

"Well, well, Toddy, I see you are up. How did you sleep?"

"I slept fine," was all he could answer.

"Coming down?"

"Yes, I'll be down in a minute."

"I got back much sooner than I'd expected. I didn't think I'd get back before this afternoon."

Toddy just nodded his head. He wished Jean would hurry up and get out of the room. He felt he could not stand being in his presence much longer.

"Come on down and have something to eat."

"Okay."

"What's the matter? Is anything wrong? You look a little under the weather."

"Oh, er, not at all. I am all right. I'll be all right."

Half an hour later all three were seated at the table. Toddy said to Jean, "Please, sir, there's something I must tell you."

"Oh, yes," interrupted Marie, "please let me tell it. You see James drank a little too much yesterday and became intoxicated."

Jean looked at both of them, and a peculiar look it was. "Did you two see each other this morning?"

Marie was the first to understand what he meant. "Oh, pardon me. Good morning, Mr. Turner," she said.

"I am sorry," Toddy replied, "good morning."

For a few moments no one said a word, then Jean spoke. "What's the matter with you two?"

"Oh, yes," said Marie, "we were talking about him drinking too much last night."

"You see, it does seem a bit difficult to understand, but when my aunt died, she begged him not to touch any strong drink. That's what killed his father and you shouldn't force him to drink if he doesn't want to," Jean scolded Marie. Then he said to his cousin, "So that's why you looked so peculiar this morning, Toddy. I wouldn't let that worry me if I were you."

"No, sir, that is not what I wanted to tell you. I was thinking it would be better if I went back to New York today."

"What?" Jean blurted out. "Nonsense, how about the big dance I told you about going to on Thursday night? You said that Stella wouldn't be home for a week. Why? What's the matter? Don't you like it here?"

"I do, sir, very much. But, er, well, I'll think it over."

"Now, young fella, no buts. I asked you to come to spend a week with me. Now you look here, I've got to go downtown this morning and you'd better be here when I get back."

With that said, Jean looked at his watch, got up, and went upstairs.

Toddy looked at Marie, who stared back at him silently.

With an "excuse me," he arose and walked to the parlour.

Jean came downstairs in a hurry and, in passing, patted Toddy on his back and disappeared through the door.

His parting words were "See you later."

Toddy knew that Marie would be along any minute, so he waited for her. He didn't have to wait very long. She approached him, smoking a cigarette, and sat down near him.

"What kind of a woman are you?" he began. "What sort of a creature is behind that beautiful face of yours?" He waited for her to answer, but she said nothing. She just sat there blowing the smoke slowly from her lips. "You have the nerve to sit there at the table with him and me knowing what happened last night. And to act so cool as though it were just an adventure."

"The greatest adventure of all," she answered. "You know, I think it's time for me to tell you what I wanted to tell you yesterday," she continued. "You are just a young man but perhaps you may understand a great deal better than old people would. From what Jean tells me you only had one girl. Please listen to me." Her voice was pleasantly pleading.

"When I was about fourteen years of age I remember one of the sisters in the convent telling me that the greatest thing in all the world is forgiveness. I have given it to you. Why can't you forgive me? You think that I am very bad.

"Your cousin is more than twice my age. I married him, yes, but how was I to know that he was a cripple? Yes, you are surprised, but that is what he is, a 'love cripple.' He was dishonest with me, and now I am supposed to suffer, just because he is a cripple.

"I am young, healthy; he is rich and a cripple. I have no one else to take care of me so . . . Then you came along. I really am unable to explain it but when you walked in that door Sunday morning, something inside of me gave way completely. I saw you both when you got out of the car, but I had no idea you were so good-looking. Well maybe it wasn't just looks, but it was as if I was drawn to you." She shrugged her shoulders. "I can't explain it. Let's put it that way.

"I knew the moment I saw you that we were going to do what we did. I knew that you were the one who could make me walk on my hands and knees, and I still know that you can make me do anything you want me to."

The change in Marie's personality amazed Toddy. She was as changeable as her eyes. He listened carefully to her and began to wonder if she was telling the truth. She had never sounded like this before.

154

"I wouldn't care if you were his brother, but I will say I am glad that you are not. I know you will not believe this but . . . " She seemed to be on the verge of crying, but she went on, "The truth is I have been faithful to him until last night."

"Please don't say anything about what happened," said Toddy, pleadingly. "I find it hard to believe you, about you being true to him, I mean."

"That's exactly what he thinks, and I don't really blame him. There may come a time when you will be like him and you'll probably think the same thing he is thinking, but honest to God, what I have told you is the truth."

Toddy tried to interrupt, but she continued, "Please allow me to finish. He is always accusing me because he knows he is going to lose me. On account of his affliction. The doctor begged him to let me get a divorce. I even pity him. I stayed with him because without me he'd be nothing. He loves the dirt I walk on, but meanwhile I must starve to satisfy his incompatibility."

"But," interjected Toddy, "why did it have to be me?"

"Why?"

"Yes, why me of all people?"

"Because I've never met anyone since I married Jean that made me feel that way, that's all. You called me a name yesterday. It was not nice for you to call me that, but I was not angry. You wanted to slap me and you almost did, but if you did I would not have felt it because way down deep in my heart I am in love with you and nothing that you may say or do can change that feeling in any way whatsoever."

"Suppose he found out?"

"He probably would kill the both of us and that would be terrible, for I know that he'd kill himself, too. Perhaps you'd want me to go away and leave him to rot.

"Oh, I know it's hard for you to understand, you are so young. Nothing like this has ever happened to you before,

155

but you know that you really love me just as much as I love you. I can tell because I am a woman. You can't look me in the face and tell me that you hate me. I know you can't."

Toddy left and walked into the dining room where he met one of the girls that came in early in the afternoon.

Marie joined them a few minutes later.

"Excuse me, Toddy. I am going to freshen up a bit and I am sure that Miss Lee would like to also. Don't you, dear, of course you do." Marie put her arm around Miss Lee's shoulder and they left Toddy to wonder about his future.

The party broke up about two in the morning and the house was dark a half an hour later. The guests had gone home and Toddy, Jean, and Marie had gone to bed.

Late the next morning, the quiet of the Mondeaus' home was disturbed by the ringing of the front doorbell. There was a knock on Toddy's door and he sleepily answered, "Come in."

Jean entered. "A telegram for you, Toddy," he said.

"I guess it's from Stella."

He took it from Jean, opened it, and read it.

"Bad news?" inquired Jean.

"Yes," replied Toddy, "her mother and her father are both dead."

Neither said a word for a while. Then there was another knock on the door and Marie entered the room.

"Well, I guess you'll be leaving us soon," she remarked, after being told the news.

"Yes, she is going directly to New York after the funeral of her father. She got there too late for her mother's."

"Did she say when?" asked Marie.

"Yes, she will arrive in the city on Sunday afternoon around three."

"So you'll only have one more day with us?"

"That's about it," he replied, and Jean and Marie left.

Chapter Twelve

Summer came to Harlem once again. Hot days brought discomfort to all tenement dwellers and those who were able to gained relief by going to the beaches. There was Pelham Bay, Old Orchard Beach, and Coney Island.

Those who had to work for a living, however, had to wait until Saturday or Sunday to go to the beach, unless they went on a weekday evening. They would go up on the roof on very warm nights, or, would walk to the nearest park, where they sometimes slept all night.

It was on one of these warm July nights that Toddy and Stella took refuge on the roof of the tenement in which they lived. As Toddy lay on a blanket that he had taken with him, with Stella beside him, he looked towards the starry sky and said, "Darling, I think it's about time we make up our minds about ourselves. Don't you think it's about time we got married?"

She did not answer at once, but after a searching stare at Toddy she replied, "Tod, see that bright sky and all those stars? Well as long as they are there, I will always love you, but something has come over you. I don't know what it is, maybe it's nothing, but you seem to have changed since you came back from Detroit."

"Changed? What do you mean changed? In what way? Are you referring to, er, lovemaking?"

"I don't know," she shrugged, "maybe, as I say, it's just

my feeling. You remember when you came back and we talked about your cousin's home and his wife? There was a certain something, I can't explain it—I dream about her. I dreamt once that I saw you walking down the street with her and you didn't even notice me. Oh," she said, embracing him, "I don't know what I'd do if I were to lose you. You still feel the same way about me as you did when we first met?"

"Of course, Stella."

"And you always will?" she asked.

"Sure, always. But why did you bring up Marie? I mean, Mrs. Mondeau?"

"Oh, I don't know. That, for one reason."

"What?" inquired Toddy.

"What you just said."

"You mean calling her Marie?"

"Uh-huh."

"That's nothing. She's a relation."

"That may be, but I've always heard that a man never calls a woman by her first name unless she lets him. Toddy, it's been three months and I have never asked you, did she ever get fresh with you?"

"Darling, what are you talking about? What chance did she have to, as you say, get fresh?"

"Only one, dear. You were only there once, remember?"

"Oh, please, let's not talk foolishness. You getting jealous of my cousin's wife, are you going crazy?"

"No, since you came back, you are not the same. How about those 'cat eyes' you talked about?"

"Now I don't want to get mad, honey, but you are acting awfully stupid and jealous."

"Why shouldn't I be?"

"What made you bring this up all of a sudden? It's rude for you to think of such a thing. Jean is my first cousin."

"Ha. Some men take away their brothers' wives."

"Oh, let's forget it. It's going on four months since I left there."

"Well, maybe you've forgotten, but she hasn't. Here," said Stella, and handed him a letter. "It came this morning. I started to open it when I saw it came from Detroit, but I didn't."

Stella smiled, it seemed to him, rather devilishly, as he took the letter.

Bewilderment showed on his face as he fumbled hesitatingly with the envelope. He wondered, *Did she open it and close it back*? He dared not examine it. All he said was, "Wonder what Jean has to say."

"It's not from Jean," Stella replied. "It looks like her handwriting—Mrs. Mondeau. I remember the birthday card she sent to you. It's the same handwriting."

"Guess I'll open it then. No, you open it," he said, jerkily, and handed it to her.

"All right," she replied, and took back the envelope and opened it.

His heart missed a beat as she tore the ends of the envelope and, in the comparatively dim light, she read while he listened:

My Dear James,

Hope you and Stella are well. Just a few lines to say that I will be in New York next Sunday for the new revue at the Ballou Theatre on Monday afternoon.

There are a few of my friends in the show. If you care to go I would be glad to have you both come up to 489 Edgecombe about three thirty and perhaps we can make arrangements for all of us to go to the show together.

159

Hope you both are well and hearty. Jean sends his best regards. He won't be able to come.

Hoping to see you both,
Sincerely,
Marie

Toddy was not able to suppress the relief. He let out a deep sigh that caused Stella to look at him. Sheepishly, he remarked, "Well, just an invitation. Think you'd want to go?"

"Do you?"

"Not particularly."

"I knew it. I dreamt it. I knew it," Stella kept repeating.

"Are you sure this didn't come yesterday and you didn't read it?"

"I did not," she answered, emphatically.

"Okay," Toddy replied with a sigh, "let's go downstairs."

Toddy was the first to awaken the next morning, and as he turned and looked at Stella, who was still asleep, he suddenly found himself comparing her to Marie.

He shook his head and murmured, "Two different people altogether."

He leaned over and kissed Stella and she moved slowly, as though waiting to be seduced.

"It's ten o'clock, dear," Toddy said. "Aren't you going to church?"

"All right. We'll go next Sunday."

"Love me?" she inquired.

"Yes, dear. Go to sleep, if you are sleepy. Why?"

"Oh, never mind," she retorted, with a shrug.

And they went back to sleep. But Toddy couldn't sleep. He tried, but each time he closed his eyes he saw Marie on that train. *If she hasn't arrived yet*, he thought, *she must be here soon.* His thoughts wandered back to that morning on that sofa in her home in Detroit.

Those changeable eyes, greenish eyes, like a cat. How he had cursed himself for falling for her seductive charms. She was a beautiful and vivacious person. Then, too, there was that liquor that she had given him. How she had fondled him and tried to make him believe that she loved him, how he had pushed her away. Now after three months, he began to wonder if she had told him the truth. He tried to wake Stella but she only groaned and continued sleeping.

It was raining hard and heavy at two o'clock that afternoon. Hard, pounding, thunderous rain. The heavens were belching loud peals of thunder, and the lightning flashed constantly in the darkened sky.

Toddy was seated in a comfortable chair perusing the news of the day.

"Want to eat now?" called Stella, emerging from their little kitchenette, wiping her hands on her apron. "Everything is ready."

"All right, Madam Cuisine. Just give me time to wash my hands and I'll partake of thy delicious cooking. How is that?" he added jokingly, as though boasting of his prose.

"Sounds okay, but I am hungry."

Toddy and Stella partook of their dinner and when he called for more cake she chided him, saying, "You'll bust."

"As long as it is your cooking that does it, it's all right by me. As they say, 38 and 2."

"If it lets up," she commented, looking out the window, "we can go to the movies, huh?"

"All right, but are you sure that you don't want to go up to Edgecombe Avenue?"

"No," she answered emphatically, "a thousand times, no."

"Okay."

The doorbell rang suddenly.

"Waal," drawled Toddy, "wonder who that could be in this rain." Rising from his seat, he went to the door.

Instinctively, Stella's eyes shot at the clock on the mantelpiece, and it told her that it was three o'clock with the three strikes. Those eyes then strayed to the door and as the door opened, Stella jumped up.

"Guess who it is, dear," said Toddy. The person entered and she saw that it was a man, and alone. "It's Jean."

"Well, ask him in," replied Stella.

No one saw the awful shock that enveloped Toddy as he opened the door and saw Jean standing there.

"How are you?" she heard Toddy ask.

"Oh, just a little wet at present. I thought the rain would burst through the windshield of the car."

"Where is Mrs. Mondeau?" inquired Stella, who by this time was at the door. To Toddy her tone sounded very exacting.

"Oh, er," Jean stammered, "she didn't come up with me."

"Darling, haven't you any manners, speaking to strange men, without being introduced?" put in Toddy. "Miss Jackson, meet Mr. Mondeau."

"I am terribly sorry," replied Stella, "but I've heard so much about you that I feel I do know you."

"That's all right, you can say the same for me. I guess I should have let you know I was coming, but I thought I would surprise you both."

Toddy passed a swift glance at Stella, and she seemed to understand.

"Won't you have some dinner?" she asked.

"Well, I am hungry, but I had intended to eat a little later."

All manner of things coursed through Toddy's mind. Up to that time he had hardly taken his eyes off Jean, hoping to see some sign that would explain his visit. Toddy began to realize that his own silence was tormenting him. *Wonder what brought him up here so suddenly?* he asked himself. Everything seemed peculiar, the letter from Marie saying that Jean would not be up and then Jean himself paying a sudden visit. A somewhat guilty feeling gripped him. He felt his nerves twitching.

Jean went in to clean up. A little later he sat down to dinner. Toddy could not find enough courage to ask the reason for his coming. *Could he have found out anything? God no, no.* He shooed the thought away. *Marie was not a stupid woman.*

At last an idea struck him. *Was Jean spying on her? Maybe she had left and he followed. but why did he come here? Or perhaps they were separated. But why?*

Toddy was very much relieved when Jean finished eating and got up from the table. Toddy led him into the parlour. He was extremely anxious to know what mystery lay beneath the mantle of deceit and pretense involving his cousin and wife. And so, when Jean pulled his chair a little closer, he knew that he was about to hear something.

Jean lost no time in beginning. "Toddy, you remember me telling you how miserable my life was. That was in April, when you were down there."

"Yes I do," replied Toddy. "We were sitting, just as we are now."

"Yes, well since you left, everything has changed. Almost everything in the house has been sold and on top of that she has threatened to leave."

James Turner listened attentively.

"There is someone in New York that she wants, Toddy."

Something within Toddy snapped. His heart must have missed a whole beat. He said, "But I thought that you both had agreed to live your life . . . "

163

"I kept my part of the bargain, but she's changed her mind. I guess, oh Toddy, I am lying. I haven't kept my part. I still love her. I always will, even if I *do* go crazy. But she's getting too bold. I can't stand it much longer. Something is going to happen, so don't be surprised."

They were interrupted by Stella, who came charging in, saying, "Now what's all the secrets?"

"Just talking about old times," put in Toddy, and Stella sat down.

"Well, it looks as if the rain has stopped," remarked Jean.

"Yes, it certainly does," agreed Stella, glancing at Toddy.

"Where is the nearest garage?" asked Jean. "I would like to have the car cleaned up."

"Sure thing. I'll go along with you," said Toddy.

"I am very sleepy," Jean continued.

Stella was seated alone in the small parlor, waiting for the two men to come back, when the doorbell rang. "Gracious," she cried, "why didn't he take his key?"

She went to the door. As she opened it, she was startled by the person facing her. Intuition told her at once the identity of the person. She stared straight and hard.

"Yes?" was all she could say at the moment.

"Oh, you must be Stella. I am Mrs. Mondeau. Marie, Jean's wife."

"Come in," said Stella, who was obviously awed by the beauty of another of her sex. "Yes," she went on, "I am Stella." She closed the door behind them.

"I waited for you both to come, but I realized the showers must have stopped you, so I thought I'd run over and drive you both down. Where's James? I mean, Mr. Turner?"

If Stella had answered immediately, she felt sure it would have been a very insulting remark. The blood rushed to her head at the mention of Toddy, but, biding her time and camouflaging her feelings as best she could, she answered albeit sarcastically, "We've had company and Mr. Turner is out at present. But he'll be back very shortly."

"Oh, don't tell me you hadn't received my invitation."

"Oh, yes indeed, but our guest was so unexpected that we really couldn't leave him," she finished, smiling.

"Of course not. Do you mind if I smoke?"

"No, not at all."

Marie took out a cigarette case, extracted one, and after lighting it, drew a long, deep breath and emitted a stream of smoke. "Why not bring your guest along? I am sure she'll have a marvelous time," remarked Marie.

"She? Oh, pardon me. It's not a she, it's a he. But I doubt that he would have a marvelous time. You see, he had driven a long way."

"Well so have I," she interrupted.

"Yes, but you see our guest is Mr. Mondeau, your husband, James's cousin."

Marie, at that moment, must have had difficulty exhaling for a sudden coughing fit ensued with the smoke pouring from her mouth in quick, jerky spasms. She finally came to herself, with Stella trying to keep from smiling. Marie's mouth gaped in a taunting circle. "You mean, my husband is here?" she asked.

"Yes, he just arrived an hour or so ago."

"Oh dear, please. I'll see you later."

As the door slammed shut, Stella laughed loudly, almost hysterically.

Soon her countenance changed to one of anger as she realized that Marie had deliberately come there to see Toddy. And that there must be something wrong. Otherwise, she would not have left in such a hurry.

A half hour later the key turning in the lock told Stella that Toddy had returned.

"We didn't stay long, did we?" Toddy asked her.

"Uh-huh. I don't know exactly. While you were gone someone came to look for you."

"Who was it, dear?" Toddy closed the door behind Jean and himself.

"A friend that you haven't seen for some time. He said it couldn't wait," she put in when she saw Jean.

"Did he leave his name?"

"No, he didn't."

"That's funny."

"Yes indeed."

Toddy discerned a slight bit of sarcasm in her tone. He turned to Jean. "You want to rest, don't you, sir?"

"Thanks a lot, Toddy. I hope some day I'll be able to do the same for you."

"Make yourself comfortable, Mr. Mondeau," put in Stella.

"Well," said Toddy, turning to Stella after Jean had closed the door to his room, "what's so funny?"

"Ha. Ha. Ha."

Toddy knew that laugh. It was characteristic of Stella to laugh when she had something up her sleeve.

"Well, darling, ha, ha. Who do you think your friend was?"

He did not answer. But he knew that it wasn't funny.

"Mrs. Mondeau, his wife," she said, pointing to the room in which Jean was.

"Good God, what did she want? Is something the matter?"

"She came to see why we didn't come to the house, or rather, why *you* didn't come."

"Me?"

166

"Yes, and as soon as I told her that her husband was here she left—and I mean she left."

He started toward the living room. Stella did not know what Jean had told him and he had to be careful not to let her suspect anything.

"He must never know that she was here," he said. "He has an idea that she is cheating on him and he is threatening to kill her."

"Oh, is he? Is he? And may I ask why you are all upset?"

"Well after all, dear, isn't he my cousin? I wouldn't want to see anything like that happen to him."

"Anyway, she is a determined creature. In one way or the other, she seems to be after you."

"Oh, stop talking foolishness," said Toddy, angrily.

"It's not foolishness, and you know it," she replied.

"What do you mean, 'I know it'?"

"Oh, I er, don't know. Anyway, I'd never leave my husband to go looking for someone else, especially if he could give me all I want."

"Perhaps she has a reason."

"Oh, you are defending her?"

"I am not defending anybody. I just say there are lots of women like her. They get married to someone much older than they are and they, you know what I mean, the spark of passion goes dead, so they . . . "

"Yes, but why has she got to pick on you?"

"She is not picking on me, dear. She's just trying to be nice, because we are her relatives."

Relatives, relationship, the words played on his conscience. He was sorry that he had said it. It seemed to stick him like a knife.

"Oh, let's stop fussing." declared Toddy. "Come on, let's go the movies. I'll leave a note for Jean, in case he wakes up before we get back."

The next morning, dawn appeared somewhat slowly for James Turner. He lay in bed and could not sleep anymore. It was about five o'clock and it seemed to him that Marie was in the room. He imagined that he heard her voice in the still room. "You know you want to see me again and I do too," the invisible person seemed to say. His mind went back to Detroit. He closed his eyes and wondered. A guilty voice inside of him said, "You ought to be ashamed of yourself. You, with a girl who loves you, lying right at your side."

But something else was fighting inside of him. Something that almost made him forget Stella. He shook his head as if to clear his befuddled brain. He compared the two. There was no comparison. Both were as different as rain and sunshine. He felt he must see Marie once, if only to find out if Stella was right in what she thought. He could hear the clock ticking on. Half an hour went by, an hour, an hour and a half. He tossed in the bed. He stole a few winks, and woke suddenly. Still Stella did not wake.

Thoughts of Marie's body tormented him. She had given herself to him. He was sorry now that he had become angry with her. He hadn't approached her, she had approached him.

He would go to her that day and tell her how he felt. He would find out once and for all what was in her mind. He jumped out of bed. He went to the bathroom, walked to the mirror, and looked at himself. He bit his lip. A voice kept repeating, "Toddy, it's wrong, it's wrong, it's wrong."

"Stella," he called, going back to the bedroom.

Still she slept. He went to the kitchenette and fixed his own breakfast. The clock said eight-forty-five. He tiptoed back to the bedroom, dressed, and started out once again. He stopped, turned, leaned over the bed to kiss her. But, as his lips neared hers, he changed his mind. Shutting the door as quietly as he could, he went out. Downstairs there was a letter in the mailbox. Taking it out he examined the writing. It was from Marie Mondeau. Opening the door he walked to the street, tearing the envelope open.

It read:

James, there is something important I must tell you. We are having a meeting at my friends' home on Edgecombe Avenue this afternoon at four. Please come. Bye, M.

Short and to the point, he thought. *Goodness, she is a darn fool. Suppose Stella saw this, she would blow up.* He walked on, tearing up the letter and depositing the remains in one of the ash cans on the sidewalk. *Well, now she wants to see me, and I want to see her.*

Toddy rang the bell at the place mentioned at four o'clock that afternoon. Almost immediately the door opened.

"Come in," said Marie.

Toddy hesitated a little, looked at her, and walked in.

"Hello," he said rather sharply.

"Hello," she answered, "I thought you weren't coming after all."

"I really shouldn't have, you know," he answered, hypocritically.

"Oh, I am so glad you did come," she smiled. "Have a seat here. Let me take your hat."

"Fine place you have here," he remarked, glancing around the room. He sat down.

"Would you care to have a glass of lemonade?" she asked. "It's so warm."

"Thanks," he replied.

"Will you excuse me then?"

She returned in a few minutes with a pitcher and into two glasses she poured the liquid.

They both drank.

Toddy noticed the tightly fitting dress that she wore.

"Aren't you a little stouter than when I saw you last?" asked Toddy.

"What?"

He repeated the question.

"Oh yes, I am, just a little," she replied.

"Tell me, Marie, why did you write that note to me? You know it was not right. Oh, it was a good thing that I came out of the house first this morning. You really should not have done that."

"But I didn't mean to . . . "

"Suppose," he interrupted her, "suppose Stella had got a hold of it. No telling what would have happened."

"I thought that you would get it first, that's why I mailed it last night."

"And furthermore, why did you ask me to come here when you knew that I had to be working?"

"No particular reason, I just wanted to talk to you, that's all."

"Well, to tell the truth, I wanted to talk to you also."

"Really, James, I can't explain my feelings. I just wanted to be with you."

"Wait a minute. Is there anyone else here?"

"Nope, not another soul but you and I."

"Oh, I don't think it's right, Marie. You know after all Stella and I are . . . I really shouldn't come at all."

"But you did come and here you are."

She got up and walked towards the window. "I wonder if you realize that I am madly in love with you. I wondered whether it was only because you were the first person I had known since Jean, but now I know I am really in love." She suddenly whirled around. "Did you know that since you left Detroit, I have been miserable? I don't know what you've done to me but I've become so wretched knowing that you were in New York. Time and time again, I wanted to write to you. I was afraid. You made me love you." She sat close to him on the chair.

"Oh God, Toddy, I am not kidding you. Right now I am the happiest person in the world. Why? Because you are here. Near to me. I seem to want you near me all the time. I dream of you very often. I decided the next best thing was to come see you.

"Darling," she continued, snuggling closer to him, "I am not a bad person, but I do crave affection. When I love someone, I love them with all my heart. I want to give them all I have, everything. And it's you I love, James. Once I thought that I was wise. I thought I'd try to make Jean jealous. I tried to make him show some affection for me, but he's forever working. Always busy. Oh darling, maybe I'll live to regret the day I ever met you, but I do love you. I know it doesn't seem real. How many days and nights I ask myself that question. Somehow I know that it's wrong and then I don't care about Jean, about Stella. It just doesn't make any difference to me who is in the way. I just know that I want you and I am going to prove to you that I am really and truly in love with you. Today, why do you think I really came to New York?"

For the first in a long time he actually said a word. "I really don't know," he said.

"You may not know, but some day you will."

Could Marie be telling the truth? He had been thinking that she was just a frivolous woman. Somehow he felt sorry that he had come. The words that she had uttered seemed to come from her very soul. He felt that she was telling the truth. He actually felt ashamed of himself. He would tell *her*

171

the truth, how he had come there to ridicule her. But it would be hard, now that he knew she loved him. He had misunderstood her all along.

He raised his head and saw she was looking at him with those same eyes that had engulfed his very being back in Detroit. He took her hands in his. Deep, deep, into her eyes he stared.

"Marie," he began, slowly and deliberately, "please listen to me. After all when one does wrong, he can be forgiven, and I want you to forgive me."

"I think we said something like that before you left, remember?"

"Yes I do, Marie. I know it's going to be hard to make you believe this but you must. First of all, I came to Jean's house to ask his advice about my relationship with Stella. You see, she was the very first woman in my life. When I saw you, er, it's hard to explain, it must have been fascination or something, but you dazzled me a great deal. I've never met a more charming person. I guess I may feel the same way at some other time about some other woman. Then I had a talk with Jean. He told me everything about you, what you were, how he met you. That is after I told him about Stella and myself. He loves you with all his heart and soul. He still does. Why, up to yesterday, he was hoping that you'd never leave him. I am nothing to you, Marie. Jean is a blood relative of mine. He is so much older than I am, and I would like to look up to him for advice.

"Please, let's look at it this way. What has happened was just an adventure, a thrill, brought on more or less by the drinks we had had. I am deeply ashamed, really, from the bottom of my heart. I don't know what came over me. Please don't think of me anymore in that way. I could never be guilty in this world of doing anything like that again. I am proud that Jean is my cousin. My mother, his aunt, was proud of him. Please try and understand me, Marie. I have made a mistake, you have made a mistake, and I guess we'll suffer for it, but try not to let it break up you and Jean, please."

"Suffer? What do you know about suffering? Oh God, if you only knew how much I have suffered."

"Please let me finish, Marie."

"All right," she said, and began to cry.

"Try it again with him. Go back to him, Marie. His life will be wrecked if you leave him now," pleaded Toddy.

"Please, please," she interrupted again, "I should have known that you were too young to understand. My dear, what you are saying is impossible. Do you realise what you are telling me? You are telling me to sacrifice my life to save Jean's. I wish you wouldn't say any more." The tears were hiding her beautiful face. She buried her head in her hands. "Perhaps someday," she said slowly, "perhaps someday you'll know why I can never go back to Jean."

"But you must," he begged. "He has worked hard to get where he is. Can you imagine how he must have worked, studied, and sacrificed himself to get somewhere? Remember the first weeks you spent together?"

"Yes, I remember perfectly. If you were only there then I would not be so miserable today."

"Oh dear, you must have been happy. He must have told you the wonderful things that he planned for you. Marie, he loves you. He hasn't told me that you left him. Tomorrow he'll be at my house. He knows that you are in New York. Why not drop in and surprise him?"

Marie was shaking terribly. The tears were streaking her face. "I'd never believed that men like you still existed in this world. Maybe you are right, but there's only one thing I want to tell you. I mean it from my heart. Regardless of what happens always remember that from the moment I saw you I fell in love with you. I'll always care for you. I see that you want to get rid of me and I am not going to try to break another woman's heart. I am sorry that I can't do what you want me to do, for one good reason."

"What's that?" he inquired.

"I can't tell that to you, but one thing I will say. If for any reason whatever you want to see me, I'll always be waiting for you. Darling, I'll always want you to think of me as a person who only wanted to find happiness with the one she loves. And don't forget me ever. I'll send you an invitation to my funeral."

"Please don't think of such things. You have everything in the world to live for."

"Yes I have," she answered, slowly.

"I hope that everything will turn out all right."

"It's all right, my sweet, I'll always have something to remember you by."

Toddy stood up, lifted her up with him, tucked his hand under her chin, and kissed her on the forehead. Her eyes were red and swollen. As he stood over her a feeling of pity came over him. Methodically, he stroked her hair with both his hands. He wondered if this was really sympathy or love that he felt. She stood there still sobbing. Toddy walked to the closet where she had put his hat. He found it and started for the door.

Still Marie hadn't said a word.

Toddy reached the door. He stopped, turned, and looked back at her. She was looking at him. From where he stood her face appeared to be drawn. Her lips were trembling a little but she said not a word. He opened the door and closed it behind him.

The stark realisation that he would never see her again loomed up before him. Still he felt a moral victory. He could not have continued to see her. He must have been crazy to even think of seeing her behind his cousin's back. Gone was the feeling of adventure that he had previously thought he possessed. He was now happy that he had come. He knew that it would've eventually happened. After what had taken place in Detroit he knew that he could never face her again. So he was exceedingly happy that everything had turned out as it did. Yet this feeling, unexplainable, came again. What was it? As he reached the street, he thought to himself, *I wonder what would have happened if something else had happened.*

Chapter Thirteen

Three Years Later

There was a great deal of excitement in the small three-room apartment somewhere in Harlem. It was Friday. Preparations were being made for a surprise party that Mrs. Stella Turner was planning for her husband. It was nearly six-thirty and Mr. Turner was expected home any moment. Stella had planted a friend downstairs to take him somewhere on the pretext that Stella would be visiting some friends and to have him return later.

As she put away the modest three-layer cake, she wiped her hands and decided to clean up.

"Well, Stella," she said to herself in the bathroom mirror, "I suppose you know that you are in love. Your face is bright, your eyes are sparkling, and you do look younger even though you've been a married woman for nearly three years."

Silently she looked at the reflection in the mirror. She remembered when Toddy had asked her to marry him. She remembered how she had wept for joy, wept for the honor that he had paid her. She had begun to fear that he was losing interest in her when suddenly one afternoon he told her that they were going to be married the next month. She had realised that living the way they had been at that time was very wrong, but she prayed to God to enter his heart and for Toddy to do the honourable thing by her. Still he would have been content to continue to live just as they had been for she had truly loved him.

She had always wondered, but never questioned, the suddenness of his decision. Now it came to her, as it had so often. Toddy had left to go to work that morning, and that night when he came home, after supper, and seated in the small living room, all he had said was, "Darling, we are going to be married next month."

Jean Mondeau had been at their house, but he did not stay. He left for a hotel and Toddy and Stella had decided to move to a larger place after they were married.

A lot of things had entered her mind but she knew that Toddy had always done things suddenly. The idea of getting married was more like going to Heaven to her, so she had never questioned him about Marie, hoping that some day he would tell her.

There were times, though, when Toddy seemed "lost," sometimes when he would suddenly sit down at the piano, which they had purchased on credit, and play a melody. Once she remembered asking him the name of the song and he just answered, "Something I made up." There were other times, too, when he would make love to her savagely as though he were taking something that didn't belong to him.

Nevertheless, she was in love with him and not once in the past two years had Marie ever been mentioned in that house. She had asked him about Jean and he would answer, quite sincerely, "He is all right."

Woman's intuition had told her that something had happened but she had never said anything about it.

The key in the door in the hall interrupted her thoughts and she hurried to get through. Coming out of the bathroom, he greeted her.

"I thought you weren't home, dear," said Toddy.

"Well, I only wanted to fool you. Say, what's the matter with you? You look as though you are sick."

"Nothing, exactly. Things are not so good downtown."

"You mean on the job?"

"Uh-huh," he remarked, throwing his coat on the chair nearest to him and walking toward the bathroom.

"Well, you haven't lost your job, have you?"

"Oh, no, things are very slow. The boss was commenting how business was getting bad. I can remember last year about this time, we had enough orders to keep us busy for the whole season."

"Oh, I wouldn't worry, dear, anytime the bosses say business is slow, it means they are doing all right."

"Oh no, if it weren't for some junk that they picked up cheap from some bankrupt firm, we would really have nothing to do."

"Please don't feel that way, dear, wait till it comes. Everybody is complaining, depression, depression. If they would stop worrying about it, perhaps it wouldn't be so bad. Val's wife was here today. Her husband is laid off, but they aren't worrying."

"Why should they worry? They must have plenty of money. Val made nearly forty a week."

"Yeah, but you know how high they were living."

"That's why I am glad we haven't been throwing any money away. Let's see how much we really have," he replied, and went into the bedroom to check the bankbook. "We have almost twelve hundred dollars."

"Yeah, but you forget we owe nearly two hundred on the furniture and almost a hundred on the piano."

"Well, let's stop worrying, just like you said, huh?"

All through the dinner, Stella did not hint about her husband's birthday, and to all outward appearances, he did not seem to remember it himself. As Stella got up to clear the table she turned to Toddy and remarked, "Oh dear, I almost forgot. Val said to tell you that your club was going to have a meeting tonight, a special meeting, and for you to be there about eight-thirty."

"Tonight?"

"Yes, dear, tonight."

"Shucks, the first time I get a chance to get some rest from school and they have to go and call a special meeting. I wonder what it's about. Didn't he tell you?"

"You know that Val never discloses club secrets," she answered.

"Okay, guess I'll see what it's about," he sighed.

It was eight-forty-five when Toddy rang at Val Steven's house on the "hill," at one of that section's most fashionable apartment houses.

"Well, James Turner, what are you doing here?" greeted Emily, Val's sister-in-law, who lived with her sister.

"Why they left word that there was going to be a club meeting here. Where's Val?"

"Oh, er," she said dryly, after a few moments hesitation, "do come in. I guess they'll be here in a minute."

"Going out?" he asked, after entering.

"Why yes, as a matter of fact I am going to visit some friends down your way. Pardon me while I fix my hair, won't you?"

"Sure."

Toddy looked around anxiously. There didn't seem to be any preparations for any meeting. The table that was always moved to the other room, to make way for the rostrum, was still in place. "Are you sure they are going to have a meeting tonight?"

"I really don't know," she answered from the bedroom. "Are you sure that Stella said tonight?"

"Sure, I just left the house."

The clock struck nine and Emily came from the bedroom all dressed.

"I am going," she said. "Do you care to wait?"

"No, I don't think so. They'll just have to do without me, that's all."

"Going home?"

"Yes, I'll ride down with you."

"Someone must have made a mistake," she said, as they boarded the bus.

Emily got off at the same street as Toddy. He told her to have a good time. He went up the stairs disgruntled and perturbed over the circumstances. He was still talking to himself as he opened the door to his apartment and was met by complete darkness.

"Damn," grumbled Toddy.

He switched on the lights and was met by all his friends, who were seated about a table filled with refreshments. There was Val and his wife and three other couples. The doorbell rang. Stella rushed to the door and in walked Emily.

"Did it work?" she asked.

"Perfectly," answered Stella. "Look at him, he is still dumbfounded."

And there stood Toddy, looking foolish. Then his face broke into a smile as it dawned on him that it was his birthday.

"Happy birthday to you," they all said.

"Well, I certainly was fooled. I never even remembered. You had me going. Shucks, I should have known there was something funny, but I, er, well, I was just fooled. That's all." He turned and said to Emily, "Friends in my neighborhood, huh?"

"Sure, aren't you all my friends?"

"Well, I'll get even sometime," he said good-naturedly. "I'll get even right now. Let's play some pinochle."

"Fine," said Val and Emily.

The party broke up about three in the morning and all had had a lovely time.

The next day was Saturday and Toddy did not have to go to work. Stella went out about one o'clock to do some shopping. He began tidying up as best he could and in an hour the place was back to normal.

He turned on the radio. The last notes of "Marie" were playing.

"Good afternoon, ladies and gentlemen of the radio audience. For the next fifteen minutes we shall have the pleasure of listening to the lovely voice of Marie Vasquez, brought to us by the makers of 'Lovador,' the new beauty cream. More about 'Lovador' later. For her first number Miss Vasquez will sing that delightful melody 'Just a Memory of You'."

James Turner sat down. He listened. He thought he discerned a slight bit of familiarity in the voice singing so sweetly. He stood up and almost ran to the radio. He turned it louder. A frown came over his face. A look of doubt. *The voice*, he wondered. He stared at the radio before him. Then he whispered as though she was in the room, "Marie. Oh no, it couldn't be her. It couldn't be Marie singing. Yet, the voice sounds just like her."

She sang three songs. Almost all three were alike. Songs of love, songs of memories and disappointments, it seemed to him.

The door opened and Stella came in. He switched off the radio. Why? He himself did not know. He shifted like a silly young boy caught in the act of doing something wrong.

"Wonderful thing, dear, isn't it? The radio, I mean. Just turn a dial and soon you have music, speeches, anything you want to hear." He realized he was just talking nonsense.

"Yes, I thought I heard someone singing rather loudly as I came up the stairs. Did you turn it off?" Stella inquired.

"Yes, she had finished."

"She? Who was it?"

"I don't know, some Jenny something or other."

Stella just said, "Oh."

A moment later she stated, "Well, I think we will have roast beef for tomorrow."

"Fine," he said, curtly.

"What's the matter with you?"

"Er, nothing, dear. Just thinking about the depression. Just wondering, that's all."

"You were all right last night. Come on, let's go to the movies."

"I am still sleepy, darling. Look at all the work I've done while you were out. I think I'll take another nap. Maybe tonight, huh?"

"Oh, I can't go tonight, dear. You know our club is having a meeting tonight. Val's wife is president and we are thinking of reorganizing the club. We are going to try to make it a savings club. You men have one, so we were thinking of doing the same thing. What do you think of the idea?"

"Fine, only don't have too many members. And don't try to start off too big, if you know what I mean."

"We are planning on having about ten members. At two dollars a month, it would be two hundred and forty dollars a year. Then after the first year we'd give a dance. Then the following year we'd have a sort of Christmas fund. In case something happens to some of the members, we'd be able to help financially."

"Sounds splendid. I hope it works."

"I thought that you'd see it that way. So it's all right for me to go then?"

"Sure, darling, it's perfectly all right."

Stella left about eight. He sat on the sofa and must have dozed off, for when he awoke the clock struck ten. He had turned the radio on before he sat down and he did not remember hearing any programs. The doorbell startled him. He got up and opened the door. No one was there and realising it was the downstairs bell that had rung he walked to the kitchen and pushed the buzzer. He went back to the door, looked down the stairs, and saw Val Stevens coming up the stairs.

"Hello, Toddy."

"Hello, boy, what brings you here?"

"Oh, those 'hens' over at the house chased me out. Say, they are organizing some sort of a club. What do you say we go out for a while?"

"Why, I didn't expect to, Val. Come on in, I am not even dressed."

"Oh, fella, it's Saturday night. Don't tell me you can't go out for a little while."

"Where to, Val? You know I am not so sure of my job and I really can't throw any money away."

"Oh, forget it. I got five bucks to spend."

"I thought that you had lost your job."

"So what. I worked for six long years. They lay me off, so I can't enjoy myself for one night?"

"You still didn't say where we are going."

"I was thinking of dropping in at the Savoy. I haven't been up there for quite a while."

"Savoy? No. No sir."

Just then the announcer on the radio blazed forth: "Boys and girls, we'll take you now to the Savoy Ballroom, the home of happy feet."

The strains of a theme song blurted out.

"Okay, Val, but not for long."

"That's all right by me."

Val looked at his watch as they boarded the Seventh Avenue bus. It was ten-forty-five. Alighting from the bus at 140th Street, Toddy and Val walked towards Lenox Avenue.

Lenox Avenue, the old familiar street. They were at the corner. Gone was the glamour of the street, however. It seemed like a neglected section of Harlem. Still, the music from the Chinese rendezvous diagonally across the avenue brought back old memories to him.

He looked up the avenue. No more was the sign of the Cotton Club. Even the people going into the Savoy did not seem to dress as they used to. Young girls were wearing ordinary street dresses. Looking up at the window he saw heads looking down. Then the music, new songs, new orchestra, but the same Savoy. But it was different to him. He remembered the thrill of his first visit. It had been just a few years earlier. He really felt awkward.

Val said not a word. He was really bent on having a night of fun.

"Now listen," began Toddy, "when we go in I don't want to be running after any dames. You can have all the fun you want so long as you don't think I am a wallflower if I don't dance."

"Okay. When are you leaving?" inquired Val.

"No later than one."

"Okay."

They got upstairs and Val lost no time picking a partner. A girl passed by him, he touched her arm, she nodded, and Val went onto the floor.

Toddy walked around to the same corner he had once warmed so often. He was looking at the couples on the floor. There were quite a number of white people dancing, doing what Toddy had learned to do some years ago. *There are some pretty girls here tonight*, he thought to himself. Still he couldn't make up his mind to dance. He saw Val jumping crazily all over the floor and his partner was following him. He walked back towards the box where one could purchase a ticket and dance with the most "charming girls" in the place, the hostesses.

But he had always avoided them. He always did. He had thought them to be "bad" girls, but somehow tonight he realised he was much older and the experience of Stella seemed to suggest to him that perhaps these girls too must have "stories." Perhaps they came from good families looking for excitement. Perhaps, like him, they had become disappointed in achieving their ambitions and had decided to forget their worries by mixing with all types. He stood there, contemplating, when a girl passed him, glanced at him for a second, whirled suddenly, and confronted him. Her eyes met his.

He gulped, for it seemed his heart was going to jump out of his open mouth. All at once, his suit seemed too large for him. His mouth was wide open, but he was afraid to say anything. He stared long, searching her eyes. Slowly he started to speak but her lips parted and she spoke first.

"Pardon me," she said slowly, "James? Toddy?"

Words would not come from his lips. He reached out and held her hand, which she had extended without hesitation. He pulled her gently to one side and stared at her some more. He had thought she was beautiful four years ago, but as he looked at her now he beheld a vision. Her hair was parted in the center and put up in a ball in the back of her head. Her mouth, that small captivating pair of lips that had once touched his in moments of supreme ecstasy, her long thin nose that divided a well-rounded face, which had nestled close to his in a never to be forgotten embrace, and that seductive, tantalising pair of eyes, now narrowed a little, made her by far the most beautiful creature he had seen in many years. The rose-colored evening gown she wore swept the rug as she took another step.

The words finally came to Toddy. "Marie, what are you doing here? What on earth ever became of you? Where have you been? I thought I heard you sing on the radio this afternoon. Was it you?"

"No, James, Toddy, if I may still call you that. I am not a celebrity. I am one of the hostesses up here."

"Here? You work here? How long?"

"For the past year."

"Well, there must be a great deal that's happened since I saw you last. Tell me."

"First you must tell me. Come, let's sit at one of the tables."

He followed her as though drawn by a magnet. As she walked before him, his eyes roamed over her body. That body that once she gave to him. He just realised that all day he had had a feeling he would see Marie. Fate, that was what it was. The radio, Val coming down, Stella going out. It was fate.

They reached an empty table and Marie sat down.

"What'll you have?" he asked.

"Nothing, I just want to sit and talk to you."

"Well," Toddy began, "What's happened since . . . "

"You first, young man. You must be a doctor by now, are you? You look so smart, so intelligent."

Toddy smiled sheepishly. He was a little embarrassed. "I am still married to Stella," he answered, hesitantly.

"Still married?"

The question seemed silly, but he realised what she meant. He thought the conversation would end if he told the truth, so he decided to tell the truth while leaving some doubt in her mind.

"Well, er, yes, surely."

"Oh. But separated. I knew it couldn't last. I didn't receive your invitation."

"I didn't send one," he retorted, and then he said, rather somberly, "I didn't receive yours."

"I did send one," she answered.

"I am glad you didn't do anything foolish."

"Oh, I didn't, dear. I did what I said I was going to do. I did have a funeral but I was alive. The old Marie you used to know is dead, just as dead as if she had been buried."

The conversation then turned to Toddy's wife. Marie said, "I tried to tell you. You wouldn't understand. You are too much of an ambitious person to be satisfied with a person like Stella. She seemed to me, from what I glimpsed of her that day, to be satisfied to be married to an ordinary person. You are not an ordinary person, but staying with someone like her would make you lose all ambition."

"I don't think I can agree with you, Marie."

"Well, maybe you can't, but anyway, I am thankful to God for what you did. I went out into the world for myself. I made more money in the past three years than a lot of people make in their entire lifetime."

"Marie," snapped Toddy, "what happened to my cousin?"

"I thought you would get to that. As I was saying, I take all I can get and give nothing in return. God made me beautiful for a reason and I am finding out what the reason is. There are so many fools in this world, it's a shame that they don't organize, a union of fools."

"About Jean . . . ?"

"Toddy, he went mad. He threatened to kill me. He attacked me one night with a knife. He had an idea there was someone else but he never found out and now I know he never will."

"So you did go back to him then?"

187

"No, after I saw you, I, er, went upstate to, er, forget. I stayed about a year. Then I took up singing. One day I went back to Detroit. He had sold the house and was living in an apartment. I went to speak to him about a divorce and he flew into a rage and attacked me. Luckily I was not hurt. Later, the doctor told me he was losing his mind. They committed him to an insane asylum about two years ago. He is still there. I went to see him but he doesn't know me. He doesn't know anyone. So, I decided to forget men. I came back to New York. Now I have everything—a bank account, a car, a nice apartment—but no man to love me."

"But, I thought you weren't that type. You told me so yourself."

"Toddy, listen to me. You are older now. I am older. I had never been in love with anyone before I met you, nor since. I have never had or felt the desire for any man but you. Besides, there is another reason."

"Marie, are you trying to tell me that you have never . . . ?"

"I am not trying to, I am telling you. I have never loved anyone else. You know, a little boy plays with all kinds of toys until his daddy bring him something that he has never seen before. He forgets all the others. If he loses that one, he is very sad and will never be happy until he gets it back again. Look," she said, showing him a ring on her forefinger, "a Russian gave me that. He comes up here every Sunday, dances with me for two hours, gives me fifty dollars just to hold me in his arms. He has begged me, tried every means to get me to tell him where I live. He promised me fur coats and a swell apartment, if I would only be nice to him, and I have never even gone out with him. Last Christmas he brought me a necklace. I had it appraised. It was worth seven hundred dollars."

"If you don't mind my saying so, don't you think it's

188

wrong to accept presents from these men? You know sooner or later your conscience will bother you."

She remained silent for a moment, then replied, "Why shouldn't I make them pay for my company? They come here, sit down, tell me that I am beautiful. 'You don't belong here,' one fellow told me. I should be always looking sweet, I should be this, I should be that. Take for instance only last week. A scout or an executive or something was up here with a party. He represented a movie picture outfit. All the women in the party were lavishly dressed. One of them was a famous actress. One of the waiters came over to the hostess's bench and told me that the fellow had seen me on the floor and wanted to know if I would join their party. I went, sat at their table, drank with them, danced with one of the men. All through the time I sat there, they kept saying, 'My dear, you are beautiful; are you really coloured?' I felt like slapping their faces. Then I realised I was getting paid for sitting there. Then this other fellow, he must have been a producer of pictures, kept talking about the price of their next picture. He asked me to dance.

"I took advantage of the opportunity to ask him about my chances in Hollywood. He tried to evade the question but I kept pressing him about it again and again. Finally, he said, 'You know that you'd photograph beautifully. You could pass for a Mexican or South Sea Island girl. They could even make you look like a white person.' I asked him point-blank, 'Why don't they use beautiful coloured girls in white pictures? Seems to me,' I said, 'every time I see a picture where they use some coloured women or men, provided they weren't famous persons, they would always get the funniest and most homely people of the race.' He smiled a little. Then his face grew more serious and he said, 'You want the truth, don't you?' I said, 'Sure.'

"He said, 'Well, if they were to put *you* in a picture, for

189

instance, people wouldn't believe you were coloured. You don't represent the Negro race.' I wasn't surprised. I knew the answer before he told me. I have heard it many times before. I tried to get into shows downtown. Sure, I could probably work as a show girl in some big Broadway coloured show for about thirty-five dollars a week, but I'd have to be 'nice' to the boss, or the manager. That's as far as I would get. So I thought everything over. I can play the piano a little. I can sing a little and I feel that, perhaps, through the radio, I may get somewhere.

"In the meantime I am taking all I am able to get. Oh, I know that some of my partners will quit when they get wise to the fact that I am not going out with any of them, but you see, my dear, there are always new ones. Of course, you realise, I am not talking about love. No, my dear, there isn't a man who could make me as happy in a lifetime as you did, darling," her voice became a whisper, "in a few minutes."

Toddy tried hard to camouflage his feelings. Somehow, his feelings towards her were completely different than those of that day when he had told her good-bye, hoping never to see her again. He tried to recollect what reasons he had had then for feeling the way he did. The only reason was that, at that time, the girl now sitting before him was his cousin's wife.

He had become a different person. Perhaps it was because she had told him that Jean was out of her life altogether. He should have felt sorry for Jean and, deep down in his heart, he knew that he did. But why this sudden change in his attitude towards Marie? Sudden? It wasn't sudden. He had known it all along. He knew after he had married that the next time he had laid eyes on Marie that he would want to talk to her. Now he had met her and he wasn't completely surprised, in fact, he was grateful, that such was the case.

"Toddy, what seems to be the matter?" she asked.

"Nothing that I can tell you at the present," he answered, wondering all the time what the result would be of this latest meeting with Marie.

"Care to dance?" she asked softly. "Oh, dear, you don't have to pay, unless you had asked me. You see, in this case I asked you."

"Stop kidding me," he said, rising.

Toddy rose and led her to the dance floor. They squirmed and twisted before they could get a fair amount of space to begin dancing. The song ended suddenly and they stood there waiting for another. Then the strains of "Marie" began and Toddy looked at her and she looked at him. The male singer in front of the orchestra was giving the song all its fervor and meaning:

"Marie, my heart is breaking . . . Marie, my heart is aching . . . for you . . . "

She snuggled closer to him. He knew that she knew what they both felt. Their eyes met. She closed hers softly and they both danced.

When the number finished, she whispered in his ear, "Will you wait for me until I get off tonight?"

Without any hesitation, as though he had been commanded to do it, he answered, "Yes, Marie, I will."

They danced, on and on, to every number. They hadn't noticed that the crowd had thinned out considerably, that the time was going; then, suddenly, the announcement came from the platform: "This will be the last set played, get your hats and coats now."

They continued to dance. They continued to dance until the last note of "Home, Sweet Home" was played. When they finally walked off the floor, her arm was about his waist and his about hers. They were unmindful of everyone else,

191

of anything or everything that lived and breathed. Down the stairs they walked to the check room.

Gone was the thought of time, of danger. Nothing seemed to matter. Up they came to the street floor. Someone said good night to her, but she didn't hear it. They walked across the street and stepped into a cab. Marie gave her address to the driver and she leaned into Toddy's arms. She raised her head and he kissed her—a long, lasting kiss. Her kisses burned his lips, kisses that were full of meaning.

Her body was warm, and she felt exultant. She put her arms around his neck, at the same time the cab turned a corner. The cab stopped. Toddy got out and paid the fare, and they went upstairs. With his arms around her, she opened her purse and gave him the key. They entered the apartment and closed the door behind them.

There are no horizons on the world of dreams. James and Marie had boarded a ship on a trip to nowhere; it anchored in the midst of an ocean of passion and ecstasy. Reality appeared when the captain ordered the ship to return to its starting point and the passengers were suddenly awakened. The morning sun lighted up the bedroom and Toddy sat up and realized that he was alone. It was nine-thirty by the clock on the dressing table and he saw a note on the adjacent pillow.

Darling, there was no reason to awaken you, you were so comfortable; I had an appointment at ten at the Savoy and I will be home by noon or sooner.

Reality dawned on James. "Val," he almost yelled. *What in hell happened to Val?* He must be sure that Val did not get to Stella's before he got there.

Stella came home from her meeting and when she realized that James was not home she called Val's. He not being at home, she surmised that James and Val had gone out together. She listened to the radio until two A.M. and went to bed.

The next day, Stella was in the kitchen when James entered and all she said was "Hello." She passed him, seemingly unmindful of his presence, walked into the living room, and pulled up the shades. Passing him on the way back she smiled rather dryly and he noticed her eyes were very red.

He felt guilty but somehow apologetic words did not seem to come to him. He said nothing; he went to the bedroom, undressed, put on pajamas, and went to bed.

As he lay in the bed with his head buried in the pillow, he heard her footsteps. She came into the room. He knew she was standing over him. He did not turn to face her.

"Don't you feel well, Toddy?" she asked.

The words felt like those of pity. He turned slowly and faced her. She fell on him sobbing heavily.

"Toddy, why did you lie to me? Where have you been all night? Why are you doing this to me? Why? Why? I haven't done anything to you to deserve this. I have been a good wife. You are doing something wrong, Toddy.

"But what is happening, Toddy? Please tell me why are you doing this to me?" she persisted.

"Stella, please leave me now. I will explain when I get up. I am terribly sleepy."

She hesitated a little and Toddy turned his head away from her. She got up and left.

Toddy slept all day. When he did wake, it was dark. He looked at the radium clock on the dresser. It was eight o'clock. He heard no one in the apartment as he jumped out of bed. He turned on the light, stared at himself in the mirror, and shuddered as he beheld the dishevelled person looking back at him.

"Stella," he called.

He didn't need to call again. He knew there was no one there. He went into the kitchen; there was no supper cooked. He went to the bathroom, back to the bedroom, dressed, and went out into the street. He went to a restaurant and ate his dinner. Somehow he was worried more about Marie than about Stella. The fact that she was not at home didn't seem to bother him at all. He boarded a bus on the corner and rode uptown.

He did remember promising Marie he would come up that night when she told him she would have a surprise for him. As he entered the apartment Marie, seemingly expected him, was dressed to go out.

"How are you today, sweet?" she greeted him.

"All right," he answered.

"Darling, I am taking off tonight, too. We are going to visit some friends up in Mt. Vernon."

"Marie, there isn't going to be any party, is there? I wouldn't mind, but tonight I want to go somewhere that's quiet. I want to talk to you."

She eyed him slyly and said, "We are going to a quiet place, dear. But, what's the matter? Is anything wrong?"

"I can't stay all night tonight. I have to work tomorrow."

"I wish they would fire you, so you and I could be together all the time."

"Where are we going, darling?" he asked.

"Why? Nervous?"

"No."

"Darling, you know I think about you so much I am beginning to be miserable when I don't see you. Honestly, darling, I love you with all my heart."

"That's one of the things I want to talk to you about."

"How many will there be altogether, darling?"

"Marie, it won't work. Something is bound to happen."

194

"Well, dear, didn't something happen?" she asked, rather coyly.

"You haven't told me everything about yourself, you know. I always had the impression that you were hiding something."

She did not answer, but she slowed the car down and pulled to the curb. She turned off the motor and stared at him.

"Where are we?" he asked.

"This is the end of the Grand Concourse," she replied.

Toddy put his arm around her neck and she came closer to him. "I want to know everything about you, everything," he emphasised.

The soft lights of the dashboard reflected back to the car and she appeared more beautiful than ever. But she was crying. It suddenly occurred to Toddy that this was the second time that day he had seen a woman close to him crying.

"Toddy," she began, "I want you to listen to me carefully." She blew her nose in her handkerchief. He waited until she had gained control of herself again.

"Darling, from the moment I was old enough to realise the truth, I knew I was not destined to be a happy person in this world. The night I met you at the Savoy, I said a few things to you that I know sounded extremely cruel on my part. Some of it was true, but not all of it. Do you know that I have tried to end my life more than once? Somehow, I've always waited. That's why when I met you I knew that there was a reason for my waiting. If something had not happened after I'd met you, I'd probably be dead today. Also the fact that I was brought up in a convent where I was taught to have faith might have something to do with my hesitation.

"I actually cursed the day I was born. Perhaps after you

195

hear what I am going to tell you, you too may understand why I feel the way I do."

Toddy took his arm from around her neck and held her hand in his.

"Will you light a cigarette for me, dear?"

He did and put it to her mouth. She inhaled deeply and then emitted the smoke in a long thin line that slowly fogged the windshield and lazily crawled to the top of the car. Toddy's eyes followed the smoke as it began to find an exit through the slightly opened window to her left.

"Darling, you know I was just out of the convent when I met Jean" continued Marie. She took another puff on her cigarette and again the car was filled with smoke. "He was the first and the only man I ever knew until I met you. But now how did I happen to be in a convent? Well, when I was seven my mother decided that she was going to be handicapped on account of me . . . "

"Handicapped? What do you mean?" asked Toddy.

Marie again took a long draw on her cigarette, then she opened the window and threw it out. Again she blew the smoke out slowly. She stared at Toddy, then she narrowed her eyes. Her long eyelashes seemed like a thin black spray, painted by an artist with a fine brush.

"Because she never married my father." The words were deliberate, pitiful, and Toddy knew that she was opening her very soul to him.

"You see, Toddy, my mother was what they called a prostitute. I didn't know then what I know now. I couldn't see how things like that could happen, but now that I am a woman, I can see perfectly. Of course, I had no idea why I was sent to a convent until I was nearly fourteen. But, to go back, my mother was a good women until she met and fell in love with a Frenchman in South America when she was 17 years old. He was a bad man and he left her pregnant.

She came to this country when I was about 6 years old. She became a bad woman and was eventually sent to jail. I was sent to a home. There a Catholic Sister took a liking to me and convinced the authorities that I would be better off in a convent. When I was about fourteen I began to work around the office and they taught me how to play the piano. I also studied to be a secretary.

"One day I was looking up something in the files and I came across my records. I didn't believe it, but I figured it must have been true. I was ashamed. For days I cried. I couldn't bear to look at the Sisters. Then, finally, I begged them to try to get me a position outside. I wanted to get away from the place.

"Of course, I wasn't old enough. As time went on they made it very pleasant for me. I stayed there for two more years and was nearing my seventeenth birthday, when, one day, the Mother Superior called me into her study.

"She asked me if I still wanted to go out into the world to work and I was very happy. The following week I was sent to the home of a wealthy man to be his secretary and to act as a companion for his two daughters.

"The first few weeks I stayed there I thought I was in Heaven. Nothing was too good for me. I lived there for over a month. Then one evening while getting ready for bed, one of the girls came into my room and began, quite companionlike, to ask me how I liked the position. I answered, 'I like it very much.' She stayed a while and we talked and talked. From then on every evening she would come in before I went to bed and talk. Then her sister began visiting my room, too.

"One evening the older sister, she was about fifteen, brought in a book. When I saw what it contained I nearly fainted. It was the most daring piece of literature I've ever seen. Of course, my curiosity was aroused. I took the book away and threatened to tell their father.

"I began to take more notice of them afterwards and found that they were 'peculiar.' "

"Peculiar?" interrupted Toddy.

"Yes! Peculiar! I happened to go upstairs earlier than usual one day and found them both indecent. They were looking at some rather vulgar pictures. I took those, too. I began to talk to them, thinking I could do them some good, when suddenly Elaine, that's the oldest, put her arm around my waist and said, 'I would like to make love to you.' She began kissing me, just like a man. I couldn't imagine anything so abominable. I became inquisitive and asked her what she meant. She told me frankly, without even flinching.

"I told her to get out of my room and backed away from her. Somehow I knew what she was saying wasn't right, but I never really knew any better, about men and things like that. Now I know better but you must understand at that time I was foolish. Well, they taught me everything there was to know. One night before going to bed I read one of the books they had and I went to sleep and had an exciting dream.

"From then on I became inquisitive. I guess I just, er, well, just didn't care anymore what they did. Then one day they showed me a picture of a naked man. I remembered I kept asking questions and, er, they told me the answers."

"But why didn't you leave when you found out about them?" asked Toddy.

"Can't you understand? I didn't know then . . . ," she replied.

"Yes, but you knew it was wrong. You said so yourself."

"I finally made up my mind to. I couldn't tell their father to his face. I decided to write him. It was on a Saturday afternoon. I'll never forget it. I opened the drawer to get some paper when the door opened and Elaine walked in with another picture. This time it was of a woman. I told her I would look at it later. When she left the room I did. Do you know whose picture it was? It was a picture of my mother. Yes, my own mother, naked and lying on a bed with her legs wide open. Night after night I cried. I became sick for days. Once I almost took poison. As I told you before, I didn't. Then I decided the only thing left for me to do was to run away. So I did.

"I came to New York. I lied to everyone. Finally, I got a job. I left the 'Y' where I was living and went to live with some very nice people. They were aged and very kind to me. I became very much attached to them and later found myself calling them Mom and Pop. Of course, I never told Jean. When I met him I introduced them to him as my stepparents. He was connected with college and all scholastic activities and I married him. But I never knew the meaning of the word love until you came to Detroit that Easter morning. I've told you before and I will always tell you, when I saw you and you looked at me the way you did, sort of surging passion enveloped my whole body. I just couldn't explain it. And, when you left me on St. Nicholas Avenue that day, I knew that somehow, somewhere we'd meet again. And, I swore by almighty God that no other man was going to touch me in this world. So, that's the history of my life, you know the rest. Now what do you think of me?"

Toddy just stared at her. He had read books in school; he had seen pictures in the movies, but he could not comprehend that all this was actually happening to him. He turned to her. He reached up, lifted her chin, and kissed her. Then he said, "Darling, I think that you are the most wonderful person I've ever met. And, also, the most mysterious. There is something about us I just can't understand, like we'd met before, in another life."

"Oh, dear, we've been here a long time. Funny no policeman has chased us."

Toddy looked at his watch, it was a quarter past eleven. "Goodness gracious, it is late. What do you say we go back?" He added, "This was a nice quiet place at that."

"No, Toddy, this is not the nice quiet place I had in mind. But, promise me one thing, whatever happens tonight, that you'll never hate me."

"Hate you? What are you talking about?"

"Promise, darling."

"I promise. But, what is going to happen?"

"We are going to Mt. Vernon."

"Oh, Marie, it's awfully late. I've got to get up."

"It won't take long, dear. We'll be back on this road home in an hour."

"All right, but please drive a little faster."

"Not too fast, dear. It's very important that we both live now."

It was a quarter of twelve when Marie stopped the car in front of a darkened house in Mt. Vernon. They got out of the car and went up a few stone steps. She pushed the button and waited. A light appeared directly above them and they could hear footsteps coming. A young girl opened the door and immediately the hall was flooded as a click on the wall told them that the girl had turned on the light.

In Toddy's mind was the big question: What in the world was the reason for waking people up at this time of the night?

"Hello, Miss Marie," the girl greeted her.

"I am sorry to disturb you so late, dear, but I just couldn't get here any earlier."

Toddy knew she was lying. She could've gotten here earlier if she hadn't talked so much in the car.

"Is your mother home?" asked Marie.

Almost immediately a voice at the top of the stairs called, "Who is it, Dorothy?"

"It's Miss Marie," answered the girl, "and a gentleman."

"Hello, Mrs. Saitch," put in Marie, "I was just telling Dorothy that I am terribly sorry to disturb you at so late an hour, but I have someone here with me. Could I come in for a few minutes?"

Toddy was bewildered. What were these people talking about? He knew that Marie was talking about him.

"Oh, it's perfectly all right, dear. Come on up," said Mrs. Saitch.

Marie motioned to Toddy and with Dorothy leading the way they tiptoed up the stairs. Then Marie entered a room whose door was slightly opened and returned almost immediately.

Mrs. Saitch came out of another room pulling a robe around her and entered the room that Marie had previously left. A faint blue light stabbed the darkened room and Marie said softly, "I won't be long."

Marie reached out and found Toddy's hand. She led him into the room and pushed him lightly onto what appeared to be a small bed. A pink blanket covered the sleeping form of a little girl. Marie slowly pulled the cover back and looked at Toddy.

Toddy looked around him. There was no one else in the room. He returned Marie's look. She pointed her finger at the crib. Toddy looked closer . . . closer. His body was now bent over the child in the crib. He was examining it. There was no mistaking those features.

Suddenly, he raised himself and stared long at Marie. She, in turn, replied silently. Her face suddenly displayed anxiety. Her eyes were beginning to water, then tear after tear trickled down her cheek. Still she continued to stare at him. Neither said a word. Both hearts were beating faster

201

and faster. With quivering lips, she was searching his very soul.

"Yours?" he whispered, almost dryly.

Marie's eyes never blinked. She stared straight at him. She trembled a little, her lips parted, and a word came out slowly.

"Ours," she replied, her lips still quivering as she spoke.

Toddy opened his mouth as if to speak, but Marie put her finger over it.

"Sshh," she warned, "you'll wake her up."

Again he tried to speak, and for the second time she used her finger to stop him.

"Let's go now," she begged, tugging at his coat. They went out the door and Marie closed it easily. Mrs. Saitch stood in front of her door, and, when she saw them come out, she walked towards them.

"Toddy, I am sorry, I forgot," Marie said. Her voice seemed very tired to him. "This is Mrs. Saitch. . . . Mr. Turner." As he started to acknowledge the introduction, he noticed a slight bit of discomfort in her manner as she weakly extended her hand.

Marie pushed him a little down the stairs. "Good night, Mrs. Saitch," she said. "I'll see you on Sunday."

Toddy did not see the finger that Marie pointed at his back while she was looking at Mrs. Saitch. Nor did he hear the words she uttered: "Her father. I will call you."

Neither said a word as Marie opened the door of the car. They both got in and Marie started driving.

Toddy spoke first. "Marie . . . now I know what you were referring to all along. That's what you meant when I saw you in New York, about always having something to remember me by. Why didn't you tell me?"

"I didn't want to use that to keep you, dear, but when

you told me that you really loved me. I thought it was about time for you to know that you were really a father."

"That's why you couldn't go back to Jean. . . . That's why you argued and argued and told me I was too young to understand."

Marie just shook her head.

"Oh, darling, I don't know what to say." He hesitated, thought of Stella, and wondered what was to happen. He'd have to tell Stella. Yes, he would tell her and she would understand. . . . he knew she would. She must. She'd have to understand.

"What's her name, dear?" he asked.

"Marie Louise. She'll be four years old tomorrow."

"That's a wonderful name," he added.

It was after one when Toddy arrived home. Stella was not in bed. . . . in fact, she was not in the house. She hadn't been in the house since he had left it. He walked into the parlor, switched on the lights, and sat down hard on the sofa. He was breathing heavily. His eyes wandered about the room. There, on the radio, was a letter. Slowly, he reached for it, opened it, and read it.

My darling Toddy,

I don't know what has happened to both of us, but somehow there is something that you haven't told me. I think perhaps you may be tired of me, so I am doing what I think is best. I am leaving. I am going to stay with some friends for a while. I knew you were lying about last night. Jim came by the house and knew of no special meeting.

I don't want to quarrel with you. If you care to tell me why you are acting this way, I'll be only too glad to listen. You can get my address from Val's wife if you care to.

Your loving wife,
Stella

James "Toddy" Turner read the letter over again, then put it back on the radio. His mind was too much on one little girl in Mt. Vernon to concentrate on Stella right at that time. After all, he was the father of Marie's child. But, he was also Stella's husband. They both loved him, he knew. He sighed deeply. He stretched out on the sofa and stared at the ceiling.

"Ma," he said, "you didn't do this to me because I disobeyed you, I know. So please tell me what to do . . . please."

Toddy awoke six hours later. He was still dressed. He left the house at eight and arrived at his job at nine, after stopping at the corner luncheonette for breakfast.

He went directly to the office. "Good morning, sir," he addressed the boss. "I am sorry I was unable to come in yesterday. I didn't feel well."

"That's all right, Turner. How are you feeling today?"

"Much better, sir."

"Here are some orders you can get out."

Toddy took the pile of papers and went to his desk in the shipping room.

"Good morning, Simpson," he greeted the foreman.

"Hello, son," replied the older man.

"What's the matter with you?" asked Toddy, seeing that Mr. Simpson was a bit downhearted.

"Laid off . . . everybody . . . today. The boss told us yesterday. Of course, he says he is giving us two weeks extra pay, and he will call us when things pick up."

"But these orders he just gave me . . . ," Toddy replied, pointing to the pile of papers on his desk.

"Back orders."

All Toddy said was, "Well . . . ," and walked away.

Those next few hours were agonizing. In less than twenty-four hours his wife had left him, he learned that

Marie was the mother of his child, and he was laid off his job.

It was one-thirty when he received his envelope. He bid the others good-bye and left.

He walked up Fifth Avenue. He walked and walked. Soon, he became conscious of the fact that he was not the only one walking. There were other people out of work, too. Depression was here. Only then had he become acutely conscious of it. Right in front of him was a man walking, ragged and unshaven. Toddy turned around as he passed him. There was a cigarette butt on the sidewalk. The man reached down, picked it up, and put it in his pocket.

Toddy shuddered, then reached into his own pocket. He pulled out his cigarettes. He lit one and put the pack back. He felt the money in his pocket. There was eighty-four dollars there. Of course, he was lucky. He did have a few dollars in the bank, but it wouldn't last without more coming in. Stella was gone. He would give up the apartment right away. The rent was due the next week. He did not go to his house. He went straight up to Marie.

"Well, you got your wish," he greeted her, as she opened the door.

"What wish?" she asked.

"I've just been laid off," he replied.

"Oh, darling, I am sorry. You know I didn't really mean that."

"Well, I have some money that will last for a few weeks while I find another job."

"Oh, darling, don't worry about money."

"There's something. Stella and I have some tied up ... "

"I am glad to know that we can see each other as long as we want to now. Darling, you're going to stay with me, aren't you?"

"I ... er ... don't think it's right ... " he stammered.

205

"Why isn't it right? You love me and I love you. You can get a divorce and we can be very happy . . . you and I and Marie Louise."

"That's a lovely thing to say, dear, but it's not so easy."

"Yes," she agreed, "It's complicated all right."

"But, darling . . . "

"You know, dear," she cut him off, "I have never read many books, but when I was in the convent, I did read a few. My darling, there are a great many men in this world who at some time or another got their start from a woman. Some of the greatest musicians in the universe had women for their inspiration, whether it was financial or otherwise. What's the difference whether a man becomes a success through the inspiration of a woman's love or through her money? You see, darling, I am speaking. I am speaking frankly."

She came closer to him and said, "Darling, I have faith in you; I really believe that someday you'll make me proud of you. I love you, besides . . . and so I'm not taking any chances, dear. Only I want you to work hard and don't let me down."

"Now what are you driving at?"

Marie parted her lips and kissed him. It warmed and filled him with a surging sensation.

"Darling, how would you like to go back to school and finish your education? You would succeed, I know you would. How about it?"

The question took him by surprise. He was lost for an immediate answer.

"Marie, please don't do things like that . . . it's too sudden. Please let me get my breath."

"All right, get your breath. . . . "

She turned and went to the bedroom. He spied her combing her hair. Was this his destiny? Was this what he had been waiting for all his life? All through his school days, he had hoped that he would be able to go to college. Now, an opportunity had come . . . but how? From a woman? Was this his lot? Would his friends look down on him if they knew that a woman was paying for his education? Unbelievable. Was his head 'being turned'?

Marie came back.

"Well, dear?" Toddy replied.

"I don't know what to say, dear," Toddy replied. "If you are sincere, darling, I will certainly not let you down. With all my heart I will be the greatest, or one of the greatest, doctors that ever lived. I've always dreamt of it. I know that I can be."

"Then, dear, it's settled. And now my happiness is complete." And she kissed him again.

"You are going to stay until I come home, dear?" asked Toddy.

"Well, er, yes, if you want me to."

Marie left at nine o'clock. Toddy turned on the radio. It was a magnificent piece of furniture adorned by a lamp. He sat down in the club chair next to it. He sank down into it. He was just in time for the introduction of some classical music. The decorations in the apartment were simple and modern. It was quiet, serene, lovely, enchanting. There seemed a sort of bewitching, fantastic atmosphere here in the small, cozy apartment that made him never want to leave it.

He got up and turned off the light. Now the room was left with the small but captivating light of the radio dial. Here was peace indeed. Lighting a cigarette, he slowly allowed the smoke to curl upwards to the ceiling. For a long time, he watched it. He was thinking . . . yes, thinking; wondering why God in Heaven had performed such miracles as those that had befallen him so suddenly.

Through the smoke, he saw himself as a small, irresponsible boy. Slowly he closed his eyes and it all came back to him: The morning he entered the hospital and his mother lay there, whispering to him, "Go to school, son, and try and be somebody."

He remembered how proud he had felt after attending his first evening in night school. Then the struggle to work and to study at the same time. Then his meeting Stella. Was it love? He had often wondered. It was really his first love affair. Of course, he had had petty romances in his earlier school days, but Stella was the first to make him realise that he was a man. He had thought that he had loved her, but how could he? If he had, he would have never felt the way he felt about Marie. He cared for Stella, but it wasn't love.

Pity. That's what it was, pity. He had found himself many times wanting to help others in distress.

He had felt sorry for her that morning when he saw the marks on her body after Mr. Devon had beaten her. He knew that she loved him. He also knew that there weren't many more like her; but that was before he had met Marie. Now he realised why he had married Stella. He had been afraid of hurting someone dear to him, his own cousin. But all during his life with Stella, he had known that someday he would meet Marie again.

He had prayed that Marie would have remained happily married to Jean and that their escapade was but a memory. But he had not reckoned with fate. He had not known that she had borne him a daughter. She was caring for it herself.

Jean was out of her life. That was no fault of his. As he sat there, dreaming of the future, he wondered if he felt the way he did about her because of the child. This he was sure was not the case. He had not known she had the child when he saw her that night at the Savoy. And he had known then that he loved her.

Now she was offering to do something for him. She offered to help him accomplish the thing that his mother had wanted him to do: to go to college and to finish his education. To become a doctor.

He opened his eyes and there was Marie beside him.

"Darling, I didn't want to wake you, you looked so handsome lying there. I kissed you, right on the lips, and you never even awoke."

She went to the bedroom, still speaking. "You see, I came home. I couldn't work tonight. The faces of the men in that place . . . the music . . . everything bored me. All of a sudden I wanted to be with you, and, er, well, here I am.

She returned to his side. She put her arm around him. "Darling, I love you so," she said, and kissed him. Her kisses surged through him like hot tea on a cold night. There was that passionate feeling enveloping him again. It always did when Marie kissed him. He, in turn, kissed her on her throat. He ran his fingers through her hair and she returned his embraces passionately.

"Please, darling, please don't ever leave me," she whispered.

The words were familiar. Stella had said the same thing to him. But how different it sounded. Marie was not begging for companionship. She was begging to be loved always. Stella was lonely. Of course, she could get other men, but Marie, she was in a position to let men slave for her, men in the higher brackets of life. And yet, she turned them down.

Marie was still holding him tightly. "Oh, my dear, I've never felt this way before in all my life about anybody. Don't ever leave, my sweet. Don't ever."

"I won't," he promised, "I won't."

And two became one.

Three Years Later

Steven Bates left his office at seven o'clock. He had to walk about three country blocks to his home. Under his arm were a few Christmas packages, all tied in red paper and green twine.

He was a heavyset man, in his early forties, and, at first glance, anyone would conclude that he was a successful man. His face was full and healthy looking; he was clean shaven, slightly bald, and his large upper lip made him appear more homely than he really was. He was a commanding figure, resplendent in his appearance, conservatively dressed, but now and then possessed of an air of femininity.

As he turned on Chesterfield Street, the house in which he lived appeared in view and he knew that Stella was home. He smiled a little as he thought of how his meeting with Stella was so different from what he had expected.

Just about three years earlier, when he had had an interest in an employment agency, he walked in one morning and saw her sitting there on one of the chairs. He'd asked the lady whom he had left in charge about her and received all the necessary details. Then he'd had to plan a way of getting her to his home and set upon such a plan. He had called the agency later and asked for a girl just like Stella, and the lady had sent her to his house. The lady understood.

He remembered when he had asked her what she was doing in Newark that she had told him she'd lived in New Jersey before she went to New York, and so she had come back to find the only work she knew. He had liked her at the outset, and gave her the job, only to find in a few weeks that he was actually falling in love with her. He had married her six months later, and she had made him happy ever since.

He had been previously married, but his wife died about five years earlier, and he had always wanted a home and family; however, Stella had not borne him any children as yet, and he was a bit disappointed.

He entered his home and called her.

"Hello," she greeted him.

He kissed her on her cheek and they both walked into the kitchen.

"More presents?" she asked, spying those under his arm.

"Well, not many more. I just wanted to show a little appreciation to some of the boys in the store. I mailed most of them, but I have a surprise for some of the others, and I plan to give them theirs personally tonight. Did you get the tree?"

"Yes, it's lovely. We can trim it tonight."

"Any more cards today?" he inquired.

"Yes," she answered, a trifle cautiously.

"From anyone I know?"

"Yes," she repeated, "you can see them later." *He can ask the darnedest questions*, she said to herself.

"Did you . . . er . . . receive one from . . . him?" he asked, hesitantly.

Somehow, she couldn't answer. The words just would not come.

"It's all right, dear. I am glad he remembered you."

He had eased her pain. Somehow she could speak again. "Oh, Steven, why do you do those things? You make it very difficult for me . . . "

"I meant no harm, dear. Listen, darling, don't you remember when I first saw you, I asked you if you had ever been in love and you didn't hesitate . . . you told me the truth. I took the chance of you forgetting him, so you have nothing to worry about. Believe me, I have been very happy with you, and I have no cause for regret, even if, deep down in your heart, you love him—the same way I feel about my former wife. Only, she's not here."

Stella did not answer, but put her arms around his neck and kissed him. "That's what I like about you," she finally said, "you understand everything."

They ate dinner, and, after the dishes were put away, they both went down to the basement to dress the tree and to prepare for the party.

It was Christmas in Harlem, too, and Toddy and Marie were doing some last minute shopping on 125th Street. Bumping into one another, being separated by others, the little children running here and there, and vendors yelling all added to the utter confusion, but without it the people would not be happy. So, after many such bumpings and separations they finally completed their shopping and, loaded down with bundles, trundled to Lenox Avenue, where the car was parked. They were home in a few minutes.

After dinner, they set about wrapping the presents. They were seated on two chairs across from each other, separated by a large table on which were paper of all colors and twine to match. Every now and then Marie would stop working and glance at Toddy. On one of these occasions she asked, "Love me?"

"You know it, beautiful," replied Toddy, rather sullenly.

"Oh come on now. There is something annoying my darling husband. Why do you look so glum?"

"I am not glum," he insisted. "I was just wondering what you and I were doing last Christmas Eve."

"Oh, darling, you couldn't forget that. The same as we are doing this year. You were home from the university for the holidays, remember? We went up to Louise and you brought me back at nine in time for work. Then you went to church."

"Oh, yes. Then I came to the Savoy and I danced with

212

you so much you told me that you couldn't make any money."

"Well, I did turn you loose about three o'clock."

"Oh, yes, it was a breakfast dance. Then afterwards we went for a drive in Central Park in the early morning in all that snow. . . . or maybe we should forget about that."

"I think so, too, seeing as you nearly killed us both," she said.

"And we almost had our first quarrel because you wanted to go for a long ride out in the country and you had to go to work at a quarter of four the next day, and I wouldn't go."

"Oh, yes, you kept telling me I would ruin my health."

"Well, go on. You do remember that you took sick in February and almost had pneumonia and had to stay home for a month."

"Uh-huh."

"Oh, darling, when I think of those things it doesn't make me feel any too good to know that you are sacrificing yourself and jeopardizing your health for me."

"Now stop. Soon you'll be a doctor. You are going to graduate thirteen months from now, see, and I told you that if I do get sick, I'll never have to worry."

"You know I can't treat you if you get real sick."

"You most certainly will. Do you think I'd pay another doctor our money as long as you are a doctor, my dear husband?"

"Look at the time. If we keep on talking we'll never get finished."

"Well, suppose you finish, dear. I have to get dressed."

"Wait a minute, there's something I want to ask you. Are you going to have another baby?"

"Oh, I felt it coming. I guess I wasn't fast enough. I was so afraid you were going to ask me that."

"Well?" he asked, anxiously.

"Yes," she replied.

Toddy drew a deep, long breath.

"Why, darling. Don't worry," she said, reassuringly. "It won't interfere with any plans. I can work another three months at least. I really want a boy. Little Louise will be so lonesome when we take her for good."

"A boy? How do you know that it's going to be a boy?"

"How do I know? Well, a little birdie told me, see."

"Aren't you going to get dressed?"

"No, I won't stay up there long. She'll probably be asleep when we get there anyway."

It was five minutes to nine when they arrived in Mt. Vernon. The young lady of nearly seven years was elated when she saw her presents—dresses, shoes, hats, dolls, nightgowns, and a large dollhouse that she went crazy over. The parting was sad again, but Marie had to go to work and she said it would not be long before they would all be together.

They arrived at the Savoy at a quarter of eleven.

"Darling, I don't feel like dancing tonight. I don't think I'll come up tonight until you are through. I feel very tired. I think I'll go to bed."

"All right, I will see you about six then. You're not going to church either?"

"No, I think I'll listen to the service on the radio. But don't be surprised to see me later. If I really feel all right after a bath, I may blow in, suddenly. So don't do much flirting."

"Oh, stop."

It was a quarter past six when Marie put her key in the door of the apartment. She was tired, dead tired. She walked into the bedroom and turned on the light. Toddy was lying across the bed fast asleep. She bent over and kissed him and

214

he jumped up suddenly. "It's all right, darling. I figured you had overslept so when I didn't see you I took a cab."

"Oh, boy, was I sleepy. I set the clock to alarm at five-thirty." Toddy looked at the clock and then said, with surprise, "So that's why it didn't alarm. Look, I forgot to pull up the alarm button."

He got up, undressed, and put on his pajamas and Marie did the same. They sat on the bed with arms around one another.

"Work hard tonight, darling?" he asked.

"Oh, no," she lied, "my partners were very considerate. They preferred to sit and talk. So I made more money, nearly thirty dollars."

"I don't believe you. I bet they danced you until you were dog tired."

"No, it was fun. What do you think? Some Frenchman told me I looked like a girl he met on the other side of the world. Somewhere in Borneo, he said. Where's that?"

"Dutch East Indies. That's the place to go—peace, quiet, harmony. No one to bother the natives. Oh boy, I'd like to live down that way. Well, perhaps someday we'll go there."

There was no answer, and Toddy reached out and touched Marie. "What's the matter?" he inquired.

"Nothing, darling. I was saying my prayers."

"Oh, I beg your pardon."

"Darling," she burst out, suddenly, "what have you done to me? Nine years ago I'd have sworn that this would've never happened to me. I mean, seeing you all over again after resigning myself to the fact that I had lost you. And, falling so terribly hard in love with you. What have you done to me?" she repeated. "I don't know what I'd do without you."

"Darling," he consoled her, "are you sure that you never felt sorry that you met me again?"

"Sorry?" she queried. "You never knew how much I wanted to see you. How many nights I craved to have you by my side. I did make a mistake in my life, but perhaps I was supposed to make that mistake. Imagine if I'd never met Jean, I'd never have met you. Not just that. You remember that night you came up to the Savoy? I've never told you this before. I was supposed to be off, but it just had to happen, darling, it just had to happen. There could be no one else for me.

"If I was supposed to fall in love with anyone else, I would have. Look at the opportunity I had. All the different men I've met—rich men, successful men, men that could give me everything I wanted—but not a single one of them appealed to me. Even after you did tell me that you were married, I didn't tell you about Marie Louise. I knew that you'd know someday. We just had to be together, that's all.

"If anything ever happened so that we had to part. I think I'd kill myself. I couldn't live without you."

Toddy said, "Darling, there's one question I'd like to ask you. When you first made that proposition to me about going back to school, did you really mean it?"

"Sure I did. Haven't I proved that I meant it? Of course I did. I love you. You have made me happy. I've told you this before. There's always a woman behind every man's failure or success and no matter where we live in this world there's always one man for every woman. Perhaps there are times when they never meet. That's my belief.

"The moment I looked at you in Detroit, do you remember? I was coming down the stairs. A somewhat peculiar feeling entered my body, like an awakening. I guess that's the way people feel when they suddenly get religion. It wasn't flirtation, it was a genuine feeling of love, of faith in a person. Jean stood there with you and yet for the moment I did not realise that he existed.

"I used the only way I knew then to make you fall for me and I lost you then. But, even if you hadn't done what you did, I'd have never forgotten as long as I lived that I had met you. That's why I want you to go ahead, to go and study, to be the doctor you want to be, and if you really want to be a good one you and you alone can do it, darling.

"I am just helping you financially, but it's up to you. I can't study for you, you know, and someday, perhaps not too far away, you may even find a cure for that disease that's threatened to kill off most of our race."

Toddy turned and kissed her and she returned his kisses.

"Oh," she whispered, "I do love you so very much."

Chapter Fourteen

The leaves on the trees had become green and soft. Flowers had begun to bloom again. Housewives were beginning their semiannual cleaning. The birds had begun their migration towards the north. It was spring.

It was on a clear spring morning that Marie awakened Toddy with a kiss while he lay asleep next to her. He woke and, seeing her pretty face above him, returned the greeting.

"It's a beautiful morning, dear," she said, looking out one of the bedroom windows of their five-room house in Mt. Vernon.

The scent of the pure rich air caused Toddy to take a deep breath.

"Yes," he agreed, "it is a lovely day and even more so with you here. I had a dream last night," he went on, his face becoming a little sad. "I had a dream last night about the baby. I held him in my arms. He was so pretty, as brown as a chestnut, eyes like yours they were."

Marie nodded.

"Plenty of hair and, why did we have to lose him?"

"Please, Toddy, don't talk about it."

Marie turned her head away to hide the tears that forced their way into her eyes. She was remembering the doctor's remark that it was either her life or her baby's.

"Darling," she whispered, "after you graduate, we'll have lots of them."

"Another thing, Marie. You know what the doctor said about you dancing. You'll have to take a rest."

"Please don't worry about me, darling. You just keep on studying and when you have succeeded, I will get all the rest I want. You have less than a year, if you don't fail."

"I won't fail. Don't you worry about that."

"Come on, let's get some sleep," Marie suggested. "It's Decoration Day, I've got to make a matinee."

When they awoke again, it was almost one o'clock.

"Darling, what do you say we go for a long ride in the country before I go in?" asked Marie.

"All right," answered Toddy. "What are we going to have for dinner?"

"I think we'll stop at the Brown Shoppe and get some of those nice barbecue spare ribs."

"All right, dear, that's fine."

After they had their barbecue spare ribs, Toddy took the wheel and turned the car up Seventh Avenue. Up to 155th Street he drove, then north up the Harlem River Drive to 207th Street. Under an elevated subway on Broadway they eased along all the way up to 242nd Street.

"Do you want a soda or something, dear?" Toddy asked Marie.

"No, darling, I just want to go and go. The farther away the better." She nestled closer to him. "Isn't it beautiful, sweetheart?" she said, pointing at the distant green hills that began to appear. "Let's go right through them; you know what I mean, the mountains, darling. I want to take some pictures of you. I want to do something today that I will remember always. It's an odd experience to look back at something that appeared so beautiful and you have nothing to touch, nothing to hold, to really see. That's why today, I don't know why I am feeling this way, but I, er, don't know, just have a feeling that I will never be able to do this again."

Toddy turned off the highway and encountered some extremely bumpy roads.

"Where are you going?" she asked.

"Darling, I just remembered a spot that I once visited somewhere along here. I hope I won't get lost. It's a very elusive spot, once you pass the 'rock' you'll never miss. . . . Oh, there it is. Yes, it's still there—that rock. See it, right there? The one that appears to be pointed."

"Oh, yes, I see it now," she replied.

Toddy turned the car directly in front of the rock. He brought it to a stop and touched Marie. "Let's get out for a minute, dear, I want to show you something," he said.

She obeyed.

Toddy's arms were around her as she stepped from the car. He freed one arm in order to close the door. The road, which led farther into what appeared to be a thicket, narrowed somewhat. They walked carefully, their eyes focused on the dry and rutty ground. On they trudged, taking time now and then to look back at the car. Soon they came to a hill and, bending their bodies to facilitate their going, they made it up the short rise in the ground without difficulty. As they reached the top, they suddenly beheld a chasm directly before them. Unconsciously Marie stepped back, for the ground there seemed to have been carved out with a gigantic shovel.

Cautiously, they again approached the rim of the precipice. Down, down, down they looked, and the bowels of the earth appeared to move closer towards them.

"Look across to the other side, darling," whispered Toddy, and Marie looked.

As she did so, she swayed a little in his arms and he steadied her.

"It scares me," she said with a groan. She raised her right hand and rubbed her fingers across her forehead.

"Let's sit down a while, dear," she said.

Toddy moved her back a few paces and they sat on the ground. She laid her head across his lap and turned her face to the sky. The soft breeze lifted small strands of her hair and held them high, then dropped them back again across her face. Toddy plucked a twig of soft grass from out of the earth and slowly pointed the root to her ear. As he touched her, she suddenly turned her head and, seeing the blade in his hand, she laughed a little.

"Ticklish?"

"No, darling. I thought it might be an insect or something."

She lifted her eyes upwards once more and Toddy leaned backwards to do the same thing.

"Sweetheart," she said, softly, "I am wondering whether you are really in love with me. I am in love with you so much so that I could die with you in my arms right now. God up in His Heaven must have made us meet one another. All this happiness can't last. I am sure of that. Sometimes I feel that something will happen to make us separate. It's too good, too heavenly. Maybe I do sound rather foolish when I speak like this, but I know it can't be forever. At times when I am so happy, I want to die in that frame of mind because I know that the day will come when we might either get too old or too used to one another to love one another like we are doing now. That's why I am afraid, afraid to think of ever losing you."

"I wish you wouldn't talk like that," he remonstrated. "I wish sometimes that I had never met Stella and that you had never met Jean. Perhaps we would feel different about one another. Perhaps if you hadn't had a child with me, you would have felt differently or perhaps if you hadn't seen me again, you would have forgotten all about me. But this I do know, deep down in my heart, I would not and could not ever forget you as long as I live."

A cloud filtered across the face of the sun and the darkness was pronounced.

"See what I mean?" said Marie rather excitedly. "Just now all was clear and shiny, and then all of a sudden, it became dark. That's the way my life is."

"But that's the way everybody's life is, dear," he interrupted.

"Perhaps, but in my mind I have a feeling. It isn't the first time. It has always happened. Every time I become happy and contented, just like I feel now, inevitably something happens."

"Marie, tell me what makes you do all this for me? Why do you sacrifice yourself so that I may succeed?"

"I love you, that's all. I suppose I am one of those unusual people whose love is greater than anything else in the whole world. When you have succeeded, I want to be able to be proud of you."

"You know, Marie, I think of you all day. Wondering when you are alone if you are ever sorry, if there's any doubt in your mind as to the outcome."

"Now the sun is out again. Isn't God's work something to wonder at?"

"Yes, it is, dear, but I was asking you a question."

"Please. Why must I do all the talking?"

"I only want to know."

"Very well then. I have wondered. I've even begged God to warn me if he thought that I was doing wrong. I've even tried to imagine other men in your place, men that could do everything in the world for me, but all my thoughts, all my anticipations, all my doubts have boiled down to one thing. You are the only man in the world for me. I am earnestly and truly aware of it. If He wills it that I am to die at this moment, I would have no cause for regret. Why? Because I have found in so short a time the things that millions wait a lifetime for. In my soul I feel that I am your inspiration and I'll always want to be remembered as such. I am the mother of the child of the man that I love. Oh, I do thank God that Stella was a woman who understood another woman," Marie paused for a moment, and then continued.

"Should I become sick, I mean if I had to go away somewhere, I would want you to do everything that you could for Marie Louise, to take good care of her." Her eyes met his and for the moment he was conscious only of his own uneasiness, as he failed to visualize any sign of ailment in her.

"What are you talking about?"

"Well, Toddy, I've always had a premonition that I wouldn't live very long and I just want to be sure that Marie Louise will be all right."

"All right, I promise, but stop discussing death so much."

"That is the greatest fault of all the people in the world. Most of us refuse to face the fact that anything could happen to us and we only think of it when it happens to others. Death is always to be thought of, my darling, always."

Like a war veteran who has seen horror and destruction on the battlefield, only to have the pictures brought before his very eyes years later, so did Toddy feel as time went backwards for him and he saw the nurse in the hospital pull a cord and put a white sheet over the face of the body of his mother.

"I wish we had brought some sandwiches. I am getting a bit hungry. Darling, I want to come out here often. It's so peaceful and quiet. For a moment I forgot all about the Savoy. Well, pretty soon I won't have to . . . "

"Much sooner than you expect," interrupted Toddy.

She stood up, brushed the dirt and the wrinkles from her coat, jumped up and down a little, and went through a few stretching exercises. Then she fell into his arms and kissed him.

They strolled towards the car and in an hour and a half, they were home.

It was five o'clock when Toddy fastened the last hook on Marie's dress. He led her to the mirror and they both stood there gazing at their reflections. "Sweetheart, you do look beautiful," he said, admiringly.

"Oh, go on," she said, brushing him aside, "you'll make me later than I am already."

She walked hurriedly to the door and Toddy followed. "I have never seen that dress before, or have I?" he asked.

"Sure you have, dear. Your memory is bad. I had this on the night I met you, but it has been a long time since I've worn it."

Toddy felt it and remarked, "Isn't it a bit warm for this kind of weather?"

"It just goes to show you that men don't know anything about women's fashions. It's brocaded silk, dear," she replied, and kissed him good-bye.

Toddy kept the door open as she disappeared down the stairs. He closed it and went to the window just in time to see her drive away. Then he sat down on the couch and began to study.

Marie greeted the doorman at the Savoy with a "Hello, Ralph."

He tipped his hat and answered, "Yuh're de furst one, lady; boss kinda peeved 'cause nobody showed up yet."

"He'll get over it," she replied.

Down the stairs she went to check her coat and then to the hostesses' dressing room to put on her final makeup. She daintily walked back up the stairs and took her place on

224

the bench reserved for the hostesses. The place was practically deserted. A few couples with all the room to spare strolled jauntily across the carpeted floor. Marie arose from her seat and with a few steps reached the rail that surrounded the dance floor. About a dozen teenage couples were "Lindy hopping" to the tune of "Sweet Georgia Brown," played by Fatty Evans and his band. The trumpets and saxophones blared away to the final note. As the boys in the band saw her they all waved and she in turn waved back.

Marie went back to the bench. She was uneasy. She actually thought she felt a dizzy sensation creeping over her. "Must be all the fresh air I had today," she said to herself.

More customers came in and as some of the men passed her they stared at her as though she were a picture on exhibition. For the first time in many months she became self-conscious. She took out her mirror and made sure she looked all right. Just as she put it back Celestine came in.

"Hello, Marie."

"Hello, Cele. Say tell me, do I look funny or what is the matter?"

"You look gorgeous, that's all I know."

The place was now becoming crowded with all types of individuals. A new band began playing and the Savoy, once again, became the "Home of Happy Feet."

There was the first customer at the hostesses' box office. He purchased his amount and walked to the bench. He gave his tickets to Marie and she went to the floor with him. As he put his arm around her she glanced at the tickets. There were three. *Cheapskate*, she thought, and continued to dance.

They had not danced ten seconds when Marie recognised him as one of the "fresh" partners. He tried to squeeze her more closely and she physically objected.

"What's the matter, babe?"

"What's the matter with what?" she flashed back.

"Gee, a guy come up here to have a good time and you dames act as though he was poison. I got money and I'll spend it if you are nice to me."

"In what way must I be nice?"

"Well, now you are acting sensible. Tell you what, you get another girl and we'll . . . you see, I have a friend up here who just came off the boat, has a lot of dough, and will spend it. Maybe we both can, er, you know, kinda get most of it. It's easy, I tell you."

"How?" she asked.

"Well, after the joint closes we can go somewhere and get high, then I know a place we can all go . . . "

"Sorry, you chose the wrong girl," she interrupted him.

"Oh, I don't think so. Your name is, er, Celeste."

"No, it isn't. I have a faint suspicion that you are a detective. Tell the truth, aren't you?" Marie asked, and put on one of those bewitching smiles.

"Uh-huh. I really didn't think you were the type, but, you see, we got a few complaints that some girls from up here were using their jobs as 'blinds' for their real purpose."

"Listen, let me tell you something. Every girl up here is really up here to work."

The music stopped and they stood where they were, talking.

Marie continued, "As I was saying, those girls that do those dirty jobs don't even work here. They are good-looking, they come up here dressed as hostesses, and they tell the fellows that they do work here."

"I am awfully sorry, but you can have the other two tickets. I'll just stay and have a look around."

"Okay."

They walked off the floor together and Marie reached the bench. Her partner must have turned away for when she

226

looked back she didn't see him. "Cele," she said, "there's a cop here that knows your name. He thought I was you and tried to trap me. Told me about some fellow off a boat with a lot of money."

Celestine immediately jumped. She said, "I'll be back in a minute," and bolted for the ladies room.

"Well," was all Marie could say.

All at once Marie became disgusted. The crowds, the place, everything in it seemed so unattractive that night. It dawned on her that she actually was beginning to hate her work. Toddy was the only man she loved. The idea of men putting their arms around her and perhaps whispering insulting remarks in her ear began to peeve her. At the same time she realised that she must take it. She could take it and she would. Another customer came towards her with a ticket in his hand. She jumped up, locked her arm through his, and went on the floor, happy in the thought that she was doing it for Toddy.

Night after night the same thing occurred; hot, stinking, distasteful creatures pawed her and danced with her, stepping on her feet, on her dress, and many times on her character, but she continued to take it.

That night, she began to feel tired much earlier than usual. It was almost two o'clock when Marie told one of the other girls that she was going to the ladies room. She had not been gone more than two minutes when a gentleman walked to the bench and asked for her.

"She'll be right back," he was told.

He waited and waited and did not see her return to the bench.

"Pardon me," he addressed Celestine, "is she dancing?"

"No, she isn't. Just a minute, I'll try and get her for you." Celestine went to the ladies room and there was Marie sitting in a chair, looking very pale.

"What's wrong, Marie?"

"I don't feel so good. I am just waiting until I feel a little better, then I am going home."

"That fellow just came in. You know, that Mr. Bromisch or Bromwich."

"Oh, shucks, he would have to come tonight," Marie said, shaking her head like a wet dog throwing off water from its back. "Tell him I'll be right out."

A dull sound in the parlor of the apartment where Toddy lived awakened him from his sleep in the bedroom. He got up, went into the other room, and turned on the light. Marie was lying on the floor fully dressed. As he picked her up and took her to the bedroom, her head cleared and she began to groan.

"Oh dear, I must have had a little too much wine. Here, that's all right, I can undress myself."

He put her down and she walked dizzily towards the mirror.

"Darling, you can't kid me, there wasn't an odor of alcohol on your breath. You are just tired from working too hard. You will collapse entirely some night."

"I'm all right, dear. It was probably the heat of the place and then that country air today, I mean yesterday."

"I think you ought to go away for a few weeks. Don't you see, dear, it's not fair for you to go on jeopardising your health for my sake? I could stop school for a while, get a job, and you can use some of your money to get a much needed rest. After you are well, I could go back and finish."

"Who said I am sick?"

"I am saying it, dear, and you know you are, too. You are even looking thinner."

"I am all right, I'm telling you. I am a little tired now and as soon as I get some sleep, I'll be fine." She got into bed and turned out the light.

"You've said that over and over. Some night you are going to be actually sorry and then it'll be too late. Why can't you listen to me just once?"

"Please, dear, let me sleep."

"All right," he said, and leaned over and kissed her.

Toddy awoke at eight. He fixed his breakfast and went back to the bedroom. Marie was sleeping peacefully. He stroked her hair gently with the palm of his hand, kissed her forehead, and went to school.

Marie awoke at one o'clock that afternoon. For a moment she looked for Toddy, forgetting that it was Monday again and that he had to go to school. Reconciled to the fact that she was alone, she began to talk to herself, saying, "Please, God, give me strength to continue. I once asked you to tell me if you thought I was doing the wrong thing. Maybe I am but please, God, I do love him, you know that."

She tried to sit up but found it difficult. A pain in the center of her back retarded her effort. She tried it again, got up halfway, but fell back in bed.

Reaching for the telephone she called up her doctor.

"Please come as soon as you can. I really must see you. No kidding this time, doctor. It's important."

The doorbell rang a half an hour later.

"How do you do, my dear dancer?" the doctor said. He opened his bag and began taking out some instruments. "I don't see why such a healthy-looking person like you should need a doctor. Sit up, or can't you?"

"I don't think I can. I couldn't before I called you."

"All right, tell me what's the matter."

"I have been feeling pretty good, doctor, if I do say so myself, but, er, lately I've begun to worry a little. Last night I fainted twice, once on the job and later in the morning when I got home."

The doctor held her wrist and took her pulse. "Yes, go on," he urged.

"My husband put me to bed and this afternoon when I awoke, about an hour ago, a terrible pain enveloped my lower . . . " she said, and pointed to her abdomen, "and I couldn't move." She appeared exhausted. "If anything is wrong, I want you to tell me the truth."

"Suppose you turn over and let me see your back, huh?"

"I'll try."

"That's fine. Now breathe, hard and often."

"Another thing I have noticed, whenever I sneeze I get a pain right here." She pointed to her chest.

"Suppose you cough a little for me now . . . Again . . . Once more, a little harder."

Marie held her hand up to her mouth.

"Still hurts?" the doctor inquired.

"Yes, it does, especially when I cough hard."

"Why didn't you call me before?"

"I didn't think it was serious."

Fifteen minutes later the doctor was replacing his tools in his bag. He had made a preliminary examination on Marie. "Well, young lady, suppose you come up to my office tomorrow? I'd like to take an X ray of your chest."

"Is there anything wrong with me, doctor?"

"Well, I don't think that miscarriage you had helped you any. One thing you'll have to do is to stop dancing. There are millions of people living who haven't a heart as good as you have, only you can't afford to take any chances; so, I'd suggest that you give up dancing temporarily."

Marie nodded in agreement, knowing in her heart she had no intention of doing any such thing.

Toddy came home about three-thirty and found Marie playing solitaire.

"Hello, darling," she greeted him.

"Hello. How are you feeling?"

"Fine, my love. Are you hungry?"

"No, I am a little sleepy, that's all."

"I am so sorry I woke you up when I got in early in the morning."

"Nonsense, you didn't wake me up. You forget so quickly, don't you? Just suppose I didn't wake up last night. You'd have been sleeping on the floor until this morning."

"Forget about that. Want to run up to see Marie Louise after dinner?"

"All right," agreed Toddy.

"I think I'll take off tonight. I haven't been to the movies for a long while. We can stay up there until seven and still have lots of time for the show."

They had dinner in an hour and left for Mt. Vernon, with Toddy at the wheel.

"What did you do today, dear?" asked Toddy, as the car sped along the Grand Concourse.

"Nothing particular."

He turned and looked at her and she returned his look with a somewhat silly smile. Every now and then he glanced at her and she unconsciously wilted a bit as though expecting a certain question that did not come.

As the car neared the end of the New York City line, another car came very close to them in turning a corner.

"Look out!" Marie screamed.

"What is the matter, darling?" asked Toddy. "You seem rather nervous."

"Oh," she gasped, "I thought for sure that car was going to hit us."

"Well, it didn't. Now are you all right?"

"Yes, but you'd better keep your eyes on the road."

He stole another glance, but Marie was staring straight ahead. Her countenance appeared grim and stoic.

"Darling," he called, in a rather loud voice.

"Oh," she yelled, "please don't do that!"

"Oh, now, you can't kid me. I know you too well there is something wrong."

"There's nothing the matter. Can't we just keep a little quiet until we reach the house?"

Toddy did not answer. He could tell there was something the matter with Marie, but decided to wait until they arrived at the house before asking any more about it.

When he brought the car to a stop before the house where Marie Louise lived, Marie opened the door and got out without saying a word. He followed her, silently.

Disappointment awaited them, for when she rang the bell there was no answer. A voice called from the porch next door telling them that Mrs. Saitch had gone out and had taken the child with her.

Marie and Toddy left word that Mr. and Mrs. Turner had called and were sorry they couldn't wait, but would telephone tomorrow.

"Do you want to drive back?" asked Toddy, a bit displeased by Marie's actions.

"No, sweetheart, I nev . . . "

"Are you angry?" he interrupted her.

"No," she said, curtly.

"Now look here, darling," he demanded, "you are going to tell me what this is all about. I've never seen you act this way before."

"Oh, Toddy, it's nothing. I was just a little upset. I was wondering if Louise was all right. I am all right."

"Where do we go from here?" he asked.

"Anywhere, dear. Let's see, there's a good picture at the

Loew's Victoria—'Back Street.' I've read the book and if the picture is as good as the book is, then it's all right."

"Love story?"

"Yes, it's about a woman who loved a man she was not able to marry or something like that. Anyway, she was the other woman in his life; he was married. But, he never stopped loving her until his death."

Marie was still crying when they came out of the theatre.

"it was sad, wasn't it?" she asked.

"Yes, it's rather odd, though. Would you sacrifice your whole life like she did for anyone?"

Marie just looked at him.

"I am sorry, darling. I realise you are doing just that," he admitted.

"Yes, sweetheart, and I'd do it a thousand times, if you were the man. Every time."

Chapter Fifteen

The destiny of man changes with every second, with every ticking of the clock. Each day and night the ever present law of God makes fresh changes against us and at times we have to be the judge as well as the witness in the courtroom of life. The places we dwell in, those in which we earn our livelihood, and those where we seek and find enjoyment are all seats in the universal courtroom. The new evidence that presents itself each day is sometimes the form of surprise witnesses, and our conscience, which is actually the pendulum, must ask for time in which to plan our defense or offense. If He denies our motion for a delay, then we are faced with the alternative of using our best judgement. Should our plan of conduction and summation fail to convince our jurors and we are convicted by the court, we may be sentenced to a long term of confinement and brooding. Through perjury and deception we may be freed, but if our conscience knows that we are guilty, we are prone to suffer a much worse sentence than imprisonment in order to pay the penalty.

The doorbell rang four times in the home of James Turner before he finally heard it. He put on his robe and went to the door. It was not yet six o'clock in the morning.

Opening the door, he saw the uniform of a telegram messenger.

"Does Mrs. Mondeau live here?" asked the boy.

"No!" yelled Toddy, angry at being disturbed at such a time. "Hey, wait a minute," he called to the boy, who had turned to go, "I am sorry, I didn't remember."

The boy eyed him doubtfully, but handed him the telegram. "Sign here, please," the boy commanded.

Toddy complied with the order.

"Thank you," said the messenger, rather sarcastically, and Toddy closed the door.

"He must think I am crazy," he muttered.

He went back to the bedroom and tiptoed in, thinking that Marie was asleep, but the heels of his slippers dug deep into the rug as she asked, "Who was it, dear?"

"A, er, a telegram," he answered, a little surprised, "addressed to you. It went up to the Savoy, and it's readdressed to here."

He handed the telegram to Marie.

Opening the telegram, she scanned it hastily, with Toddy solemnly looking at her expression. Astonishment swept over her face.

Words from the Bible

As thou knowest not what is the way of the spirit nor how the bones do grow in the womb of her that is with child, even so, thou knowest not the works of God who maketh all things.

Truly the *light* is sweet, and a pleasant thing it is for the eyes to behold the *Sun*.

But if a man live many years and rejoice in them all, yet let him remember the days of *darkness* for *They shall be many*.

All that cometh is Vanity.

"What is it, dear? You look as if you had seen a ghost?"

"Toddy, do you know who this is from?" Her words were slow and deliberate.

"I don't know, I am sure," he answered.

"It's from the hospital where Jean is. He is terribly sick; he must be . . . dying. They want to know about his relatives . . . He must be very bad . . . Here, read it. What do you think I should do?"

It was a message from the land of "forgotten men." Yes, Jean Mondeau was forgotten. It was probably this reason why Marie never mentioned Jean all through her manifestations of love for Toddy. He wondered, now more so, if there wasn't a repentant reason in Marie's mind; perhaps that's why she had lavished so much of her affections on him.

"Toddy, do you think I should really go to see him?"

"Well, he must be very bad, dear. I think the least you can do is to go to see him . . . soon . . . very soon . . . Today, if you can."

"Toddy, I wonder if you, er would be able to go with me?" she asked, hesitantly.

"Marie, to tell you the truth, er, I don't know whether I should go or not. This is probably too deep for me . . . I can't make up my mind about that. You know, somehow I'd always had a premonition that something like this would happen, and I've wondered what I would say."

"Darling, I don't see why you should feel badly about it; after all, I am really the one who has done wrong . . . from the very beginning. You remember that day in Detroit, how you slapped me? How angry you were then? How you wanted to leave and go away as soon as you were able to? Now, how can you blame yourself for what has happened to both of us? I wouldn't take it that way. Please go with me, please."

"When do you want to go?" he asked.

"Oh, darling, that's so sweet of you. Let's go now, huh?"

236

"I hope I'll be back in time to go to school."

"You know, Toddy . . . I think this is the last time we'll ever be able to see him," said Marie, as they went out the door.

"I am not going to see him, Marie. I'll wait in the car for you."

"All right, if that's the way you want it. I wouldn't force you to."

As the car turned into the entrance of the institution the stigma of fear and pity came over Toddy. Pity, because he knew that Jean had no one else in the country; he couldn't reconcile himself to thinking that Jean was actually out of his mind. Fear, of himself; he wondered how he would feel when he faced Jean. No, even if he contemplated going in, he was now more sure than ever that he did not want to see Jean Mondeau.

Toddy stopped the car and Marie got out. "Sure you don't want to go in?" she asked.

"No, darling, I'll wait . . . here. You don't mind, do you?"

"Of course not, my darling. I understand."

She left the car and Toddy watched her disappear behind the large iron-gate door of the institution. He then sat back in the car, closed his eyes, and began to wonder. His eyes opened slowly. Through the window to his left, he looked, and as far as his eyes could see was God's green country. Long blades of grass waved in the cool breeze and small black patches of the shadows of trees stained the scenic beauty of the flat panorama. The leaves of the trees shook with defiance at the wind that blew through them.

He raised his eyes heavenward and there was the blue sky above, dotted here and there by small patches of white clouds, which appeared to change their shape with the wind. Sometimes they seemed to hinge together and to form a new land of their own surrounded by rivers and lakes.

Slowly, he turned his head to the right and there was an imposing structure of stone that housed an abundance of people who had lost every sense of reason. Men and women who for some purpose or other were once part and parcel of their fellow beings. Men and women of all classes; atoms of a great kingdom who could not or may never again appreciate the wonderful existence of the goodness of living.

He thought back and there before his eyes was the past again. The events that he thought were responsible for his cousin's dilemma were unfolding before him. Among memories coming to him was that one thorn that stood out before all the others: that visit to Detroit. Oh, if that had never happened! If Jean had become sick and Toddy had met Marie afterwards, he would never have felt the way he did at that moment. That was the blot that blurred the portrait of happiness on which were painted James Turner and Marie Turner.

Like a sudden pointing finger he realised that he had stolen his cousin's wife. He had felt that perhaps in all his life (he had never really had any unhappiness after the death of his mother) he had never done anything wrong. Now he wondered, Was this wrong? Would he suffer some day? Would some great disappointment overtake him in his climb to attain success? Had he done wrong by leaving Stella? (Oh, no. She was happy, she was satisfied, she had remarried. If she had been bad, if through his action some disgraceful event had happened to her, if she had done what some other women had done when they had lost their love, then perhaps he would have felt deserved of some suffering.) He only wanted a chance to get ahead and he had found someone who believed in him, someone who had helped him and was still helping him to achieve the goal he was striving for. Had he been selfish? Marie had agreed to aid him in attaining a higher education, had aided him in getting a divorce from his wife by posing as a third party, by taking a chance of being branded as an outcast, as a prostitute. He knew that he had loved her and that she had loved him. But had he been selfish?

What if a friend of his had told him that a girl was doing the same thing for that friend? Would he look upon them as he expected them to look upon him? At times there had been doubts in his mind as to whether or not he was doing the honorable thing, however, Marie constantly buoyed him up by her argument that women were aiding men all through the ages. Perhaps he was due for untold suffering. He believed in God. He knew that had He not wanted him to be successful He would have stopped him before his time—or was this the beginning?

"The path to success is always hard," he had been told many times. But so far he had had it very easy.

Marie opened the door so suddenly that he was a bit startled.

"Well, dear?" he said, rather dryly.

"Come on, darling, let's get away from this place. We can talk later."

The car had left the environment of the institution and Marie began speaking.

"Toddy?"

"Yes, dear."

"Your cousin is not exactly dying, but he has to go away. It seems according to the doctor those tumors that he has developed into some sort of disease. They said it might be cancer and they were checking to see if he had anyone, a near relative, that, er, had any money."

"They don't think he'll live?"

"Well, the doctor says it may not be fatal for perhaps a great many years."

"Did you see him?"

"Just a glimpse, Toddy. I shuddered when I looked at him. He looks terrible, his face sunken and only a shell. The real reason they wanted this nearest relative, Toddy . . . was in the event of, er . . . for research purposes, and experimental work. I didn't exactly let them know . . . well, I did tell them I had remarried, but I didn't let them know it was to one of his relatives. . . . I didn't think you'd want me to."

Toddy kept his eye on the road. He did not answer. Marie went on. "So if they find no one else the State will give them permission to use his brains."

Toddy just sighed, and Marie thought it better not to continue on the subject.

Toddy stayed home that day. He just couldn't go to school. The skies, which had been so beautiful in the early morning, were now grey and stormy. Rain was falling. With small pelting sounds the rain pattered against the windows. It seemed to enter the house and his muddled brain and to create more puddles, making such a drenching that he could not wade through.

Marie was in the kitchen. Toddy walked over to the piano. He opened the cover and clamped his arms on the keys. The notes took effect, and soon the strains of "The Lost Chord" were being played by him.

Only a week earlier the Glee Club, in which he sang a moderate alto, had earned special merit from the music professor for the way they sang this number. Softly he began to sing.

"Seated one day at the organ"—low ominous rolls of thunder were heard in the distance.

"I was weary and ill at ease"—a stab of lightning tore through the unshaded window and for a moment he was unable to discern the white keys before him.

"And my fingers wandered idly.

240

"Over the noisy keys.

"I knew not what I was playing.

"Nor what I was"— crash! came a roaring peal of thunder that shook the house to the rafters. Bang! echoed a chord on the piano made by both his hands. It sounded like a jumbled shaking of many cowbells all at once. He stopped playing, walked to the door, opened it, and was met by a flash of lightning that sent his hands to his face to shield himself, at the same time backing up and pushing the door with his foot.

"Gosh, what a storm," he muttered, as he went back to the piano. He sat down, then jumped up suddenly—something was wrong; he was tormented. He pulled down the shades. He was losing control of himself. He kept wondering why should he feel this way. Premonition. Impending danger, like a captain of a liner at sea in a hurricane—suddenly, there loomed before him another ship—It was too close. He was unable to avoid the collision. Then it happened: "Crash!" But he was not at sea. There was no thunder. That noise had come from the kitchen.

"Marie," he shouted, running—and there she lay, on the floor. Water had splashed all over the room and an empty pan lay on the floor.

"Marie, Marie," he called, rubbing the palms of her hands. He flew up the stairs, pushed open the bathroom door, and jerked open the cabinet. Grabbing the smelling salts, he went down the stairs three at a time. He opened the bottle and held it to her nostrils.

"What happened, dear?" he asked, as her eyelids parted and her hand went to her forehead.

"I, er, don't know. I was just putting some water on the stove and before I could say anything or even realised what had happened everything went black."

"Put your arm around my neck. I'll take you upstairs."

241

"I'll be all right."

"Yes, I know you will, but put your arm around my neck," he said, insistently.

He picked her up and took her upstairs, where he laid her on the bed and called the doctor.

Doctor Simmons turned to Toddy after examining Marie. "She'll be all right; she is just tired." He winked at Toddy and walked out of the room. Toddy followed the doctor as they walked downstairs towards the living room.

"Mr. Turner, your wife is not very well. I told her that when I was here before," explained the doctor.

"You were here?"

"Yes. She called me up and I gave her a preliminary examination. I asked her to come to my office for a thorough X ray and she never came."

So that's why she has been so nervous lately, thought Toddy.

"Did you tell her anything was wrong?"

"Yes, I did. She told me not to hide anything from her. I told her that her heart was a bit weak and that she should stop dancing . . . and, you know that's not all."

"What do you mean, sir?"

"She's going to have a child."

"I am not surprised. She's been acting very irritably for the past few weeks and I guessed as much . . . but I don't like the way you said 'that's not all.' "

"Your wife cannot go through another period of childbirth. She is very weak; she has an unnatural cough. That may or may not mean complications, but this much I can tell you—she won't be able to withstand much pain." The doctor paused, and then asked, "You love her, don't you?"

"More than anything else, sir."

"Well, I should have made myself more plain to her. I am going to be honest with you. If you continue—let's see,

242

how may I put it—if you continue to physically love her as much as you have been doing, she might become extremely ill."

"You mean . . . ?"

"Yes," answered the doctor.

"Oh, I think I understand."

"Try not to be too affectionate. Her resistance to disease is very poor and she needs to conserve all the strength she can muster."

"But, doctor, she's the one that, er, is always desirous."

"Yes, I don't doubt that. That is all the more reason why you have to use more control. You'll have to tell her in your own way, as gently as possible, and I do hope she'll understand. And remember, under no circumstances must you ever have anything to do with her for the next month. You understand that clearly?"

"I do—perfectly."

"I'll call back tomorrow. If she's able, let her come over to my office. Good-bye then," said the doctor.

"Good-bye, sir."

As Toddy let the doctor out of the house he wondered how he would tell Marie what the doctor had just told him.

The rain was still pounding on the roof of the back porch and Toddy decided to continue preparing the dinner that Marie had started. He was peeling some apples when he heard footsteps coming down the stairs.

"Marie, you get right back upstairs," he ordered, as she poked her head through the door.

"But, darling, do you think I am going to stay upstairs all by myself? You haven't been up to see me since the doctor left. What did he say to you?"

"He only told me how sick you really were and I didn't see any reason to disturb you. That's the only . . . "

"The only what?" she interrupted.

"The only, er, reason I didn't want to bother you, dear."

"But I *want* you to bother me, my love. Are you by any chance getting tired of me?" she asked, jokingly.

"Oh, now, don't be silly. You know fully well you are not at all well. If you were you wouldn't have fainted, now would you?"

"Anybody can faint sometime . . . "

"Yes, but I kept telling you to stop dancing for a while, but you wouldn't listen. Now you have got to stop."

"Oh, so the doctor has been saying something to you."

"Yes, he has . . . and lots more."

"Well, I can't stop dancing now. Perhaps in a few months, I promise. I came down to ask you to get an iron ready for me; I want to press a dress."

"What for?" asked Toddy.

"What do you mean, what for? I've got to get ready to go to work."

"Are you going crazy? Oh no, dear, not tonight. Do you realise that you are a sick woman? You go right back upstairs and get to bed," he commanded.

"Oh, darling, puh-lease."

"Marie, do you know that you are going to have a baby? The doctor told me."

She pouted, smiled, stuck her head a little further into the kitchen, and whispered, "I know it."

"Yes, but you don't know how serious it is."

"Sure it's serious. I had one before, remember? Oh . . . ," she murmured, and swayed a little.

"See, you are still dizzy. I told you, you are going upstairs right now," insisted Toddy.

"All right, I will go on one condition, that you come up soon."

"All right, I'll come up soon and I will bring you some dinner, too."

244

"All right."

A little while later Toddy took her dinner upstairs as he had promised. She was lying in bed reading. "A new book, dear?" he asked.

"No, I was looking through some old books I had in the bag and I liked this one the best. I remember back in Detroit I started it, but for some reason or other I had to stop, and I never got around to it again; but since I can't go to work I might as well read."

"Not a bad idea," Toddy remarked.

"Will you kiss me, darling?" asked Marie.

"All right, but promise to go to bed?"

"Yes, I promise." Toddy kissed her, and then she said, "Ah, that's so good. Guess I won't lose anything if I don't go to work."

"What do you mean?"

Marie just winked back at him. And Toddy got up. In doing so, he knocked the book from her hand and in picking it up a sheet of paper fell on the floor—he picked up the paper and read:

My Last Request

I am writing this as a personal favor to you, dear. If I die before you, please have my body taken to the place where I was born and bury it beneath the brown clay on the banks of the River Outeau, in the village of Veille Case on the island of Dominica in the British West Indies.

Although my father and mother have died long ago I beg to be near them in the end. May God bless you for it.

Your loving husband,
Jean

Toddy handed the note to Marie and she read it. They looked at each other in complete silence. Finally Marie said,

"I've always wondered why he asked me never to part with this book. This is the reason. Well, I don't think it's possible to grant his wish."

"Why?" asked Toddy.

"When he wrote that, darling, he never thought he would ever lose me. At that time he probably had a great deal of money and he hoped to acquire more. Now, where would the money come from to do that?"

"Marie, after all, that is his last wish and I wouldn't be very happy if I knew we could grant it and didn't."

"Darling, you do forget that he is still alive, and he may be for some time."

"Yes, I know, but tomorrow I'll have to go to the hospital and tell them who I am and stop them from doing what they are planning."

Later that night, Toddy lay close to Marie in bed with his arms around her. He had kissed her good night and was almost asleep. A slight tugging on his arm caused him to open his eyes and he peered into the darkness of the room around him.

"Toddy, do you still love me?"

"Always, darling. As long as I live, I will," swore Toddy.

"I don't want you to say that so many times; I want you to love me and comfort me. I wouldn't trade my place right now here in your arms for all the money in the world."

Marie reached over and searched his face with her hands. She found his lips in the darkened room and kissed him. "Darling," she whispered and then, noticing his frigidity, said, what's the matter?"

"Nothing, dear. I am a little sleepy, I guess."

Marie pulled her face away and moved rather boisterously to the other side of the bed. Toddy knew by her silence that she was peeved. He knew how sensitive she was when scorned, but he was trying his utmost to avoid her as quietly as possible.

When he awoke the sunlight was beaming in the window. He turned and looked at the clock. It was five minutes past seven. He looked at Marie. She was lying there apparently asleep, her beautiful face nestled in the crease of the pillow, and he tried hard to penetrate those eyelids that were so tightly shut. He tried to move from the bed when a brown arm encircled his neck; he lost his balance and fell back in the bed. Marie was staring at him and looking extremely bewitching.

"So, you weren't asleep?" he asked.

"I couldn't; all night I couldn't sleep. Why did you act that way last night?"

"I didn't act, dear. I was just asleep. I fell off to sleep right away," explained Toddy.

"But you aren't sleepy now" she purred and kissed him. The touch of her warm lips on his seemed to burn his very soul and she continued to draw the very existence of his being from him. His arms went around her and that burning sensation of real, true love enveloped him. She raised her head a little in the manner of a woman who is starving for love and affection. She kissed him again and again and then opened her eyes. They were open enough for him to penetrate those grey-brown "cat eyes," whose beginnings lay deep down in her heart, and he was lost. Everything was forgotten: all the warnings of the doctor; his conscience; everything that surrounded them save this lovely, desirable, delightful, unappeased woman so close to him—his wife.

Toddy reached the classroom at three minutes past nine after taking all sorts of chances while driving.

He was back home at four and Marie was in the kitchen preparing dinner.

"Darling, what are you doing out of bed?" he asked, concerned.

"I am not sick anymore, my dear. I am well and I don't see why I have to stay in bed."

"Oh God, what am I going to do with this woman? She refuses to be sick," remarked Toddy, with exasperation.

"I was doing some checking today, dear, and guess what I came across? We actually have more money than I'd figured. My insurance policy has almost matured and I am sure we can get quite a bit of money on it."

"Yes, I knew that things were getting bad but I didn't think it was as bad as all that."

"What are you talking about?" asked Marie, with surprise. "I didn't say that we were broke. I was just thinking about the baby. We have about three hundred dollars and my policy should bring about seven hundred."

"Goodness, that reminds me. I, too, have a policy—not one, but three of them. Imagine I forgot all about them. They must have lapsed years ago."

"Why did you have to let them lapse?" she asked.

"To tell the truth, I couldn't keep them and I forgot all about them. My mother took them out when I was no more than about four years old, but I know they are paid up for at least eleven years. I think I'll run down to the company Saturday and find out all I can about them. They must at least be worth a few hundred, just in case . . . "

"Just in case what?" interrupted Marie.

"Oh, dear, I, er, don't mean anything, but you've got to look ahead. It's much safer to feel a little secure; don't you agree with me, dear?"

"I suppose so, but I don't see why you are so much worried about the baby."

"You know I have stiff exams tomorrow and all next

week and I really have to buckle down and do some study-ing."

"Yes, my dear, I think I understand. I should leave you alone, is that what you are trying to tell me?"

"No, don't misunderstand. Aren't you supposed to go to the doctor today?"

"I am going to wait until Saturday when you are home so you can go with me."

"Okay," agreed Toddy.

Chapter Sixteen

Toddy completed his term successfully. He passed all his subjects with high honors and was lucky in acquiring a position for the summer holidays. The Harlem Drug Company, which had a great many stores throughout the metropolitan area, had given him a chance as an assistant in one of its upper Manhattan stores.

It was in the middle of July, and Toddy was glad for more than one reason that the summer had come. Marie had not worked for the past five weeks following a collapse one night after which she had had to be brought home. True, she was receiving money every week from her health and accident insurance policy but there were bills to be paid and Marie was growing. This necessitated the purchase of new clothes and their money was quickly dwindling.

Jean in the asylum was gradually weakening and there seemed no hope for his recovery. The doctor told them that there was little chance he would last through the fall of the current year, and Toddy hoped that he would be able to comply with his cousin's last request.

It was on one of these hot July mornings that the telephone rang in the store and as Toddy answered it his face took on a sad aspect, it was from Doctor Simmons.

Toddy bridged a gap of almost fifteen years, when a hospital doctor had called him and told him to come up right away. Now another doctor was telling him the same thing. Marie, his wife, the woman he adored, was ill. The woman who had all faith in him, whose sacrifice had enabled him to look forward to a great future, whose love for him had been so overwhelming as to cause him many times to sacrifice his own normal duties for her was now so sick that she had to be taken to a hospital.

Toddy thanked the doctor, then walked back to his boss at the prescription counter and told him what had happened. He was permitted to go at once and, having the car parked outside, he lost no time in getting to the Mt. Vernon General Hospital. He was then led to a room where Marie was resting.

He entered the room slowly, his hat in his hand, and walked to the bed.

"Marie, darling, what happened?"

"Oh, my love, I didn't know that I was so sick. The doctor says that I am awful sick and I may have to go away. Darling, I've got to leave you?"

Toddy fell on his knees at the foot of the bed.

"Sweetheart, please tell me what has happened. What are you saying, please tell me?"

"I was ironing this afternoon and one of those fainting spells came over me again, and I just managed to get to the telephone and call the doctor. I must have fainted while talking to him for when I became conscious again I was on the bed and he was standing over me. He said I should go to the hospital and that I wasn't to call you until I was there. Later, I heard all the doctors talking; they said that I only had a fifty-fifty chance. They are going to operate on me."

"I'll find out, my dear. They'll tell me just what is wrong, but I wouldn't worry, dear. You are okay. Just keep on believing that you are all right. I can't go on without you, darling. Don't you know how much we love each?"

But Marie fainted again.

"Marie! Marie! . . . " Toddy exclaimed, frantically.

251

"Nurse, please, someone, please." He jumped up and ran to the door. He brought a nurse back with him, who administered something to her. Marie opened her eyes and the nurse left. Two doctors then came and looked at Marie and then looked at Toddy.

"You are her husband?" one asked.

"Yes, I am," he answered.

"Well, would you mind stepping outside for a moment?"

Toddy followed the doctor, but not before he looked back over his shoulder. Marie's eyes were moist and she was sad.

Then one of the doctors spoke to him. "Young man, your wife is a very sick woman. She has a tumor that must be removed and she is also pregnant. Very odd, some woman have taken a tumor for pregnancy—in fact, some doctors have too—but in this case your wife has both. Now here's the situation: We've got to operate and I might as well tell you she is not very strong."

"You mean that she might die?"

"To tell the truth . . . yes."

"But she can't die. Listen, you two, I am studying medicine in school; I will graduate next spring if I can continue. And, doctor, there isn't one life at stake lying in there, there are three. If she dies, I will follow her."

"Oh, come now, you just told us you are studying to be a doctor. That means you are studying the ways to save lives, not to take them. Isn't that right?"

"Please, gentlemen, what I am driving at is this. Oh, I could go far back, very far back, and tell you all the things that led to this, and still it would be very difficult for you to understand. I'll say only this: You've got to save her . . . and here's how. I am sure that if she were to see me before and after that operation, she'd live, I know she would. You know what I mean. I want to be standing over her so that when she opens her eyes and sees me you won't have to worry about her living. I am sure it would mean a great deal toward her recovery. So please, if it is at all possible, let me be near her."

The doctors looked at each other; then they returned to Toddy. His face was wet with tears. One of the doctors said, "Buck up, young man. You can be there. We'll try to help her as much as we can, but please do not go in now. You see, she knows that she is sick and coupled with the fact that she loves you so much it might create a false picture in her mind that might tend to hurt her. So, wait a few minutes and the nurse will let you know when we are ready."

"Thank you, gentlemen," said Toddy, bowing.

Three hours later Toddy saw a great feat performed before his eyes. He knew a picture of the operation would stay in his mind as long as he lived.

Time and time again his heart almost stopped as the doctors and nurses worked with perfect precision. Nothing he had ever learned in class on dummies, no experiments that he had ever took part in, took more grit and heartwarming determination than he was witnessing. And it was Marie lying on the table.

She was finally led out of the operating room, after three-and-a-half hours. Toddy watched her. He was struck with awe and pride as he realised that someday he probably would be rendering the same service on some other person.

Toddy again went to the doctor to find out what the prognosis was.

"Doctor, do you think she will make it?" he asked.

"She has a good chance of survival, but she will have to go to a much warmer climate, preferably tropical. The growth was not malignant."

"You are not trying to tell me, doctor, that she has tuberculosis?"

"She is in an early tubercular stage, and complete rest, clean wholesome food, and an abundance of fresh air will be absolutely necessary in order for her to regain her health; of course, you realise that you must have nothing whatsoever to do with her . . . until she has recovered."

"Yes, sir, I know. I have been told before by Dr. Simmons."

"I am happy that you understand everything. Be careful. She is a very sick young woman and, might I add, that she is very beautiful so if you want her to be with you—and I am quite sure that you do—you'll have to take good care of her."

"I could never in this world do as much for her as she has already done for me, sir, but I'll do the very best I can. Thanks a great deal for what you have done, I do appreciate it from the bottom of my heart. Some day I am going to be a doctor. I graduate from medical school shortly," Toddy informed the doctor.

"Well, you have my best wishes. Good luck to you."

"Thank you, sir. Good-bye."

"Good day," replied the doctor.

The feeling of fear that Marie had sacrificed her life for him brought tears and sadness to Toddy's heart. Doubts about the feasibility of continuing his medical career began to prey upon his mind as he tried ever so hard to project into the future. The tentacles of life's mighty explosive web began to coil about him.

He knew there was emptiness in his home as he drove along the street. There was no reason to go home. The world was empty. God had punished him. This was his sentence for the crime that he had committed. They both had committed a crime and they were both paying for it. There could be no other reason for the sudden avalanche that moved on him as he tried to thread his way in the pathway of life below. He didn't remember turning on his street but suddenly he was there. Upon entering his home, he walked over to the nearest chair and sat down. He took off his hat and laid it on the table nearest to him. He just sat there, lost, trying to envision the effect of this tragic stigma that had befallen him. Slowly he raised his head. The ceiling was there as it always has been, but Toddy did not see it. He penetrated the ceiling, the roof, the air, the sky, yea, even the heavens above and there he saw the Great Man staring at him. "Lord, if it's thy will let it be done."

Toddy awoke the next morning and called the hospital. Marie was as good as could be expected. Years ago, the same thing had happened when his mother was sick in the hospital.

He went out about eight o'clock and before going to work at the drugstore he ordered some flowers from the florist across the street. The man there said that he would send them up as soon as his boy came in.

That day at the drugstore was an agonizing one for Toddy. Time and time again he would stop in the middle of his duties and stare into space. The proprietor on more than one occasion told him to "buck up," but Toddy felt that no one living could ever understand. He also knew that no one would ever be able to estimate the extent to which two people in love would go to prove to each other how much one loved and adored the other.

Two weeks passed and Marie became strong enough to leave the hospital.

All preparation had been made for Marie to come home on that Sunday. Toddy awoke early and gave final instructions to the nurse, whom he had hired for a period of two weeks.

255

He was asking the telephone girl what ward Mrs. Turner was in when a man came up to him and inquired if he was Mr. James Turner. Unconsciously Toddy answered in the affirmative.

"Well, well, well," the man sighed, as though he had finally cast off a heavy burden.

The man went on amid Toddy's ignorance of what the man wanted. "Is Mrs. Turner, the lady in the hospital, I mean the former Mrs. Mondeau, is she your wife?"

"Now wait a minute. I am in an awful hurry and I hope this is not some sort of sales talk, because I am not interested," replied Toddy, sternly.

"Sales talk? I'll say it is—if you are the person I am hoping you are." The man delved into his brief case and took out a picture. "Do you recognize this?" he asked Toddy.

"Why, it's a picture of my mother and . . . and it looks like . . . my cousin Jean . . . "

"Jean Mondeau?" the man shot back.

"Yes," agreed Toddy, in a tone of complete surrender, as he realised that the man did want something. The man was very methodical about everything. He shuffled some other papers, brought out another photograph, and handed it to Toddy.

"Know that person?"

"Yes," answered Toddy, "that's the same man in the other picture—my cousin Jean."

"Yes, sir, you are the fellow," said the man, and handed him a card. Toddy read: "North American Inheritance Ltd.; Buffalo, New York; Branches in all the world; Mr. Bradley, Ag."

"Here is a card and a letter for you, sir. We have been trying to locate you for almost two years. We located this man," he said, pointing to the picture, "but he is in an asylum and not eligible to make use of it. Then we continued to

256

search the hospitals and yesterday morning we found the name of Turner here in this one. There were over four hundred Turners; however, none of the others could be you. To tell the truth I didn't believe we had actually found you. . . . "

Toddy had opened the letter and he did not hear the last words that the man had said. The letter read:

Dear Mr. Turner:

We have information very beneficial to you concerning the death of one Mr. Paul Mondeau in the island of Dominica in the British West Indies. We are pleased to inform you that you have been left a considerable sum of money by this man, who evidently is a distant relative of yours.

However, inasmuch as we have to prove legally that you are the right person we would expect you to appear at our office in the State in which you are located not later than thirty days after receipt of this letter.

We hope to see you as soon as possible.

Very truly yours,
N.A.I. Ltd.
P. Schules, President

Toddy's eyes were agape with astonishment. He thanked the gentleman for the letter and told him he would see him as soon as he received whatever was coming to him.

He turned and asked the telephone girl the question he had asked when he had entered the hospital.

"Third floor," she answered.

"Thank you," he replied, and it occurred to him that she had said the same words before. Toddy decided not to say anything to Marie about the inheritance until she was home.

On the third floor there was a small information booth and with help from the girl there Toddy located the room in

257

which Marie was. On entering it he found her dressed, seated on the chair. "Hello, darling," he greeted her.

"Hello, Toddy," she replied. She was weak and appeared very much worried. "How are you?" she asked.

There was a strange tone in her speech, but Toddy attributed it to the fact that she had been in the hospital for such a long time.

"Are you ready to go, dear?" he asked.

Marie just nodded.

A nurse entered at that moment. "Well, Mr. Turner, your wife is all ready to go home now. Take good care of her; she was a very sick girl, you know."

"Yes, I know she was; I am going to take care of her."

"And you, lady," said the nurse, pointing at Marie, "you remember what the doctor told you and care . . . "

"I'll try," answered Marie, cutting the nurse off.

"All right, dear," said Toddy, "let's go," at the same time putting his arm around her. A wheelchair was brought in for Marie. "I can walk, dear," said Marie. "Take the bags, please."

They went down in the elevator and out into the driveway, then home.

"Well," said Marie, on entering the bedroom of her home, "it seems like I've been away for years. I am tired."

"You better go right to bed. There will be a nurse here in the morning to take care of you."

"Nurse? I am all right. I won't need any nurse . . . ever," protested Marie.

"Marie, what's wrong? Oh, I know that you've been terribly sick, but you don't seem to want to get well. Oh, I mean, you are giving in so." Toddy felt exasperated.

"I haven't given in, my dear. I am suffering from TB. Didn't the doctor tell you that I'd have to go away?"

"Yes, but Marie, look at all the other people in the world

258

who are suffering from worse than that; and they are not as despondent as you are."

"I am not despondent, my love; I am reconciled to my fate."

"See what I mean—the way you are talking now?"

"All the good I try to do in this world," lamented Marie, "I try to help those that I love . . . I try to make a little happiness for myself while I am living, and I do thank God that I have found all the happiness that I could have had in my lifetime. And now I am going to die. I may linger and be a pest and a nuisance to everyone and I wouldn't want that. Oh, Toddy, it's no use . . . We have had all our lovely days and nights together. I couldn't bear going away from you for months. As the doctor says, it should be a year before you can make love to me. I couldn't wait that long, darling. I just couldn't bear it."

"Sweetheart," begged Toddy, "please don't talk like that. I will wait for you. I will work hard and long to make you well and happy again. Please don't talk like that again; you make me feel terrible. The nurse will be here in the morning and then we'll find a way to make you better—in the best possible manner."

He kissed her on her forehead and she hugged him tightly.

"Darling, I am going to get some sleep. Will you go to the store and get some soup for me?"

"Certainly."

"Darling, come here before you go. You know I still love you, don't you? You know I would never want to hurt you for anything in the world, I would never want to see you suffer at all . . . What I mean is, dear, I am your wife and I am unable to be your wife all the way . . I wouldn't mind if you found someone else."

"Oh, please, Marie, don't speak like that. Please.

Please," begged Toddy and then said, "I am going to get your soup" as he left the room.

Toddy opened the door of the car, which was parked in front of the house, then looked up the street. He decided that the distance to the store did not warrant a drive so he shut the door and began walking.

Had he looked up at the window of his bedroom he would have perceived Marie's face peering at him through streaming tears.

He returned in twenty minutes and put the contents of two cans of the soup on the stove to be heated. He then went upstairs to speak to Marie about the letter that he had received at the hospital that morning.

Marie's underthings were thrown across the back of a chair and her shoes and hat lay on the floor. Her light coat was at the foot of the bed. She was lying down fast asleep. Toddy tiptoed over to the bed and bent over to pick up her coat. He stood still watching her. Her eyes were not closed very tightly. Her hospitalisation had caused her face to become thin. Her cheekbones were extremely prominent, and the color that once glowed from her face was missing. He walked over to one of the windows in the room and noiselessly opened it a little. He tiptoed back out of the room and went to the kitchen to get the soup for her.

Marie was still sleeping when he reentered the room. He put the plate containing the soup on the dresser-bench and sat down in the chair at the head of the bed. He hated to wake her—she slept so soundly. Although she looked thin, her beauty had not vanished. He had made up his mind about what to do with the money. True, he had no idea how much it was but he guessed it would take care of her for at least a year.

The soup was getting cold and he decided to awaken her. He touched her face, but her skin did not move; he

260

leaned over and kissed her. As his lips touched hers all color left his face and his heart seemed to stop; slowly, silently, afraid to even whisper, his trembling hands eased up to her eyes. He pushed up her eyelids and then emitted a loud scream. He jumped up, covered his mouth with his hands, and stood there frozen with fear. He picked up the telephone and called the doctor. "Please come right away. Something has happened to Marie." He stood there with the phone in his hand, still staring at his wife's face. He cried, "Marie! Oh, Marie! Marie! What have you done?! What have you done?! Oh, God, what has happened?"

His trembling lips tried to speak, but words could not come. His eyes wandered about the room . . . to the window, where the breeze gently pushed the curtain into the room . . . to the dresser, where he saw what appeared to be an envelope. He ran across the room and his legs were weak and nonsupporting. He reached the dresser, took up the envelope, tore it open, and read:

My darling,

This is going to be very hard on you I know but all the time I was in the hospital, I thought this would be the best way. You see I knew my condition before I went to the hospital, and when I overheard the doctor speaking to you I knew then that I was incurable.

Perhaps I would have gotten well, still, my dear, I also knew that I would have been an impediment, and that you would not have been able to continue your studies. For, sweetheart, I knew that you would have given up everything in the world just to take care of me; and that's exactly what I didn't want to happen. Please don't scold me in your heart; don't think I am not aware of what this means to you, but I want you to know that although my great love for you over-shadows everything else in this entire world, I would not let

261

it stand in the way of your becoming the great doctor I know you'll be.

You have made me very happy and now I don't want to make you unhappy. I've seen everything, I have had your love, I have given you a child, and I am contented.

Continue to study with all your heart, for me—remember that I'll be with you always and when the Dean hands you your diploma next year, I want you to remember that that is exactly what I wanted. To some people who do not understand what true love is, what I am about to do may seem silly to them, but those who have suffered in order to love will be sad but understanding. This is the only way I know to make you see that I've always meant what I said about "sacrifice." I am sure, my precious darling, that we'll meet again somewhere. If God, because I am about to take my life, refuses me into Heaven I will wait outside the gates for you.

May He bless you always. I'll be looking down, or up at you, hoping and wishing that when you die your name will mean something glorious, and be worthy to all others.

Take good care of our baby and whenever she asks for me, just tell her I have gone away to pray for her to be a good girl. Good-bye, my own sweet darling, till we meet again.

Your ever sweet little baby, Marie

Tears obliterated the sight of the words and only by constantly pushing them away with his fingers was he able to read. Everything that she'd ever done came to him in quick succession. It was then that he lowered his head and saw the empty glass on the floor.

Marie was dead. . . . He knelt down and, with his fists beating his temples, he cried aloud, "If I had only used the car I would have been back in time!" Slowly he arose, covered her face with the sheet, and went out of the room, and picked up the telephone once again.

The hardest thing on this earth is to learn to accept

death, for the final sleep is certain to change the plans of man and beast.

Time, however, is the great equaliser and as the minutes and the hours plod onward toward the fulfillment of one's destiny, the days that follow become, once again, "As it were in the beginning."

Toddy realised that Marie would have wanted him to continue with his studies. There were days and nights when he was unable to think.

At first nothing mattered. The person that meant everything to him was now gone forever. Of course, there was his daughter, but the main concern that lay ahead for Toddy, was his education.

Paul, his uncle, had left him a little money, and the future was secure as far as finances were concerned. He was determined to make every effort to become a great doctor and one of the world's best surgeons.

He would endeavor to take his cousin Jean back home to Dominica as he had requested in the letter to Marie.

There were many items—evening clothes, jewelry, letters, and personal belongings—to be checked and sold or given away.

Four Years Later

In the office of Dr. Satell, chief of the medical staff of the General Memorial Hospital, Dr. James Turner was seated in one of the leather chairs reading a magazine. The door opened slowly and Dr. Satell walked in. He was a man in his early sixties; he had one false leg as evidence of an altercation with a native man in a jungle in far-off Africa many years ago.

As he walked into the room Dr. Turner stood up to greet the elder man.

"How do you do, Turner," he replied. "Sit down, my lad, sit down," and Dr. Turner did.

"Turner, I sent for you because I want to take you with me on a trip. I have taken leave and I could use a man with your ability and courage."

"I would like nothing better, sir. I consider myself honored. Thank you very much. When are you going?"

"In about three weeks, but tell me," said Dr. Satell, changing the subject, "you've been here a year now and, pardon me, but I've noticed you haven't been with a woman or gone out with one in all that time. So what makes you such a woman-hater?"

"Woman-hater?" replied Toddy, taken aback. "I am not a woman-hater, sir. Do you mean because you have never seen me with one?"

"Well, yes—to put it that way—that's what I mean."

"Doctor, the answer to that would probably take about two hours, sir, so suffice it to say that I could never fall in love with another woman, and I don't think it's fair to lie to them."

"Ah! there has been one?" queried Dr. Satell.

Toddy did not answer immediately.

"Yes, sir, there has been . . . That's why I am here. I'll tell you about it sometime."

After Marie's death, James Turner had moved to the city once again. He had buried her modestly and with the balance of the money from her insurance he invested in some U.S. bonds. The money he had received from the North American Inheritance Co. Ltd. amounted to over twenty-nine thousand dollars and so James Turner continued to do what Marie had wanted him to do. Marie Louise still lived in Mt. Vernon with Mrs. Saitch and was growing up to be an attractive young lady. She was now nine years of age.

"Do you think they'll move out of port in this fog, doctor?" inquired Dr. Turner, as both men stood on one of the decks of the big liner, which appeared to be stranded at one of New York's largest piers.

"It seems to be lifting. It's not as thick as it was when we came on this morning," replied Dr. Satell.

The engines had been constantly pounding their way through the floor on which they stood and officers walking back and forth with brisk nervous steps gave the impression that the ship was about to embark.

"I'll be back in a moment," said Dr. Satell, and Dr. Turner was left alone, not truly alone, for there were many more passengers on the ship, but he felt alone for he knew no one but his fellow doctor. As he leaned over the rail he felt happy that Marie Louise's welfare was arranged for. She had wanted to come to the boat to see him off but he'd decided otherwise.

The gangplank was coming down. Young men in uniform had been crying, "All ashore that's going ashore," since early that morning, but while the ship stayed in port the plank was never put down. The last long blast from the steamer's whistle gave warning that the ship was about to put to sea. Dr. Satell returned.

"Well, we are going," he commented.

"Yes, sir," answered Dr. Turner. The thrill of his first trip on an ocean liner was somewhat subdued by the memory of the ritual he would have to perform.

As the boat turned towards the open sea only a faint glimpse of New York Harbor was visible. The Statue of Liberty was blinded by the patches of fog that swooped across her head like windblown smoke. Constant horn blasts of small boats could be heard and the bells on the buoys rang as the backwash of the boats plied near to them, creating parallel waves that seemed to divide the waters of the bay. Soon the skyline was lost to view and a faint, thin

265

stretch of land, which was gradually diminishing, was all that remained.

Dr. Satell turned to his younger colleague, who was deep in meditation. The chill in the air caused both men to turn up the collars of their coats.

"Well," said Dr. Satell, "this time tomorrow we'll be well out to sea, and all the expectations and dreams that you've envisioned will begin slowly to unfold before you."

The younger man turned to him and, without exhibiting the slightest amount of interest, calmly answered, "Yes, sir."

"From what you told me last night, I know you've done the right thing, and I am sure you did just as she wanted you to."

"I think so, sir."

Dr. Turner took from his pocket a small bottle and uncorked it. He then emptied the contents in the waters below with such dignity that Dr. Satell studied him with awe.

"What are you doing, Turner?"

"Well, sir, to anyone else I would be ashamed to explain it—for reasons of my own—but I think you can understand. I've taken a little dirt from my mother's grave and some from my wife's and I've mixed them together. I've always said that if I were ever to leave this country I would try to join their resting place together. My mother came to this country through this same entrance, and so did Marie, my wife, and in my will I have begged, if possible, for this same ritual to be performed after I am buried."

Dr. Satell shook his head. "I understand," he said.

Toddy leaned over the rail and made the sign of the cross. Turning to his colleague, he said, "I think I'll go to my cabin, sir."

"Good idea."

They walked together and disappeared below the deck.

The years continue to go on and on. Some men get older, some die, and others are born. Some achieve their goals, others fall by the wayside.

It was four years later when a freighter chugged slowly up the Hudson River in the City of New York, bearing an assortment of animals from all over the world. Not animals for the zoological gardens but animals treated for all known diseases of the brain. Small rodents and large chimpanzees were among the assortment that Dr. Turner had brought back to America with him. He came back alone, for Dr. Satell had died in Africa, but he left behind one of the greatest pupils and brain specialists in the world. Dr. Turner had concentrated on the study of the brains of animals and humans who had gone berserk. Now he was considered an authority on the subject. In fact, one experiment that he had performed on the brain of a man in far off Torno Island who had suffered a complete lack of memory due to an accidental head injury would always be referred to by doctors and scientists throughout the world as an outstanding achievement in the annals of the medical world.

Dr. Turner had only returned to the United States for one specific purpose. Ever since he had learned of his cousin's insanity years ago he had thought of contributing more to the study of problems and the causes of the loss of mind. In Africa he had begun to delve deeper into the mysterious intricacies of the human mind. He had kept in touch with the hospital in which Jean was a patient and had learnt that Jean had continued to linger on and that his condition had become somewhat modified to the extent that he was given a longer lease on life.

There were a great many contributing causes to Jean's downfall, thought Dr. Turner, and with more time to think after Marie's death, he concluded that the best he could do was to aid him in regaining what little could be salvaged. Of course, now that Marie was gone he no longer had a guilty conscience. He just wanted to help as best as he could his own cousin.

Jean had never known that Toddy had been responsible for Marie's leaving him.

There were many times like this when he had begun reminiscing on his past experiences to find that there were many links in the great chain of theories and that any one of them could be used to foster his argument that no one person could be blamed or could take credit for his attainment of success.

If Jean had not invited him to Detroit perhaps he would have never met Marie and in all probability he would have never been a doctor. But supposition would not enter now into his next professional endeavor. He would operate on Jean, who had continued to live despite all Toddy's colleagues' predictions that he had been doomed to die more than eight years earlier.

The momentous occasion arrived and on this Monday morning when the person of Jean Mondeau, weak in mind and body, was rolled into the operating room, Dr. James Turner prayed in the antechamber:

"Oh, God, I have asked Thee a great many favors and Thou has granted them with all Thy goodness. Remember, Lord; the suffering that this man has gone through, remember the suffering that he will go through if this attempt to resurrect his mind fails. Assist me, O Lord, in this undertaking and guide my hands and fingers and all those that work with me. Keep us from faltering for thine is the kingdom, the power and glory, forevermore. Amen."

Twelve hours later Jean Mondeau was wheeled out of the operating room, alive, and with a chance for a successful recovery. With congratulations from the assistant doctors and nurses still ringing in his ears, Dr. Turner slowly walked to his office. He slumped into the nearest chair and thanked God silently but earnestly. He had done his best.

A knock on the door interrupted his meditation and he spoke.

"Come in."

One of the nurses who had worked with him entered the room. "I came in to say, doctor, that we all are proud of you, for more than one reason, but we were not surprised. We knew you'd come through perfectly."

"Thank you very much. Thank you," he answered, without raising his head.

"You'll pardon me, doctor, but there's something I'd like to ask you, if you don't mind."

Dr. Turner looked at the speaker for the first time since she entered the room and said, "Oh, it's you, Byrd; yes, what is it?"

"I've heard a lot about you. I've heard that this was where you first came—from medical school—and I've seen you the past few days. I am a woman and I've never seen a man, or I should say a doctor, work with such fervor and firmness as you did in that room just now. When I handed you those instruments there was something in your work that told me you were not just operating on another patient. There was the precision, the will to do something for some particular reason."

"Yes, there was that," agreed the doctor, getting up and walking to the window, "but I can't explain now. I've got to wait and see. Yes, I've got to wait and see . . . "

"Do you know him, Doctor?"

Dr. Turner whirled suddenly and faced the nurse. "Do I know him!" he yelled.

The nurse cowered and said, "I am sorry, doctor."

"I am the one that should apologise, my dear. I am

terribly sorry I yelled. Forgive me. Yes, I do know him very well."

"I think I'll go, doctor."

"All right. And don't forget, come in and see me, anytime."

Three days later Jean Mondeau was removed from intensive care and put into a bed as a recuperating patient. The day arrived when Dr. Turner was to make his examination of Jean. He was a bit worried on his arrival at the hospital. Everyone seemed to sense the importance of his visit.

An attendant who had greeted the doctor and received a rather brisk answer turned to another and said, "The doc seemed worried this morning."

"Yeah," replied the other, "I do hope his patient is okay."

"I wouldn't worry too much, that guy knows his stuff," retorted the other.

"I know, but once yer crazy, yer crazy. Takes more than an operation to put a cracked nut together."

Nurse Byrd was waiting for the doctor in the patient's room. Another doctor accompanied Dr. Turner to the room.

"Would you mind, doctor, waiting here? I would like to go in alone," exclaimed Dr. Turner. "I'll call you later."

He turned to the nurse. "You wouldn't mind?" he asked.

"No, not at all," she answered.

In the few remaining moments left before Dr. Turner reached Jean's bedside, he prayed.

Finally, he opened the door to the outer room. Farther on was the door to Jean's room. The suspense of these moments was exacting.

Dr. Turner swallowed, put his hand on the doorknob, pulled it slowly, and entered the room.

There was a nurse seated, reading. He motioned for her to leave and she obeyed. He was alone with Jean.

Suddenly, he was not a doctor; no longer did he feel any professional reason for being there. He was there only to see a man like himself who was lost and whom he hoped would be found. It was Toddy standing there looking at Mr. Jean Mondeau, his mother's brother's child, whose wife he had stolen.

Jean's face was turned away from the doctor's view. Toddy moved across the room and faced Jean. Jean slowly raised his head and a smile creased his face. Apprehensively, Dr. Turner smiled back. Neither said a word.

Jean was staring at him, examining him. Dr. Turner returned the stare. It seemed that he could not force himself to wink. Jean continued to stare. He looked at Toddy's clothes; then his eyes began to blink and continued blinking incessantly.

He tried to rise, his head bandaged with a white cloth that covered his forehead almost to his eyes. His hands rose towards his face as he slowly tried to rise from the bed.

His eyes were bulging. They seemed twice as large as they were when Dr. Turner had operated and also when he had entered the room.

Jean was trying to open his mouth. He was trying to speak. . . . He was trying to smile, then his smile changed to an expression of amazement. His mouth opened wide and as clear as the sound of a new string on a violin Toddy heard the words, "Toddy Turner," and he leaped to Jean's bedside.

The patient murmured, "It can't be . . . it can't be . . . it can't be . . . oh, no." Then he turned his head away, tossed it back just as suddenly, and said, "Tell me, aren't you . . . James . . . Turner? My aunt's nephew?"

Tears poured down Dr. Turner's face. He was proud and happy and as he reached out and stroked Jean's forehead, he whispered, "Yes, Jean, I am Toddy. I helped you to get well. I am a doctor now."

271

Jean replied, "I haven't seen you since that day at Stella's house."

"Yes, I know," answered Toddy, "that was a very long time ago."

A month later the specialists at the hospital concluded that Jean Mondeau would never recover from his illness completely, but that he would be able to lead a normal life and with a long rest and complete relaxation he would progress more and more.

There were times when Jean appeared to be normal; he remembered most of the events that took place before his breakdown. He had asked Dr. Turner many times about Marie and the doctor had told him the truth—that Marie had died. Jean had accepted this news without any visible sign of emotion.

Finally, Jean asked the doctor to take him home as the report from the hospital showed that he had recuperated enough to be able to take care of himself, and the doctor had made preparations to do just that.

A few months later Dr. Turner and Jean Mondeau were on an ocean liner in the Caribbean Sea bound for the island of Dominica. Jean Mondeau was seated in his cabin when the third blast of the steamer's whistle brought memories of fifty years earlier.

He walked towards the porthole and peered out into the waters of the river—the same river he had looked at a half century before—only this time he was leaving America instead of coming in.

As he stared into the waters he saw his Aunt Celia, his mother and his father, Marie, and his grandfather. All gone now. There was no one but Toddy. All his dreams and ambitions had dissipated.

"What happened?" he wondered aloud. He knew how hard he had tried. He thought that the Lord had been good to him. He had "lived," but was it possible that some sort of a curse had befallen him?

The first day was uneventful; the sea was calm and Jean stayed in his cabin most of the time resting.

On the third night of the trip Jean was restless. He found it difficult to sleep. It was four o'clock in the morning when he decided to visit Dr. Turner in his cabin. Jean knocked at the doctor's cabin door, and waited. . . . He knocked again. . . .

Toddy opened the door and rather slowly motioned Jean in.

"Doctor," began Jean, "I am sorry to have disturbed you at such an early hour, but I am unable to go to sleep."

"Come in," said Toddy, but Jean made no effort to enter the cabin.

"Toddy, I wondered if you would mind going up on the deck with me?"

"Of course not," replied Toddy, "I'll be ready in a moment."

"Thank you, Toddy; thank you," answered Jean.

A few minutes later the two trudged up the small staircase leading to the upper deck. As Jean reached the top stair he suddenly stopped and held on to the rail, seeming to tremble, unsteady. Dr. Turner threw his arms around Jean.

"Are you all right?" inquired Toddy.

"Yes, I am sorry," replied Jean. "I am glad you understand."

The brilliant circle in the sky above the ocean brought back memories to Jean; the moon was full.

They walked towards the rail. They both stood still, and Jean looked down at the water below.

The moon was directly overhead and Jean raised his head and peered into the Heavens and pointed towards the eastern horizon.

"Dr. Turner, it will be dawn very soon," commented Jean.

"Yes, Jean, very soon."

"You know, Toddy, to you this is just another dawn, just another day, and to most everyone that moon is just a fixture. To lovers, a sort of aid to their romantic endeavors. To mariners a great help in time of peace, but dangerous in time of war for both participants.

"Ah, but to me it's a stamp in my memory that won't come off. You see, Toddy, I was about seven years old—a very long time ago. I stood at the rail of a ship, just as we are doing now, almost at the same time in the morning. That was long before you were born."

There was a bit of a tremor in Jean's voice and Toddy moved closer to him lest Jean might become melancholic.

"It's all so clear to me now," Jean went on, "I was a little bit full of ambition. It seemed to be such a short time ago that your mother died."

"My mother?" questioned Toddy.

"Oh, yes . . . oh, I don't mean when your mother, and I came to America. I mean when we were going to her husband's birthplace. He lived on another island before he met your mother. It was called Antigua.

"He was a grand person; we came on deck early in the morning, just before sunrise. It was on a Sunday morning. He said a prayer, so did your mother. I did too, in my own little way," said Jean, and then became silent. "That's it! That's it!" he continued, "we were all seeing this whole thing through you," and Jean began to laugh rather mockingly.

"Why are you laughing, Jean?"

"At this. This final ending to my life . . . to our lives. I was the one who was supposed to come back as a successful person—a lawyer, a doctor—and now look at me. It's you instead. You! Who wasn't even thought of then. You are the one accompanying me after saving my life. What a quirk of fate. Oh, Toddy, I am so proud to know it's one of us who made good." He clasped the doctor's hand in his.

The doctor and Jean both looked into the great stretch of water and there, with Toddy in his heart knowing everything about Jean and with Jean hardly knowing anything about the doctor, it was one of the most important chapters in the doctor's life.

Jean exclaimed, "Yes, I am glad it is one of us that became a doctor. The Lord works in a mysterious manner."

Toddy answered, "Yes, he certainly does."

The moon ran towards a dark cloud and darkness ran across the ocean. For a few moments there was nothing to see, then the full face of the moon appeared once again and pushed away the shadow.

The ship plowed onward.

Far to the east a faint film of light gradually came upon the horizon and the two men stood at the rail, silently, each one in his own heart pondering the outcome of the voyage . . . staring at the birth of a new day.

As Dr. Turner looked at the ship dividing the billowy waves, the foam spurting in the air reminded Toddy of his fight for success. He had reached his destination because of a wonderful crew of one, named Marie.

Toddy looked on as Jean made the sign of the cross, as though completing a prayer. As Dr. Turner stood there he wondered if Jean would ever again ask about Marie or if she'd gone completely out of his mind. He did not want to mention her name for if Jean had really forgotten about her it would serve no purpose to awaken his curiosity.

Jean had taken something from his pocket and was staring at it. Dr. Turner waited. Evidently this had been the reason for the early morning trip on deck. Jean handed it slowly to the doctor and Toddy looked at a somewhat faded picture of a little girl.

"Toddy," he began, "this has been with me always. I must have put it away with some other things I had in Detroit, before I became ill. I came across it while packing for this trip. I don't think I'll need it anymore." He handed the faded photograph to Toddy.

Toddy took the picture and glanced at it rather casually. His eyebrows narrowed. For the next few seconds he was suddenly confronted with a catastrophic decision.

He imagined himself at the helm of a ship in the dark of night when there appeared before him an object that was not discernible at first glance.

You know there *is* something there and you are at the mercy of fate. You have to think very fast and, if at all possible, you try to avoid what seems to be a certain collision.

Toddy did not look up right away as he glanced at the picture before him. Had he done so he would have been unable to hide his astonishment. His heart began beating rapidly, for he realised that the picture that Jean had just put into his hand was identical with the picture that his mother had left to him in an envelope along with a letter over thirty years earlier, when he had come home from the hospital after she had died.

"Jean," asked Toddy, calmly, "where did you get this?"

"Your mother gave it to me a very long time ago. My grandfather gave it to her that day before he died and asked her to try and find that girl, as he was sure that she was somewhere in America. Your mother had a couple of them made and she gave me this in the hope that I might help to find her."

Toddy's heartbeat seemed more pronounced as the silence on the deck of the ship was broken only by the division of the great ocean and the sliver on which these two men stood.

"Why did he want her to be found, Jean?"

Jean sighed, raised his hand to his forehead, looked woefully out into the ocean, and answered.

"Toddy, my grandfather went to South America after my grandmother had died and he met a Spanish girl who later gave birth to his child. He came back to Dominica without them and later, when he tried to locate them, he found they had gone to America."

"This picture, was it taken in South America?"

"I'm not sure. Your mother said it was a place named Cayenne, not far from Panama. Why, have you met someone that resembles her?"

"No. No," the doctor lied, "I don't think so."

Jean then took out another picture from his pocket and handed it to Toddy.

"I had three more taken by a studio about ten years ago. The others must have gotten misplaced or lost. You keep them when you go back to the States. You might just meet someone that knows her. You see, Todd, she is my mother's half sister and your grandmother's half sister, too, and, "Jean continued, "Toddy . . . "

But Toddy interrupted. "Jean, is this a picture of my aunt who is also your aunt?"

Jean did not see the ghastly expression on Toddy's face, for the doctor had turned suddenly towards the rail and said, inwardly, *Oh my God. Jesus have mercy on us.*

He turned to Jean and said, "I'll try to find her when I return to the States." He was visibly shaken as he walked away from the rail.

He started towards the stairs that led to the cabins below and Jean followed.

"I think I will get a few more hours sleep," remarked the doctor. "How about you?"

"Yes," Jean replied, pointing towards the east, "we'll have to go soon anyway." He added, "We'll never see the sun this morning."

The doctor's eyes followed Jean's pointing finger.

"It's going to rain," Jean went on.

"Rain? Nonsense. Why, it's so beautiful, a little breeze, a few clouds perhaps . . . "

"Yes, clear now, but here in these waters many things happen that one least expects to happen," answered Jean, prophetically.

Dr. Turner bade Jean good morning and they went to their respective cabins, but Dr. Turner was completely shaken.

Would God do this to him? Did Marie take her life solely because she was deathly ill or did she find out about her identity when and if she saw a copy of the picture that was in his pocket?

Dr. Turner sat on his bed, reached into his pocket, and took out his wallet, and extracted two pictures. One his mother had left for him after her death, and the other he had found with Marie's belongings after she had committed suicide.

He then put them with the pictures that Jean had given him. All the pictures were of the same person—the mother of Marie!

Marie, he said to himself, *Jean's wife. Marie, later my wife, the mother of my child, the daughter of my grandfather's child.*

Dr. Turner took out a pen from his pocket, reached for a sheet of paper, and began to write:

"Marie was conceived when her mother was sixteen years old in Cayenne, South America. She came to the

United States when she was ten years of age. She entered the convent when she was fourteen. She met Jean when she was nineteen, and she met Toddy for the first time in Detroit when she was twenty-four. Marie, the mother of his child, was the granddaughter of Pierre Mondeau. Marie and his mother were sisters sired by the same father!"

Was it at all possible that Jean had become mentally ill because he knew? Perhaps he did find out, wondered Dr. Turner.

Dr. Turner left his cabin and walked over to Jean's. Somehow he felt that Jean was not asleep. He knocked on the door.

"Come in," came the answer.

Dr. Turner pushed the door and both men faced each other, but neither said a word.

Dr. Turner broke the silence. He did not want to mention Marie's name but he had to. "Jean, did you ever meet Marie's mother? I mean, did she ever mention anything about her mother?"

After a long pause, Jean said, "No. Come to think of it, she did mention once that she preferred not to talk about her. . . . I don't think that she was very proud of her."

It was the first time that Marie's name had been mentioned in conversation between them on the ship.

Jean did not seem a bit perturbed when Toddy asked him about Marie. In fact, it appeared to Toddy that Jean had known all along about Marie but did not know about her and Toddy.

"Jean," Toddy began, "perhaps we should discuss . . . "

He was interrupted by Jean. "Toddy, please allow me to say something. You have saved me and you have saved my life; if there is anything that would cause any problem I would rather not hear it. I would like to go home and spend my last days there." He turned away and said, "See you in the morning."

Toddy returned to his cabin and went to bed.

The next morning Jean Mondeau awoke at nine o'clock, dressed, and walked to Toddy's cabin. He knocked twice but when he received no answer he beckoned towards the white-jacketed steward in the corridor.

The steward opened the door and they entered. The realisation that the bed had not been slept in caused consternation as they both stared at each other.

The search for Dr. Turner began on the huge vessel.

The captain ordered a complete investigation and after a few hours decided that the missing passenger was not on the ship.

The S.S. *Belvedere* continued on the voyage to the Caribbean islands but the article in the obituary column of the *New York Times* the following Sunday explained everything:

"Dr. T. Turner, a well-known surgeon who was accompanying his cousin to the island of Dominica in the West Indies, disappeared from a cruise passenger ship somewhere between the island of St. Thomas in the Virgin Islands and the United States. A thorough search of the ship was made and no trace of the doctor was found.

"Dr. Turner performed an operation on his cousin Jean Mondeau a year ago for the removal of a tumor on his brain which was successful.

"A note found in a sealed envelope in his cabin quoted from a Shakespearean passage:

The evil that men do lives after them. The good is oft interred with their bones.

followed by a passage from the scriptures:

280

There is more joy in Heaven for one sinner doing penance than on ninety-nine just.

"Jean Mondeau, the doctor's cousin, suffered a severe stroke which left him completely paralyzed on his arrival at the island of Dominica.

"The authorities disposed of his body in accordance with his wishes which were left in a letter in his cabin. It stated that his remains if he died before or on arrival in the island were to be buried close to those of his grandfather Jean Pierre Mondeau in the cemetery in the small village of Ville Case in Dominica.

Ten Years Later

Marie Louise, the daughter of Marie and Dr. Turner, was adopted by Mrs. Saitch after the death of her natural parents and she had been living with the Saitch family in Mt. Vernon for the past fifteen years.

Marie Louise was told by Mrs. Saitch of her adoption and she began to ask many questions about her ancestors as she grew up.

She was constantly tortured by the fact that no one knew why her father, a well-known and successful surgeon, had disappeared from the ocean liner on which he was accompanying his cousin Jean Mondeau on a return trip to Mondeau's birthplace to be with his grandfather forever.

The trust fund her father had left made her independent financially and it was enough for her to be able to continue her education.

She was a college student and for the first time she had felt the urge to investigate the circumstances that led to the events which caused her only known ancestors to be unrecognizable. So she had convinced her stepmother to accompany her on a trip to the Caribbean during her summer vacation. She had decided to visit the homes of her grandparents after she had acquired proof that her maternal and paternal grandparents came from the islands of Dominica and Antigua in the Caribbean.

She applied for and received a passport to visit these islands on her next summer vacation and she took her adopted mother with her on their first cruise to the West Indies.

She came to the realization that the few hours she would spend on the islands would not permit any lengthy search, would only be a preliminary investigation that might lead to further trips to the islands.

Marie Louise wrote to officials in the islands of Antigua and Dominica and the information received from the Hall of Records in the islands did not satisfy her, but she figured her first visit would open the road for further investigation later.

After visits to at least three travel agencies her stepmother and Marie decided on a ten-day cruise on a Home Lines ship.

The cost was $3,770 for two and the ship's itinerary included stops at St. Thomas, Virgin Islands, Martinique, St. Martin and Antigua. Dominica was not on this itinerary and other plans would have to be made. Marie Louise and Mrs. Saitch left New York on their visit to the Caribbean.

The cruise ship *Atlantic* left the pier at four P.M. for the Caribbean. First stop, St. Thomas, then to St. Martin the French and Dutch Island, then to Martinique and Antigua.

Marie Louise had written to Antigua to enquire about her grandfather and had hoped on arrival to gain some knowledge of her paternal ancestors.

On her arrival at St. Johns, the capital of Antigua, the records did not divulge any information that would enable her to contact anyone still living who would be able to aid her in her quest for information about her grandfather's early beginnings.

The short time allotted her on the islands was not enough to enable her to contact anyone and she decided to return to the islands and stay for at least three days on the islands of Antigua and Dominica, the home of her maternal grandparents.

The next two years were spent in acquiring information, and she finally received information that encouraged her to visit the islands again.

With the assistance of the travel agent she was able to make plans to take a plane to Antigua and stay for three days and nights in a hotel, then on an interisland plane to visit Dominica for three days, and then fly to Puerto Rico from where she would fly back to New York.

The island of Dominica had become independent and natives, although blessed with a deep harbor in the capitol, Roseau, and an abundance of fruits that were aided by the volcanic soil, were economically poor. The mountainous surroundings of the island did not attract foreign investment and the tourist trade was not enough to balance the economy of the island.

Marie Louise visited the island of Dominica by plane from Puerto Rico. After a stay of a day in Roseau, she finally acquired the services of a guide who accompanied her to the mountain villages of what was once Macondee, Veille Case, and Libya but she located no one nor could she meet anyone who knew of her ancestors.

In her search, however, she came upon an old woman, a descendant of the Caribs. She was almost 100 years old and she remembered the tale of an obeah woman who had treated a well-known man in the village of Veille Case for a disease in his leg which had had to be amputated.

This man it seems had been cursed by a woman in

Cayenne, South America. He was a great man. He owned a lot of land, was a big church man, and was buried in the cemetery up on a hill a long, long time ago. He had a brother who had died years later. His name was Manuel. The obeah woman had given him a crude sketch of the woman.

The man who walked around with a wooden leg—named Mondeau. He'd had eight children. All had died except one daughter who had gone to another island and never came back. Her brother and sister died in a hurricane in Portsmouth a long, long time ago.

Before Mondeau died, the obeah woman told people in village, he had made money in South America, found gold there, and had a child by a Spanish woman. That's all the Carib woman knew.

Marie Louise told her stepmother when she returned to the U.S. the tale told her by the old Carib woman.

A year later, Marie Louise boarded a plane to Antigua to try to locate someone who knew her grandfather's people.

The island of Antigua had also become independent but the main product of the island, the sugarcane, had dwindled and the island had become wealthy due to the development of the tourist trade.

Magnificent homes were built. Expensive hotels, cottages, and companies all invested in the island and the deep harbor and landings where the largest ships could dock made Antigua one of the wealthiest of the Caribbean islands.

Marie Louise delved into the city records and found the name of Turner, a child born to a white man and a black woman. He had left Antigua for the U.S. at the age of twenty-eight and had never returned.

Marie Louise again returned to the U.S. Records in the State of New York showed the death of a James Turner, husband of a Mrs. Turner in New York City, Harlem—the victim of a murder.

Marie Louise was all alone and, after ten years of searching, she had come to the conclusion that she had no relatives left in the world. Her mother, her father, her grandfather were all gone. Her maternal grandmother had deserted her mother. After a brief consultation with her adopted mother, she decided to make one more trip to the West Indian islands in an attempt to find out about her ancestors.

Her trip to Dominica would be by plane from Puerto Rico after a plane trip from Kennedy Airport in New York.

There were eight passengers on the plane bound for Dominica. She turned her head to face a passenger who had touched her on the shoulder as the plane became airbound.

"I beg your pardon but somehow I have a feeling that we have met before," the young man said. He continued, "Believe me I am not trying to be fresh but I am sure I have seen you before."

"Perhaps you have," Marie Louise answered. "Are you from New York?"

"Yes, I am going to visit some relatives in Dominica. Are you also visiting someone in Dominica?"

"Yes," Marie answered, "this is my third trip. I am trying to locate some relations whom I have never seen."

"In Dominica?"

"Yes."

"That's a rather funny coincidence. I am doing the same thing."

They both stared at each other. Then Marie Louise spoke.

"My father's name is James Turner. My great-grandfather on my mother's side was born in Dominica in a place called Veille Case. What was your father's name?" she asked.

"James Turner. His nickname was Toddy," replied the young man.

Marie's left hand closed her open mouth as she stared at the young man before her—he appeared to be about her age.

"Your father was born in the U.S.?" she asked, utterly amazed.

"Yes, about fifty years ago."

"Your mother's name would not be Stella?"

"Yes!" exclaimed the young man.

"Great God in Heaven," cried Marie Louise covering her forehead with her open palm. "My father's name was James," she hesitated, then continued, "Turner. My mother's name was the same as mine—Marie . . . I am your half-sister!"

The young man stared at her. "Your father was a doctor?" he queried.

"Yes! I was brought up by my adopted mother and she told me that my father as a young man was married to a girl named Stella and she bore him a son. Then for some reason they were divorced and he married a girl named Marie, whose mother was born in South America but who was the daughter of a Frenchman named Mondeau who was born in Dominica. Marie, my mother, was married to a Jean Mondeau. Jean Mondeau's aunt was your grandmother. My mother, Marie, was your grandmother's sister."

"The same father . . . ," began the young man, but Marie Louise cut him off.

"My great grandfather's name was Mondeau—and yours had the same name—Mondeau. My father and his cousin, Jean Mondeau, were on a ship bound for the Caribbean. Jean Mondeau was married to my mother and he became mentally ill. He was operated on by my father and a year later they both were booked on a ship going to the Caribbean. My father disappeared from the ship and Jean Mondeau suffered a stroke and died later on the ship. According to the records I have just discovered he's buried near his grandfather in the village of Veille Case."

"So Jean Mondeau was married to a child sired by his grandfather?" asked the stunned young man.

"Yes, and his grandson married the same girl," answered Marie Louise.

Marie Louise made the sign of the cross and bowed her head in prayer.

Fifteen minutes later the small plane crashed in the Martinique channel. There were no survivors.